W9-CCK-336

CONCEPTS, EVENTS, AND HISTORY

L. B. Cebik

University Press
of America™

Copyright © 1978 by

University Press of America, Inc.™

4710 Auth Place, S.E., Washington, D.C. 20023

Printed in the United States of America

ISBN: 0-8191-0639-9

Library of Congress Catalog Card Number: 78-64825

FORWARD

The material in this volume is the result of working and rework-
ing some fundamental ideas over a number of years. Some of the ideas
appeared in the following journals: "Colligation and the Writing of
History," *The Monist*, 53 (1969); "History's Want of Authority: Some
Logical and Historical Speculations," *The Southern Journal of Philosophy*, 8 (1970); "Collingwood: Action, Re-enactment, and Evidence,"
Philosophical Forum, 2 (1970); "Narratives and Arguments," *Clio*, 1
(1971); and "Events and Past Events: Some Ontological Considerations," *Ontological Commitment*, ed. Richard H. Severens, (University
of Georgia Press, 1974). To these journals and publishers go my appreciation for permission to use material from the articles. In addition, thanks go to the following publishers for permission to quote at
length: Cambridge University Press for A. C. Danto, *Analytical Philosophy of History* (1965); McGraw Hill Book Company for R. G. Collingwood,
Essays in the Philosophy of History, ed. William Debbins (1965); Oxford
University Press for R. G. Collingwood, *The Idea of History*; and
Princeton University Press for Haskell Fain, *Between Philosophy and
History*.

Those to whom I owe philosophical debts are too numerous ever to
do complete justice, but Bruce Waters, Ivan Little, O. K. Bouwsma, Bob
Dewey, and Bob Hurlbutt deserve special mention, if only to say that I
have not forgotten--or at least not everything. In addition, this volume owes much to the skills of Mrs. Dolores Scates, who prepared the
manuscript and interpreted my handwriting; my debt to her is also
great. Thanks also go to Ms. Barbara Moser for a variety of services
to this work. For any errors of judgment, analysis, or argument that
remain in this work, I shall take unhappy responsibility in hopes that
there are some correct and useful ideas among the remainder.

Contents

INTRODUCTION

No one, so far as I know, has ever explored in depth the role of accidents in doing philosophy. Yet, accidents just might constitute the springboard for many a philosophic study. Perhaps a chance encounter with an anomaly within a certain conception, perhaps a surprising inference from an argument that appeared originally not to have implications for a particular subject or field, perhaps an emphasis upon an ordinarily unstressed word within a well-worn phrase: all these and more might give rise to philosophical studies. In a very non-serious way, one might say that an accident gave rise to this study.

The function of an introduction is, in part, to spell out the particular circumstances, both methodological and accidental, which have played a role in the origination of a study. Readers sometimes find it useful to be aware of and to understand the peculiarities that give a study its individual impetus, direction, and flavor. Philosophical studies, as separate pieces of writing, each have their own slight histories, and the present investigation into certain aspects of history is no exception. Part of the history of this study includes, besides the usual methodological precepts, its accident of emphasis.

The present study into history owes more than anything else to an emphasis which I have come to place upon certain words that occur, but pass unnoticed, in various descriptions and definitions of history. To cite one of the authors of these descriptions and definitions, Danto speaks of historians' concern "with events in their past, or with, in certain cases, events in their present."[1] Stover, as a second example, states that "historians are commonly looked upon as specialists in ascertaining and reconstructing particular happenings of the human past."[2] Walsh, for a third, thinks of the historian as one who constructs a "significant narrative of past events."[3] If we turn to Collingwood, we find that he takes the object of history to be "*res gestae*: actions of human beings that have been done in the past."[4] In partial agreement with these exemplary statements, Cohen remarks that "in general current usage the term 'history' is restricted to an account of past events, no matter what the field."[5] In all these descriptions, reports, and definitions, there occur words like "event," "action," and "happening." Whatever else may differentiate the writers cited, they do agree that the doing of history presupposes or simply supposes a concern for events and actions. From this we might infer, if we did not already have overwhelming evidence in the writings of historians since Herodotus, that historians would make essential and extensive use of event and action concepts in their historical accounts. It is, then, the continual reference to events and actions in philosophic analyses of history which has most struck me and which consequently forms the central concern of the present study.[6]

1

The emphasis which I have come to place on words such as "event" and "action" in descriptions of the historical enterprise thus provides the main subject and theme for this study. Since I tend to view philosophy as a field of conceptual studies, the main subject can be expanded and explicated in terms of a series of questions having roughly the following form: a. What is the nature of event and action concepts as historians use them? b. Does the nature of event and action concepts have any implications for the way in which we describe various activities on which historians agree? In other words, does an account of the language historians use entail anything for historical methodology? c. Does an account of event and action concepts together with its entailments for historical methodology supply material which might help answer some of the traditional questions in the philosophy of history?

In what follows, I shall propose an account of event and action language which I hope does descriptive justice to such language as it is used in historical writing. The account will have methodological implications, and these implications will, in turn, suggest some partial answers to traditional questions in the philosophy of history. Among the traditional topics for which the account will have implications are historical facts and evidence, historical truth, the selection of events for inclusion in historical accounts, the purpose and objectivity of history, and the role of the narrative form in historical writing.

The topics just mentioned will fill the chapters of this study. It is important to note, however, that just as a particular starting point provides criteria for the inclusion of subjects in a study, it provides as well criteria for exclusion. The central interests of this study exclude mention in any systematic way of problems and questions which lie beyond the range of the implications of the account of event and action language. Moreover, even those *parts* of the problem under study which go beyond the limits of the implications of the account of language will not be dealt with in detail. To illustrate what is meant by these remarks, we must get ahead of ourselves a bit: the account of language will concentrate on those aspects of event and action concept use which are involved in the justification of an assertion that an event or action has occurred. The account will not, except in passing, attend to the uses to which assertions of the occurrence of events or actions may be put. (The main reason for this restriction is that there is a great deal which needs to be said with respect to problems in the philosophy of history that rests upon just the assertion of the occurrence of events and actions. So much needs to be said, in fact, as not to allow many extensions into further uses of those assertions. This restriction does not, of course, deny either the possibility or the utility of exploring those extensions.) To give just one example of an excluded subject, the restriction precludes any detailed discussion of explanation theory as it relates to history. Most theories, especially the varieties called covering law theories, conceive an explanation assertion to be one which relates two or more events in cer-

tain ways.[7] The assertion of the occurrence of the events related in
an explanatory statement is presupposed. Precisely the presupposition
and not the explanatory assertion itself holds central interest for
this study, and for this reason, theories of explanation fall outside
the scope of the investigation. For similar reasons, problems such as
freedom vs. determinism, progress and development, et al. will also be
omitted.

In principle, the plan is to carry the implications of the account
of event and action concepts only so far as they can be taken without
introducing further theoretic elements which themselves would require a
large scale justification, that is, to confine the study to the application of the account of event and action concepts to those matters for
which the account has direct implication. In practice, however, nothing goes as well as in principle. The dividing line between inclusion and exclusion, so clear in principle, becomes blurred as soon as
one attempts to draw it in fact. For one reason, even to speak on certain matters is to presuppose that certain other things hold true of
one's subject. Moreover, practical considerations of orderliness and
unity dictate that in some places discussions must extend beyond the
strict limits imposed on this study. The remarks on the notion of historical truth in Chapter III is one such instance. Ultimately, I suppose, I must leave it to the critical reader to decide whether I have
taken matters far enough or too far.

The criteria of inclusion and exclusion peculiar to this study may
well lend it an air which is not intended. Modern analytic studies in
the philosophy of history have made great progress in their efforts to
understand and describe rather than to prescribe and dictate the nature
of history. In contrast to early works in the field, most recent work
has attempted to bridge perspectives precisely, I believe, to avoid unwarranted prescription. (The attempt, of course, does not guarantee
freedom from error, but it is the attempt which interests me at this
point.) Danto's *Analytic Philosophy of History* can claim roots in both
positivistic and ordinary language analysis. Dray's *Laws and Explanation in History* balances with adroitness a Collingwoodian humanistic
and rationalistic tendency with an appreciation of modern British analysis. Stover's intentionally pluralistic *The Nature of Historical
Thinking* attempts to understand both the standpoint of "natural order"
and that of "living in the world." Even Hempel's *Aspects of Scientific
Explanation*, a classic treatise generally taken as a paradigm of contemporary positivism, cannot fail to strike the attentive reader by its
willingness to consider seriously suggestions for alternatives to his
own point of view. Numerous other works could extend this list into a
critical bibliography. The feature which marks all of them is an attempt at balance, whether it be a balance of philosophic methods or a
balance of perspectives on the elements of history which their authors
take to be philosophically relevant.

By contrast, the present study may appear quite unbalanced by virtue of the fact that it takes one standpoint and operates at one level.

To reiterate, the restrictions imposed by the nature of the study yield an account of event and action language as related to history and permit one to draw implications for problems in the philosophy of history only from that account. Thus, it may be useful to note here that the narrowness of the study is not intended to foster the belief that its author holds his standpoint to be the only one proper or possible. Indeed, my sole claim would be that the standpoint employed is simply a useful one. Nor would I suggest that problems which are not mentioned are either unimportant problems or pseudo-problems. Again, my position would be that they are problems which fall outside the scope of materials upon which the present investigation allows intelligent comment. It is perhaps a worse fault to comment on everything simply because it is there to be commented upon than it is to be silent even where reasonable comment is possible.

Whether the claims which I have been concerned to make and justify by way of introducing the present work can in fact be justified will be a partial function of the case which the following chapters make. In addition, it will be a partial function of the willingness of the reader to accept, at least for the duration of the study, the presuppositions on which the study rests. The presuppositions lend themselves minimally to a bi-fold division: substantive assumptions and procedural presumptions. A word of comment may be in order about the main members of each group.

Primary among the substantive presuppositions is the view of philosophy which underlies the entire work. The philosophy of history is not itself history, despite the fact that various kinds of histories have been called philosophies of history. Today, it is common to speak of "speculative philosophy of history" to label histories which make use of overriding conceptions or theories within which to locate the events of the past. The works of Toynbee, Spengler, Hegel, *et al*. have well-earned the label. Within the present context, however, philosophy of history covers what has been called "analytic philosophy of history," in contrast to speculative philosophy of history. The range of considerations covered by the term "analytic" can be further delimited by noting that philosophy of history investigates matters of justification within history. The distinction made by Rudner and others between the context of justification and the context of discovery spells out well what I take to be the realm of relevant philosophic work.[8] Philosophy of history does not yield historical fact or speculation; that belongs to discovery, and discovery belongs to history proper. Philosophy of history instead investigates the structures of historical accounts and the structures of the means by which they come into existence; its aim is to find and formulate the "logic" of the activities which go into the production of historical accounts. Thus, it is the structure of justification with which this study is concerned.

Although this supposition may seem to be obviously appropriate, it has not been, and is not now, always adhered to by philosophers of history, even by those who appear to fall somewhere within the analytic tradition. Fain, for example, argues that "if one wishes to do philosophy of history in a proper way, one must lay aside one's historical prejudices." Something more than the analytic techniques of philosophy seems necessary to the philosophy of history because, as Fain would have it, "analytic philosophy of history seems to contain nothing but leftovers from the philosophy of science."[9]

Fain's comments are cogent only to the extent to which we are willing to associate with the philosophy of history one analytic approach or perhaps a small number of approaches, namely those associated with the philosophy of science. Then, we must define what can count as a justificational structure only in terms of those approaches. However, Fain's view breaks down if one is willing to divorce the concept of justification from some particular theory of justification. If we separate the concept from particular theories, it becomes possible to explore the question of justification by asking what will in some case in question constitute the validation of a given set of historical results. And we can ask the question without presupposing that either the answer must meet the terms of some theory or else the historical results shall be incapable of validation. It may be true that the most discussed form of justification (the covering law theory or theories of explanation) has been one in which the context of justification and the logic of science have been coincident, but the connection of the two is not *a priori* a necessary one.

The alternatives to allowing an investigation into the context of justification with respect to history without prior commitment to a theory of what sorts of things will count as justification are not very attractive. We can, of course, yield to a prior commitment, in which case Fain's criticism would seem compelling. We can, as well, turn to something other than the context of justification, e.g., to the context of discovery. If one interprets the context of discovery to include the products of the activities in which historians engage, one runs the danger of reducing philosophy to history. On the other hand, if one interprets the context of discovery to include the conditions of the historian which yield his product, one runs the risk of reducing philosophy to a variety of psychology. Given alternatives such as these, the option selected herein, i.e., treating the context of justification as a proper ground of philosophic investigation without *a priori* commitment to a theory of justification, appears to be the soundest.

Beyond this supposition, which determines the perspective and influences the method of this study, there are other substantive assumptions which underlie the work of the following chapters. First, I shall assume that occurrences of event and action assertions are numerous enough to constitute a significant part of historical activity. More controversial perhaps is a further assumption, namely, that the historian's assertions of present and past events and actions sufficiently resemble ordinary or non-historical assertions of present and past events and actions to allow an analysis of their nature which makes use of both historical and non-historical examples. For the initial stages

5

of this study, I shall hold for limited purposes that there is no essential difference between identical assertions to the effect that an
event E occurred at time t and place p when made by a historian on the
one side and by a non-historian on the other. In Chapter III the question of historical "evidence" will arise, and questions concerning the
difference between the historian and non-historian, if there is a difference, are best withheld until after consideration of that fundamental concept.

Finally, I shall assume without further ado that history is cog-
nitively significant, that it is a form of knowledge. In part, this
assumption is what enables one to explore history philosophically in
terms of a context of justification, for only if history has some cog-
nitive significance does mention of a context of justification become
sensible. Specifically, the assumption rejects any pervasive scepticism with respect to historical knowledge, cartesian, russellian, or
otherwise.[10] Rejection of a pervasive epistemic scepticism does not,
of course, rule out all scepticism, some forms of which may have a
vital utility. Fain seems to hit the point squarely when he writes,
"Skepticism about historical knowledge is useful when it manages to
arouse an interest in criteria of intelligibility of historical concepts."[11]

The terms of Fain's useful sort of scepticism, however, are better
met by the question, "How is historical knowledge possible?" than by
the question "Is historical knowledge possible?" The latter question
gives an appearance of completion with a simple "yes" or "no" answer;
moreover, it appears to force the inquirer to one of the two options.
The dangers of oversimplification inherent in this situation should be
obvious. The former question concerning the how of historical knowledge demands a different sort of account, one of both argument and
description. Furthermore, an inadequate account does not prejudice the
question of whether historical knowledge is possible at all, since the
inadequacy may lie either in the accountant or in the subject. It is
my impression that "how" questions, regarding this or any other philosophical matter, have always been much more productive, though far less
exciting and flamboyant, than "is it possible" questions. Anyone who
undertakes to answer a "how" question must nonetheless understand the
risk he takes, insofar as any such question presupposes that whatever
he deals with is possible.

The procedural presumptions of this study number three of note.
Mention of them may amount to needless omens as to style, but they appear worth noting at least briefly. First, the style throughout this
study is assertive, as befits what is intended to be an account which
describes and follows the implications of description. Nonetheless,
the intent of the whole is more to be suggestive than anything else.
Even the most rigorous of arguments, when viewed within the totality of
concerns to which it is and might be related, ultimately only suggests
for those who follow and might see some use for the argument.

Second, in accord with the exploratory nature of the questions which gave rise to this study, the style will be discursive rather than strictly argumentative. Many positions and assertions by past investigators have seemed to be nearly correct or to be correct but inadequately expressed when viewed from the perspective of this study. This has occasioned an exploration of those positions in conjunction with the exploration of the subject matter under study in each chapter. The aim of these dual studies is to find the relation of the positions to the subject matter, as well as to find a mode of formulation which does justice to both. Chapter III, in which Collingwood's conception of historical evidence for an event is explored together with the notion of criteria which justify the assertion of an event, provides a case in point: Collingwood's position needs explication and then juxtaposition with the conception of event and action language developed in Chapter I. Only after such a procedure is completed can the implications for the historical enterprise be adequately drawn.

Finally, and possibly because of the first two procedural presumptions, the approach to any given author may appear ambivalent, at once for and against his positions. This aspect of the study is intentional and paradoxically regrettable. The work of Dray, Walsh, Collingwood, and Danto, which appears prominently in the critical analysis of the various chapters, has contributed much to the philosophical study of history. The present inquiry might be interpreted as (in some small part) an attempt to preserve what is best in the relevant portions of their work. On the other side of the coin, the necessity of reformulating their positions from the standpoint of this study involves some critical stripping from the relevant positions those associations which are either antithetical or simply not germane to the work of this investigation. All this can be done, of course, without in the least affecting the validity of the work of each writer when given his or her own starting ground. Thus, the effect will be, on occasion, to leave the reader with the impression that criticism has occurred which fails to reach the heart of a philosophic position. And that is as it should be, since the intent throughout is not to undercut or destroy a position, but rather to use what it is possible to use from that position, necessarily reformed so as to be compatible with the essential elements of this study. The amount this study owes to the writers cited above and to others noted throughout the following chapters should not be underestimated.

These introductory pages have so far recorded the central subject and theme of this study, its criteria for the inclusion and exclusion of topics, and its operative presuppositions. With this perspective on the whole of the project, we can sketch in more detail what the individual chapters seek to accomplish.

I. The principle contention which underlies the entire study is that we have devoted insufficient analytic attention to the use of event and action concepts, despite the importance of their use in historical accounts. The first chapter focuses on event and action concepts in order to establish certain fundamental elements of analysis which will contribute to an understanding of the problems in the philosophy of history that are raised in succeeding chapters. Section one attempts to justify the proposed investigation by showing that the solution to certain problems in the philosophy of history in part rests upon an analysis of the use of event and action concepts. There is a potentially major hindrance to an analysis which is adequate to history: modeling the analysis of event and action concepts on the analysis of object concepts. The second section calls into question the application of notions like "whole-part," "classification," and "reference-description" to the analysis of event and action concepts in order to show in what ways the analysis of such concepts must differ from the analysis of object concepts. The proposed analysis of event and action concepts appears in section three. It is suggested that the warranted or justified use of event and action concepts rests upon the fulfillment of criteria. The association of a criteria set with a concept constitutes a linguistic convention in which the fulfillment of the criteria provides sufficient "grounds" for the use of the concept in factual assertions, although the criteria set does not provide a definition for the concept. In order to clarify the proposed analysis, section four distinguishes two ideas from ordinary uses of event and action concepts: one is the notion of a "conceptual proposal," which encompasses both the introduction of new concepts and the alteration of existing conventions; the other is the notion of a label which has a singular application. The final section, a sort of appendix, shows the sources of the major elements in the critical view of event and action concepts, especially those elements which derive from metaethical studies.

II. The sketch of the criterial view of the use of event and action concepts presented in the first chapter presumes that the relation between a concept and its criteria cannot be reduced to or adequately analyzed in terms of some other relation. Since the presumption is central to the treatment of issues in terms of the criterial conception of event and action language, the second chapter examines the possibilities for analyzing the criterial relation such that one may substitute for it a more traditional relation. After separating the questions of meaning and use for the purposes of this study, the chapter examines the following candidates for substitution: 1. definition, 2. reference and description, 3. classification, 4. wholes and parts, 5. sufficient conditions, 6. necessary conditions, 7. probability and induction, 8. hypothesis and evidence, 9. normic connection. In each case, the proposed analysans is found wanting in one or more respects. Nonetheless, the discussion will prove useful insofar as the contrasts it elicits between the criterial relation and the various candidates for substitution will informally precise and circumscribe the notion of conceptual criteria.

III. The most immediate application of the proposed criterial conception of event and action concepts ranges over certain uses in history of the notions of "evidence," "inference," and "truth." Be-

8

cause Collingwood's position on evidence and inference replicates within a different terminological framework the implications for these topics of a criterial view of language, his views can serve as a starting point for the explication. Besides noting agreements between Collingwood's position and the one proposed herein, the chapter also notes divergencies, e.g., on the notion of re-enactment. Specifically, the first section explicates Collingwood's view of history as an evidential and inferential activity. The second examines the relation between evidence and the facts inferred from evidence: Collingwood views the relation as essentially pragmatic, i.e., based upon an interrelationship between questions and the evidence which permits answers to them. In the third section, Collingwood's departure from his analysis of evidence and inference in order to embrace the theory of re-enactment is sketched in terms of three factors: a. his conception of history as a whole, continuous process, b. his theory of historical imagination by which one interpolates between known events to provide the whole, and c. his separation of what happened in the past within the special category of thought and what historians infer to have happened. Avoiding the theory of re-thinking, section four explores the coincidence (over a relevant class of cases) between the evidence-inferred relation and the criteria-concept relation for events and actions. The following section goes on to show that the realm of thought, which Collingwood had held to be distinct, may be treated in the same manner as the realm of events and actions, thus allowing one to dispense with re-enactment altogether. In this regard, two examples of Collingwood's re-thinking are re-analyzed as cases of "conceptual expectation" (to distinguish such cases from other forms of expectation). Collingwood's distinction between "certain" and "permissive" conclusions, noted briefly in the first section, opens the question of truth with respect to historical inferences. Section six outlines the implications of a criterial view of language for the conditions of truth of event and action assertions. One major consequence is that truth and falsity with respect to event and action assertions do not adhere to the principle of the excluded middle. The final section deals with the sense in which one can say that an entire history is true, specifically contrasting Collingwood's conception of history as a coherent whole with the application of the concept "plausibility" to historical writing.

IV. Three topics which bear too close a relationship for separate treatment form the core of the next chapter. The historian's selection of events for inclusion in his account and his purpose in writing a history have both been associated with the debate on the question of history's objectivity. Although farther removed from the starting point of this study than the subjects of Chapter Three, these topics find relevance to the extent that they involve consideration of conceptual proposals and of the interrelationship of question and method. The first section of the chapter traces the trends in the history of philosophy which lead to Dray's attempt to find a place for non-objectivity in history via the need in a purely descriptive history to select events with respect to their "intrinsic" importance. In the next section, I argue that the elements of non-objectivity which Dray in-

9

cludes in a descriptive or non-explanatory history as a result of the need in such a work to create unifying concepts belong to the context of the discovery or genesis of those concepts. Attention to the justification of these conceptual proposals provides grounds for a relevant possibility of objectivity. The third section explores the relation of purpose to objectivity. By distinguishing internal purposes (goals) from external purposes (uses) of history, one can separate those factors of historical use and abuse which are necessitated by historical method from those which follow contingently. The factors usually characterized as non-objective fall into the latter category. In the last section, positions which argue for history as non-objective by stressing the role of personal, subjective factors in the selection of events for historical accounts are rejected because of their dependence upon reference to personal facts and processes. Ignoring the interrelationship of method and purpose, they amount to genetic accounts of written histories rather than inquiries into the justification of those histories. Only in the latter context does the question of history's objectivity appropriately arise.

V. The present practice of history is marked by the widespread, if not predominant, use of the narrative form. The fifth and last chapter of this study attempts a contribution to the investigation of the narrative form in history by showing that narrative structures are generated by virtue of certain features of concepts and of statement forms. As a necessary preliminary, the first section of the chapter rejects three major theses which have from time to time been associated with historical narrative: a. that history is to be identified with narrative, b. that narrative and explanation have a necessary connection, and c. that a historical narrative must have a central subject. Separation of narrative form from the control of these theses provides freedom to explore narrative as a structure for a certain mode of discourse and to explicate elements of concepts and of sentence forms which supply what shall be called "narrative organization." Using and expanding upon suggestions made by Danto, sections two and three attempt to elicit the features of "past-referring terms," tensed sentences, "narrative sentences," and "temporal structures" which permit time progressiveness and continuity of content, the foundations of narratives. Since the "narrative-organizational structures" noted in these sections supply structural elements of narratives, but do not themselves amount to complete narratives, the fourth section attempts to distinguish among various relations which may occur within a narrative and which provide criteria for successful narratives. The relations to be distinguished include narrative consistency, the relation of non-narratively expressed facts to narrative-organizational structures; narrative congruency, the relation between two (or more) narrative-organizational structures; narrative unity, the relation of narrative-organizational structures to an entire narrative; and thematic unity, the relation of a narrative to a central theme or subject. One major consequence of delimiting the structural elements designated by the relationships mentioned in section four is that narratives need not be, nor need they contain, arguments. Insofar as argument is essential to

10

some pursuits in which historians engage, e.g., proving a thesis or illustrating a theme (not to mention certain forms of explanation), it becomes necessary to investigate the conditions of compatibility between narratives and arguments. The condition of compatibility, that there be produced or producible a series of statements narratively consistent with the story and argumentatively consistent with the operative mode of argument, suffices not only to establish a relation between narrative and argument, but as well to explicate the manner in which theses, morals, and arguments may be said to be drawn from narratives which do not themselves argue.

Two things are or should be obvious from the outline of the chapters to come. First, the cases made in Chapters Three through Five hinge upon the plausibility of the conception of language offered and defended in the first two chapters. Second, the nature of the work is philosophic rather than historical. There is for the working historian very little, if anything, which can in any way alter the day to day activities that constitute the doing of history. However, the fact that this study recommends itself to philosophers does not automatically entail that it does not lend itself to historians. The reason perhaps parallels the reason that a historical study intended for professional historians need not pass the philosopher's eyes unread and unappreciated. Beyond the appreciation of history that one might gain as an amateur, the work of history may also provide insight into problems in the philosophy of history without saying a word about them, but only by illustrating or exemplifying their solution (or their failure to be solved). Work upon the problems which make up the philosophy of history may not benefit from the reading of a hundred more histories, or it may benefit from reading just one more, or even a part of one. The historian in turn can benefit from the philosophy of history in perhaps the same proportion: a hundred may be wasted time; one may prove in some way useful to his understanding of his discipline. (This is not to claim that the present study is the useful one or even one of the useful ones.) What such studies do is not history, although their existence is dependent upon history. Nor is what they do a substitute for history. Russell was quite right to say that "there are things to be learnt from history,"[12] but I think we must add that not all of them are historical.

NOTES

[1]Arthur C. Danto, *Analytical Philosophy of History* (Cambridge: At the University Press, 1965), p. 19.

[2]Robert C. Stover, *The Nature of Historical Thinking* (Chapel Hill: University of North Carolina Press, 1967), p. ix.

[3]W. H. Walsh, *An Introduction to Philosophy of History* (London: Hutchinson University Library, 1958), pp. 31 ff.

[4]R. G. Collingwood, *The Idea of History* (New York: Oxford University Press, 1956), p. 9.

[5]Morris R. Cohen, *The Meaning of Human History* (La Salle, Ill.: The Open Court Publishing Co., 1961), p. 8.

[6]Philosophers and historians have not universally referred to events or actions in their descriptions of doing history. If one is impressed by Hegel's account of, say, Universal History, which shows "the development of the consciousness of Freedom on the part of Spirit," then one might well concern oneself with the role of "development" and related concepts in history. (Georg Wilhelm Friedrich Hegel, *The Philosophy of History*, trans. J. Sibree [New York: Dover Publications, Inc., 1956], p. 63.) Or, if one eyes Oakeshott's remark that "the historical past is a world of ideas, not a mere series of events. . . ," then one might seek out the role of coherence in history, or perhaps concentrate on what it is to be past. (Michael Oakeshott, *Experience and Its Modes* [Cambridge: At the University Press, 1933], p. 110.) In short, what one chooses to emphasize or what one comes to emphasize (with or without good reasons) does determine the subject and direction of his philosophical inquiry.

[7]These remarks do not indicate a commitment to any particular theory of explanation, and other notions of explanation which hinge upon single event assertions will be mentioned at appropriate places in the study.

[8]Richard S. Rudner, *Philosophy of Social Science* (Englewood Cliffs, New Jersey: Prentice-Hall, Inc., 1966), pp. 5 f.

[9]Haskell Fain, *Between Philosophy and History* (Princeton: Princeton University Press, 1970), p. 206. Cf. p. 216, where Fain says, ". . . speculative philosophers of history are preoccupied with the kinds of problems that cluster around the narrative aspect of history, whereas analytical philosophers of history are primarily interested in the establishment and explanation of historical facts and have naturally approached this matter with an eye to how facts are established and explained in science." The association of science and history with regard to establishing facts may be natural when taken as a phenomenon in the history of the philosophy of history, but it would take a separate argument to show the association to be logically "natural," i.e., logically necessary.

[10]René Descartes, *Discourse on Method*, trans. Laurence J. Lafleur (New York: Liberal Arts Press, 1956) Part I; Bertrand Russell, *The Analysis of Mind* (London: Macmillan and Company, 1921), pp. 159 f; see Fain, *Between Philosophy and History*, pp. 133 ff. and all of Chapters VII and VIII and see Danto, *Analytical Philosophy of History*, pp. 76 ff. and all of Chapter V for extensive treatments of the question of scepticism.

[11]Fain, *Between Philosophy and History*, p. 138.

[12]Bertrand Russell, *Understanding History* (New York: Philosophical Library, 1957), p. 17.

CHAPTER ONE

Event Concepts and Criteria

The principle contention which underlies the entire
study is that we have devoted insufficient analytic attention
to the use of event and action concepts, despite the importance of their use in historical accounts. The first
chapter focuses on event and action concepts in order to
establish certain fundamental elements of analysis which
will contribute to an understanding of the problems in the
philosophy of history that are raised in succeeding chapters.
Section one attempts to justify the proposed investigation
by showing that the solution to certain problems in the
philosophy of history in part rests upon an analysis of the
use of event and action concepts. There is a potential
hindrance to an analysis which is adequate to history:
modeling the analysis of event and action concepts on the
analysis of object concepts. The second section calls into
question the application of notions like "whole-part,"
"classification," and "reference-description" to the analysis
of event and action concepts in order to show in what ways
the analysis of such concepts must differ from the analysis
of object concepts. The proposed analysis of event and
action concepts appears in section three. It is suggested
that the warranted or justified use of event and action
concepts rests upon the fulfillment of criteria. The
association of a criteria set with a concept constitutes
a linguistic convention in which the fulfillment of the
criteria provides sufficient "grounds" for the use of the
concept in factual assertions, although the criteria set
does not provide a definition for the concept. In order
to clarify the proposed analysis, section four distinguishes
two ideas from ordinary uses of event and action concepts:
one is the notion of a "conceptual proposal," which encompasses both the introduction of new concepts and the alteration of existing conventions; the other is the notion of a
label which has singular application. The final section,
a sort of appendix, shows the sources of the major elements
in the criterial view of event and action concepts,
especially those elements which derive from metaethical
studies.

The main contention of this study is that philosophers have paid
insufficient attention to event and action concepts as they are used by
historians. Those who attempt to investigate, set, and solve the

issues which collectively bear the label "philosophy of history" can hardly avoid dealing with and making use of event and action concepts. Yet, it appears to be the case that philosophers of history have concentrated their attention upon subjects other than event and action concepts. They have attempted to construct theories of explanation of past events and assumed that the notion of an event was clear enough to allow them to confine their attention to the notion of an explanation. Others have inquired into what it is for an event to be past, and again they have concerned themselves little for what it was for an event to be an event. There are many topics within the philosophy of history which presuppose the notion of events or actions; yet few philosophers of history have made any effort to inquire into the nature of event and action concepts.

The burden of this study will be to see what implications (if any) the nature of event and action concepts has for history, specifically for certain problems within the philosophy of history. As the means to that end, this first chapter (and in part the next) will attempt to clarify the use of event and action concepts within the context of historical accounts. These contexts are similar enough to ordinary contexts to permit the use of both historical and non-historical examples. (By "ordinary contexts" I mean simply those contexts which do not belong to one or another discipline. We may also call them conversational contexts or contexts of everyday life.) The clarification will consist of an attempt to describe adequately what I take to be the essential features of the use of event and action concepts. An adequate description will be one which both describes accurately and distinguishes what is described from other sorts of things with which what is described may be confused. The essential features of the use of event and action concepts will be those features which I take to be important with respect to the selected problems in the philosophy of history for which the features may have implications.

The last point, that essential features are stipulated to be those having a relation to the problems which give rise to the inquiry into the use of event and action concepts, bears an element of circularity. The circularity, however, is far from fatal. Rather, it circumscribes the limits of this study. I shall not claim to have produced a complete analysis of event and action concepts, and likewise, I shall not claim to have solved or even investigated all the issues in the philosophy of history. Not every facet of the use of event and action concepts is relevant to problems in the philosophy of history, nor is the solution of every problem connected with history dependent on a prior analysis of event and action concepts. Nonetheless, the interrelationship between the analysis of event and action concepts and the particular issues of the historical enterprise chosen for study does not relieve this investigation of the requirement that its outcome must be consistent with the most reliable facts and the most cogent theories which lie outside its borders.

Within the confines of this study, the interrelationship between the analysis and the problems does make the choice of starting points somewhat arbitrary. One could choose to examine critically the problems of the philosophy of history and then to show how a certain conception of the use of event and action concepts allows one to solve (or dissolve) those problems. For this investigation, I have chosen the opposite procedure. In this chapter, I shall set out a conception of event and action language. In succeeding chapters, I shall attempt to vindicate the particular conception elaborated by showing how it bears upon certain topics in the philosophic study of history. Here at the outset I shall restrict myself to showing that certain problems in the corpus of issues which make up the philosophy of history are dependent upon an analysis of the use of event and action concepts and to a preliminary characterization of what I mean by "the use of event and action concepts."

I. Event Concepts and Problems in the Philosophy of History

The following appear to be typical of statements appearing in historical accounts, despite the fact that they are taken from one of the earliest historians.

a. After dark . . . there was a very violent rainstorm. . . .[1]

b. Aristides accordingly went in and made his report. . . .[2]

Notice that, even though the statements are abbreviated from their original form, they still must be classified as complex event and action assertions, respectively. Omitting the complexities--"after dark" in a. and "accordingly" in b.--the statements represent examples of the use of event and action concepts by a historian. Sentence a. asserts the occurrence of an event, a rainstorm, by the use of the concept "rainstorm"; sentence b. asserts that Aristides performed two actions, a going in and a reporting, by the use of appropriate forms of the relevant concepts.

In speaking of the use of an event or action concept, I have not attempted to distinguish the notion of a "concept" from the notion of a "word" as it might occur in a phrase such as "the use of an event or action word." The use of "word" rather than "concept" would be open to several objections, similar to those which gave rise to the notion of "proposition" in logic as preferable to "sentence." Just as two sentences (or phrases) may be used to express the same proposition, so too may two words be used to express the same concept. Synonyms (which are determined to be synonyms within a given context) represent an obvious case. In a less obvious case, given a suitable context, "John ran through the streets" may be equivalent to "John sped on foot through the streets"; in this case "ran" and "sped on foot" may be taken to express the same concept. Moreover, just as the same sentence used by different speakers on different occasions may express different propositions, so too a single word used in different assertions may express different concepts. Ordinary language analysis has devoted much effort to distinguishing among multiple uses and to tracing down the allowable inferences of each use.

Despite these qualifications, it makes no difference in many instances whether one speaks of the use of a word or the use of a concept. If one remains cognizant of the dangers of ignoring the qualifications, no difficulties for the present investigation will ensue. Moreover, treating "word" and "concept" as interchangeable under these restricted circumstances permits one to avoid the unnecessary and speculative question of what a concept is if not a word. I can think of few circumstances in which the question could arise, and the present study is not one of them. It is sufficient to note that within the language there are event and action concepts and that they may be used in factual assertions to the effect that a certain event or action occurred. The central question for this investigation concerns the nature and justification of precisely this sort of use. History is, at least in part, a discipline which attempts to make factual assertions to the effect that certain events and actions occurred, and on this ground alone, the central inquiry of this study would be justified. Nonetheless, it is possible to show that there are specific issues and problems within the philosophy of history the solutions to which rest on a prior analysis of the nature and justification of the use of event and action concepts in historical assertions.

The range of potential problems in the philosophy of history which one might use to warrant the investigation into event and action concepts may extend well beyond those sketched below. Only those which occasioned this specific study will be mentioned. Moreover, the treatment of them in this section intentionally avoids specific criticism of any philosophic position. Instead, the brief sketches aim only to establish the relationship of the problems to the question of the use of event and action concepts.

Foremost among the problems is the nature of historical evidence. Most treatments of historical evidence have been confined to generalities concerning either the necessity of basing historical assertions upon it or the categories of items which make up the totality of what historians use as evidence.[3] Little work has been done on the question of the relation of evidential items to the facts asserted on their basis, except perhaps as that relation bears on the question of the past: the events are asserted to have occurred in the past but the evidence used to justify the assertion is in the present.[4] Concerning the specific sort of relation which exists between the types of items used as evidence and the types of things asserted, hardly any discussion exists.

If I am correct in taking statements a. and b. above as typical of the sorts of assertions a historian makes, then what he asserts is at least in part the occurrence of events and actions. Such assertions necessarily make use of event and action concepts. It would seem plausible that an inquiry into the justification of the use of event and action concepts in factual assertions would provide, if not the key, at least a clue to the relation which holds between evidential items and the assertions of the occurrence of events and actions which are based upon those items. Moreover, inquiry into the justification of event and action assertions should also supply some clue as to the grounds upon which such statements can be said to be true. To the extent that a historian wishes to make true statements and to the extent that the statements he does make assert the occurrence of events and action, the inquiry into the justification of event and action assertions would seem to be a necessary condition of understanding at least one relevant sense of historical truth. Analyses of historical evidence and truth which do not first examine the nature and justification of the use of event and action concepts run the risk of presupposing an inaccurate account of the use of these concepts.

A similar case can be made that any solution to the question of historical objectivity depends upon an inquiry into the use of event and action concepts. Generally, however, essays on historical objectivity have concentrated on other matters. Some have dwelt upon human fault, whether accidental or endemic.[5] Others have insisted upon comparing certain general features of history to features of the sciences or other disciplines and activities.[6] It is true, on the other hand, that some studies have attempted to eschew psychologistic, epistemic, and comparative approaches in favor of a methodological approach confined wholly to an examination of history. Thus have arisen the attempts to link the question of objectivity to the historian's selection of events for his account and to the aims of history.[7] What may be needed is one further step.

The aims of history and the selection of events for a historical account are linked to the extent that the events selected for use in an account will be those which in some sense further the aims set for the entire account. Therefore, one might ordinarily approach both the questions of aims and of selection from the point of view of the whole, i.e., by seeing the sorts of aims historians might have. However, any selection of events must be restricted by the events from which one *can* select, by the combinations that can be used in furtherance of an aim, and by any restrictions which may be imposed in virtue of the nature of the justification of the assertions that the events in question occurred. Consequently, an inquiry into the nature and the justification of the use of event concepts would appear to be a precondition to formulating correctly and adequately the conditions of selection and thereby the conditions of objectivity.

Even more direct is the dependency of the analysis of historical narrative on the inquiry into the use of event and action concepts. Analyses of historical narratives have primarily concentrated on the gross features of narratives.[8] The unity of narratives and their func-

tion to tell stories are among the most noted features. A unified narrative which tells a story, however, amounts in part to a sequence of
events and actions which are asserted to have occurred, and further
asserted to be related in certain ways. To the extent that assertions
of events and actions constitute an essential part of a narrative, the
analysis of narratives depends directly upon the analysis of the use of
event and action concepts. Any analysis of historical narratives which
ignores the investigation of the use of event and action concepts runs
the risk of error or distortion in ascribing structural features to the
narrative.

These brief arguments, designed to show at least in outline the
dependency of certain problems in the philosophy of history on the
analysis of the use of event and action concepts, presuppose too much
to be truly effective. They suppose, for one thing, that the reader
views the problems cited from the same perspective and with the same
familiarity as the author, and only accidentally can this be the case.
If the argument sketches perform any useful function, it is perhaps
only to convince one that there are good reasons for examining the use
of event and action concepts. The nature and extent of those reasons
will appear in detail within the chapters of this study devoted to each
specific issue. For the present, the best course may be to concentrate
upon event and action concepts and upon their analysis.

II. Event and Object Concepts

The particular conception of the use of event and action concepts
which this study will explore arose and gained its initial plausibility
in consequence of certain difficulties which have characterized past
treatment of event and action concepts. The root difficulty centers
around the fact that theorists, consciously or unconsciously, have
treated event concepts either on an object model or in object terminology.

Nagel, for example, rejects the idea that Rickert's individualistic historical concepts could increase simultaneously in both scope and
richness of meaning unless that increase amounted to a whole-part relation rather than to a linguistic relation of extension and intension.[9]
However, the relation of the so-called parts to the so-called whole
seems to shift when one moves from objects to events. A window is a
physical part of a house, one which it may or may not have. The overthrow of a government, while not encompassing all that goes into a
revolution, seems part and parcel to be the revolution. Without an
overthrow of government, we might still have a revolution, though we
should want to know on what grounds we could call whatever occurred a
revolution. At the same time, we would hesitate to say the overthrow
of government is a condition for a revolution. First, one might allow
the possibility of either without the other. Second, we should need an
explanation of in what sense overthrow is a condition. Unlike the case
of machines, wherein the loss of a part raises questions of operation,

18

the loss of an event's "part" raises the question of justifying the use of a concept.

The Dray-Walsh notion of colligation provides another example of concept treatment which prompts a total re-examination of events. Walsh, in his own account of the generalizing feature of colligation, stresses the teleological relation to be found among historical events. Just this inner relation supposedly permits the colligation of events under concepts of policies, plans, purposes, and movements. In fact as in narrative, events are related by one or more "dominant ideas" which make them intelligible.[10]

Walsh's suggestions raise serious questions regarding the notion of an inner connection or relation. One may grant an internal as opposed to an external relation to actions; which is to say, one better characterizes the relation between a plan's goal and the steps of the plan as analytic rather than empirical. Not a law or an inductive generalization, but in some sense the meaning of "plan" itself makes automatic the move from speaking of a goal to speaking of steps toward it or from speaking of steps to speaking of a goal. Insofar as plans have goals, no harm accrues from calling this class of concepts teleological. However, many of the concepts Walsh deems relevant to colligation have no goal and no steps. A renaissance is a movement with direction (an ever increasing interest, say, in art) but without goal, i.e., without some point at which one can say that one has arrived and that the movement need go no farther. Social institutions and mores can have goals, but unlike the goals of plans, fulfilling them does not terminate activity. Should a university seek to provide a liberal education, one class of liberally educated graduates does not end the university's educating activities in the way that success in achieving the goal of conquering Europe would necessarily terminate conquest-of-Europe activities. In consequence of examples like these, seeing an internal relation as inner, that is, inherent in events themselves, may involve a confusion between the characteristics of events and what events acquire by virtue of conceptualization. There seems nothing *a priori* and outside some one or another context of. assertion to force one logically either to see an act as simply an act of a particular sort or to see it as part of something else, e.g., a plan, policy, or movement. If the so-called teleological relation does not carry the weight of necessity, then one must investigate further, and perhaps elsewhere, to find the nature of the relation between the acts and the plan for which they are steps.

Dray's account broadens the scope of colligation. The historian, Dray suggests, reorganizes, synthesizes, and, especially, classifies when he sees "a collection of happenings or conditions" as amounting to an event of a certain higher order.[11] What sort of classification colligation accomplishes remains dim. At the lowest level, to apply any concept at all is to classify, insofar as the application links the present case to others warranting the application of the same concept. Beyond the fact of using the same word, nothing in the case so far legislates how the classification occurs. Since the collection of happenings consists of "x, y, and z," that is, a number of disparate and separately characterized events, the notions of genus and species disappear into irrelevancy. Dray's own example from Ramsey Muir, that the enclosure of agricultural lands, the beginnings of industrial production, and improvements in communication and transportation amount to a "social revolution,"[12] reveals the disparity of kinds of events and thus the inappropriateness of calling "social revolution" a genus. Yet, the suggestion that the colligatory relation is one of wholes and parts suffers the same doubts it encountered in Nagel's problem. Indeed, the notion of part-whole has so many uses--physical position, function, temporal order, just to begin with objects--that it cannot help but to raise rather than to answer questions. If enclosure acts are part of a revolution, then one may still relevantly ask how the parts relate to the whole. Such a question simply repeats the earlier request for the relation between the events colligated and the colligatory concept.

Moreover, Dray lays great stress upon innovative cases of colligation, cases in which a historian uses metaphors and analogies to create new classifications and organizations.[13] Such a stress leads one to think of historical labels, such as "The Renaissance," with all their suggestive power. But labels, like brand names, while suggesting their contents, do not necessarily refer to them either directly or indirectly. For all the desire one may have that a given label, historical or otherwise, identify what it labels, it does its work so long as it minimally allows one to distinguish the labeled item from others. Concept status requires more than this. But, how much more in part depends upon what relation the events cites as "x, y, and z" have to the concept applied to them. Precisely this question Dray leaves open. That colligation applies equally in Dray's account to "The Renaissance" and to "social revolution" implies at least that the notion of colligation does not constitute a finished or even a nearly finished analysis of historical concepts.[14]

One more example may go farther in raising doubts about trying to handle event language in terms of object categories. In most modern formulations of logics capable of treating objects, one encounters expressions of the order "There exists an x such that x is. . . ." For many theoretical purposes, such expressions hold no danger. However, when such expressions carry over from logical theory into the philosophy of history, dangers abound. If we let E be an event, then we may speak of descriptions and redescriptions of E, and perhaps, with Danto, of "rules of redescription."[15] Such expressions presuppose that "E" denotes something for the description or redescription to be of, a supposition seemingly harmless with objects, but awe-inspiring with events. Notes Danto, "phenomena *as such* are not explained. It is only phenomena as covered by a description which are capable of explanation."[16] Although Danto correctly relates explanation to the concepts in terms of which one asserts the occurrence of an event, one may question his supposition that there are two things:

20

a. the event/phenomenon/action and b. the event/phenomenon/action-covered-by-a-description.

Description and reference take on dark shadows of vagueness when applied to events. A policeman asks witnesses, "what happened?" (For surely "something" happened.) A replies, "There was a tragic accident." B says, "The black sedan ran a red light." C offers, "A lot of good metal turned into scrap." (Bearded C always was a bit of a poet and trouble-maker.) If we take Danto and others like him seriously, we may want to say that they all saw the same thing, as if "the same thing" carried the force it has when we apply it to cases such as this one: A says "I see the pigskin," and B notes, "I see the inflated, egg-shaped, leather-covered ball," and C remarks, "I see the football." Any difference between the event and object cases popular accounts usually ascribe to the complexity of the former. Or they put the problem of witnessing events, like seeing beauty, in the more than metaphorical eye of the beholder. Between complexity and subjectivity, many a soluble problem has disappeared into mystery. In the object case, however, for all three witnesses to have seen the same thing requires one or more identifiable features common to the perception of all the speakers. That is, "inflated, egg-shaped, leather-covered ball," "pigskin," and "football" are analytically related for the given context. In the event case, the policeman's problem is that running a red light, turning metal into scrap, and being a tragic accident are not analytically related. There is no common subject or item having definable qualities such that the notion of "analyticity" (or its correlate "syntheticity") can find application.

Consequently, if the twin notions of reference and description apply at all to event and action concepts, they apply only after some assertion of a particular event's occurrence has been made. Once one has said, "An accident occurred at Main and Broad," then one can refer to the accident and describe it as tragic. Prior to the original assertion, the common request to *describe* what happened amounts only to the request to tell or say what happened; it is a request for the assertion of one or more events. Fain appears to be making a similar point when he notes, "One's knowledge *that* something took place often supposes a knowledge of what it was that took place."[17] That Fain is not willing to make a universal statement seems to stem from the fact that on occasion we are in a position of speechlessness; we know something happened but we cannot say what or are unwilling to say what. (These cases do not render my argument unsound, because they are not to be explained by reference to an indescribable E; rather, we must note that in all such cases we can say something. For example, we can say moment by moment what occurred. What we cannot say is what happened such that the event or action concept used will encompass the entire time span.) Nonetheless, it remains the case that reference and description occur only after one has an event to which one can refer and which one can describe.

This account, of course, presents a logical priority; the language itself allows, if it does not encourage, blending both assertion and further description in a single assertion. One might well say, "The accident at Main and Broad was tragic," or, "A tragic accident occurred," in answer to the question, "What happened?" Following initial assertions, descriptions and references applicable to one asserted event may not be applicable to another. Descriptions, for example, which fit an accident may prove inapt to running a red light.

Is the accident, then, a different event from running the red light? Are they the same event? Or parts of a single event? Or perspectives on an event? Such questions contain philosophical traps to the extent that they seemingly provide phenomenal levers by which to raise the problem to metaphysical heights. Running a red light and turning metal into scrap may be said to refer to the same accident in a suit brought to court by an insurance company. In traffic court, where the purpose may be only to determine a traffic violation and to assess responsibility for the accident, talk of scrap metal might be disallowed. The concern resides with the accident and its causes, not with its results, which "are another matter." Thus, the notions of "same" and "different," of "whole" and "part," of "perspectives" appear to derive their sense and applicability more from the context within which and purpose for which questions and statements occasioning their use might arise than they do from some common referent. Put another way, nothing prior to the assertion of an event provides the necessary constancy of reference to warrant the notation "E" or to give univocal meaning to "same," "different," etc.

Similar problems arise as soon as one begins to probe the traditional difficulty of trying to define event concepts. Definition has so long proven to be such a trying task that hardly anyone dares mention it nowadays. Attempts at ostensive definition leave us flailing the air in search of something to end the line begun at our fingers. Dictionaries devote more space to examples than to definitions. Events and actions admit so many exceptions that Aristotelian definitions *per genus et differentia* consist seemingly of qualifications alone. We routinely get by with calling murder a species of killing and political revolutions a species of revolution, but we never try examples like "running" (too many genuses?), "renaissance" (too few or none?) or "reclamation" (?).

What plagues attempts to define event concepts parallels what shatters attempts to apply the notation of object-relevant logical theory to events. Fickle events and actions lack the constancy of reference to stand clearly delineated univocal definition or even clearly differentiated multivocal definition. The problem is not that we cannot find something to supply a referent for a primary as opposed to a secondary meaning of an event word, but rather that the absence of reference prior to the use of an event word prevents any relevant application for the word "meaning" at all. Not that event, action, and related words are meaningless; they have meaning and are used meaning-

22

fully. However, so long as meaning carries with it the burden of definition, event words defy all attempts at adequate analysis.

Such considerations as these suggest strongly that as long as object language and any logical system or terminology successfully applied to it remain the operative categories within which to treat event words, little if any progress on issues involving events can occur. What such issues need is a conception of event and action language which will provide a conceptual foundation for understanding historical activities without introducing either unpalatable distortions or subjective mysteries. The following pages are an attempt to provide at least the beginnings of such a conception.

III. Criteria and the Justified Use of Event Concepts

Fundamental to the conception which will meet the needs outlined above is the notion of criteria. In explicating his conception of "explaining what," Dray coined the formula "x, y and z amount to a Q."[18] The formula comes close to expressing precisely the criterial relation wherein "x, y, and z" constitute linguistic criteria, the fulfillment of what warrants the asertive or factual use of the concept "Q". Dray's formula, then, also amounts to a linguistic convention, where "convention" has the sense of a non-arbitrary but changeable rule of language. Because conventions rarely come in for formal statement, that is, we have no rule book--not even the dictionary--in which to find expressly given rules, all statements about conventions run the risk of exception and incompleteness. Nevertheless, features general to most of the classes of concepts to which the present conception applies can be noted.

For example, the criteria which warrant the use of a concept tend to vary with the context of use. The violent overthrow of government, as a criterion for political revolution, seems relevant in cases such as France or America. However, the level of violence and its nature in these cases cast serious doubts on its relevance to certain cases of revolution in South America. Consequently, criteria for concept uses find themselves clustered in sets, each set relevantly used in one or more contexts. One should not take the notion of criteria in too formal or even serious a manner, i.e., in support of the idea that one could enumerate and demarcate sets and their contexts in a final way and prior to questions concerning a particular instance of concept use. The notion of criteria set has its most proper application in cases where one would germanely distinguish one context from another and thus one set of relevant criteria from another--as in the case of distinguishing the French from certain Latin American revolutions.

Criteria sets and contexts very often show no clear boundaries. Sometimes, criteria within sets overlap in the fasion of set A containing x, y, and z, set B w, x, and y, set C v, w, and y, etc. Thus, we may call a woman vain who spends hours before her mirror preening her hair, and we may call a man vain who spends much time adjusting his clothing prior to a public appearance. These cases overlap to the extent of involving the expenditure of time (better spent elsewhere) upon personal appearance, but they also contain significant differences. In addition, what count as criteria, as in these cases, coincide not merely with physical facts, but also with social mores and other rule governed aspects of behavior and action. The cessation of wearing clothing or the institution of fashionable baldness would preclude the use of the term vanity on the grounds given in the example. Of course, not just social mores may condition the criteria for a concept's use. Discovery, innovation, technical development and other factors all play a role in establishing the criteria set or sets relevant to particular contexts. The very occurrence of new contexts themselves may influence the use of concepts, with or without conscious effort or decision on the part of the users.

In ascertaining the relevant criteria set, one must attend not only to the context of use, but also to the purpose for which a factual assertion is made. The multiplicity of possible criteria sets rests not only upon the number of contexts in which one may relevantly use a concept, but as well on the number of purposes one may have in using the concept. A maid enters her mistress's room and sees a bloody knife, a punctured, bloody corpse, and a room disordered by struggle. Her telephoned assertion of murder to the police is justified, even if the police find it was all a hoax made of ketchup and a store window dummy. The criteria applicable to the assertion of murder by the police not only differ from those applicable to the maid, they differ for various police purposes. The criteria set which justifies the cop on the beat's asserting to the homicide squad that a murder occurred at a certain address (the maid's) varies from that required to justify a request for an indictment against a person. Motive, for instance, plays an important role in the latter case, but is generally irrelevant to the former. Sherlock Holmes often used the concept "plan" on the basis of a series of events. Scotland Yard rarely disputed these assertions, but denied their utility. However, Holmes' purpose was usually to prevent a crime, whereas the Yard stuck to apprehending criminals. The differences of purposes here determined both the criteria set and the concepts used in factual assertions. Of course, one may subsume the notion of purpose under the rubric of context, but to the extent that the latter term sometimes fails to get us beyond the conditions in which an assertion occurs, separate attention to the purpose of an assertion becomes useful.

The expression "the factual or assertive use of a concept" is not intended to focus upon event, action, or other similar concepts to the exclusion of facts which one may use them to assert or assertions which express facts. It makes little difference whether one takes as his unit of analysis the concept as used, e.g., the concept of "crossing a river" in "Caesar crossed the Rubicon," or some assertion of the form "A river crossing occurred." The Caesar statement presupposes in a Strawsonian fashion the warrant of the river-crossing assertion on appropriate grounds, which is also to say that the use of the concept "crossing a river" is warranted in the Caesar statement. Indeed, to argue that one should take apart the assertion "Caesar crossed the Rubicon" to get a collection of assertions, such as "there existed a man named Caesar," "there existed a river called the Rubicon," "a river crossing occurred," "the crosser was Caesar," "the river crossed was the Rubicon," is at once to note the relevant cases of concept use and to note the facts that a historian might question in appropriate contexts, namely, those in which he has sensible doubts about the fulfillment of criteria. In short, the historian's assertion of fact amounts to no more or less than his use of a concept in a given context on the warrant given by fulfilled criteria.

That historical fact often amounts to the warranted use of an event or action concept in an assertion in no way reduces any part of the historian's task to a matter of linguistics (and certainly not to a *mere* matter of linguistics). The fulfillment of criteria which give warrant to the use of an event or action concept is an empirical task. The historian, or anyone else using event or action concepts to assert facts, must see that the criteria warranting a certain use, warranting a certain assertion are fulfilled. If Becker's claim, that every historical "fact" really sums up a myriad of others,[19] has any credibility, it lies within a sense commensurate with this analysis.

The notion of criteria, while not altering the historian's task, does aid in understanding many of the areas of potential and actual historical debate. Even where non-controversial concepts come into play, several grounds for contest may exist. A historian may argue against another that one or more criteria are not fulfilled and that consequently a certain assertion lacks justification. For example, he might argue that since no government was overthrown, no revolution occurred, despite a change in leadership and policy. Should such an argument be applied to a Latin American revolution, the historian against whom the argument is raised might reply that the violent overthrow of government is irrelevant or not a criterion in the given context. His antagonist had based his argument on applying a criteria set in the wrong context (or a wrong criteria set in the context).

Arguments to the effect that cited facts do not fulfill the criteria for an assertion often take on an air of great subtlety. For example, the records of Hitler's build-up of armed and naval forces, his diplomatic and military maneuvers in Austria and Czechoslovakia, his *blitzkrieg* in Poland, and his writings, especially *Mein Kampf*, might in the hands of some historians count as the justification for the assertion of a Nazi plan to conquer Europe.[20] Then there enters an A. J. P. Taylor who argues that, if we take the assertion of a plan seriously (i.e., as more than an ideal, a hope, a dream), then we must conclude that Hitler did not so much plan to conquer Europe as he fell inevitably and step by step into doing so.[21] Hitler's maneuvers and other activities count for both claims: the only genuine plans, however, were not the loose sorts of assertions in *Mein Kampf*, but just war college plans commonly produced in all western European nations. Taylor's claim thus amounts to a denial that the facts sufficiently warrant the use of the concept "plan" in the present case.

Because debate often rests, not on all the members of a criteria set, but on one, the temptation arises to believe that the crucial fact alone constitutes a sufficient ground for the assertion in question. The next easy step would be to define the questioned concept in terms of the crucial criterion, and the object mode of handling events and actions would have crept back into play. Criteria, as such, are neither qualities nor conditions of events. The fulfillment of criteria constitute sufficient grounds for the use of a concept, where sufficiency is judged by reference to a convention.

The expression "sufficient grounds" seems better to characterize the relation between criteria fulfillment and concept use than does the expression "sufficient conditions," especially in view of the conventional nature of the warrant which is provided for a given use. Linguistic conventions amount to rules of practice rather than to laws of uniform action, and as such are rarely verbalized. In historical as well as in other writing, one uses event and action concepts for the most part without justification. Only when a use is questioned or when an issue hangs critically in the balance does the writer or speaker begin to explore his justification for an assertion. Broadly speaking, he has mastered his language and uses it naturally, that is, without concern for justifying any particular parts of it except those matters of decision subject to active debate or question. Consequently, early attempts to fend off critical questions concerning one's assertions usually founder, go around in circles, and otherwise skirt the issue until the parties of a debate can elicit the context and criteria specifications necessary to the disposal of the question. The furor raised over Toynbee's challenge-response thesis, far too long for reproduction and too complex for exemplar summarization, can be instructive with respect to the amount of flapping and flogging which occurs while the opposing sides slowly refine the exact terms of an issue.

That one can elicit those elements of criteria and context which suffice to settle disputes does not imply that one needs to or can produce an entire criteria set. The examples used to illustrate the notion of criteria often mislead to the extent of suggesting, openly or tacitly, that the given list of items represents the full convention. Alston, in his treatment of the conditions for various word uses, leaves the impression of having generated complete lists.[22] Any list, however, is incomplete. The very use of the term "context" suggests this fact. For just as the distinction between cause and condition rests on the pragmatic grounds of particular cases calling for explanation, so too the distinction between criteria and context leans upon the kinds of questions raised with respect to a particular assertion. One man's criteria may become another's context, not according to taste, but by virtue of the justification required in a given situation. Questions concerning the enclosure of lands in relation to

26

Muir's assertion of a social revolution may not call for the mention of improvements in communications and transportation, while questions about the beginnings of industrial production may necessitate the mention of those improvements. Still other questions, perhaps concerning the implicit migration of the labor force, may involve all three and still others. Nevertheless, although no criteria set achieves theoretical completeness, criteria sets can and do attain in practive relevant completeness, i.e., they contain the elements necessary to the solution of a given problem. Conceptual debates demand for their resolution only the latter sort of completeness. Insofar as a specification of further criteria would not contribute to deciding a given issue, such a specification—even carried to the point of theoretical completeness—would remain a superfluous and pointless achievement.

Many times, conceptual debates do not achieve a resolution, but instead reach only a standoff. One important sort of impasse results from the use of what Gallie has termed "essentially contested concepts."[23] With concepts like "champion," "art," "democracy," we seem, for one vested interest or another, unable to agree upon criteria of application. We can agree, perhaps, that should one set be used, government X is a democracy; should another set be used, government X is not. Disagreement continues over which set of criteria should be used. At this point another kind and level of supporting reasons comes into play, reasons which may include the consequences of referring to or classifying the government in question as a democracy. The standoff reached in debates such as this one does not preclude the use of essentially contested terms in historical narratives. To the extent that history can be regarded as a rational pursuit open to germane argumentation, the use of essentially contested concepts only demands recognition of the criteria upon which a given use leans for warrant and the reasons for selecting the one criteria set over others. Given an impasse with respect to contested concepts, productive argument can only concern the supporting reasons for the contending criteria sets; anything else amounts to challenge or rhetoric. Insofar as this sort of situation does permit the recognition of its nature and demands, however much verbal brickbats may attempt to obscure them, its existence deals no low blows to history's objectivity. Nonetheless, as a later part of this study will explore, claims for history's value-ladenness or subjectivity rely in large measure on such unresolvable issues for their plausibility. The bellowing of wounded historians adds a convincing touch to conceal the objectivity of which history is capable, as distinct from the objectivity to which historians display a willingness to adhere.

Another case of multi-tiered argumentation may occur whenever one critically justified assertion rests on another. For example, suppose that the relevant criteria for the assertion of the occurrence of a revolution includes the replacement of one ruling group with another. Further suppose that the name and aims of the ruling group change during other sorts of events that go into making a revolution. One historian might argue that the changes warrant the assertion that there is a new ruling group and that it, along with the remaining facts, warrant the assertion of an occurrence of a revolution. An opposing historian may reply that, although the name and aim of the group had changed, the personnel of the ruling group remained significantly constant, perhaps belying a greater concern on their part for personal power than for ideology. Thus, he would conclude, the ruling group had not changed, and no genuine revolution took place; that is, one has no warrant for asserting that there was a change in the ruling group and therefore none for asserting that there was a revolution. For want of a nail a kingdom was lost, and many a historian has felt the chagrin of its paraphrase: for want of an ever so minor fact, the thesis was lost.

The existence of multi-level arguments involving criteria and the criteria of criteria effectively blocks any attempt to apply to events the object relevant categories of definition and description. Criteria neither define nor describe the events whose assertion they warrant. Event concepts might even be called ascriptive (but for the lack of anything to which one may ascribe them) rather than descriptive, since criterial events, objects, and conditions (i.e. the events, objects, and conditions which fulfill criteria) do not equate with the concept used on the warrant they supply. Moreover, what follows from the use of a concept does not follow from the assertion alone of facts which would fulfill the criteria for the use of the concept. The correctness of this claim does not rest upon distinguishing verbal levels or domains. The notion of domains may be useful in some contexts insofar as it permits one to distinguish between or among areas of discourse which make use of concepts in a cohesive manner but with little or no overlap of concepts from one area to another. The notion has proved useful in connection with the question of reductionism by enabling, for instance, a distinction between "social" and "individual" concepts.[24] It is initially plausible to suggest that what follows from a social fact (from the assertive use of a social concept) does not follow from a corresponding individual fact (from the assertive use of an individual concept), since one has substituted predicates which presuppose no facts about the social domain for those which do presuppose facts about the social domain.

Whether the distinction among domains can contribute to the present analysis at all seems doubtful for at least two reasons. First, the failure of a fulfilled criteria set when treated as simply a collection of facts to have the same implications as an assertively used concept which received warrant for use from that very set holds true regardless of whether the concepts designating a set of criteria do or do not belong to the same domain as the concept for which the set comprises criteria. Second, criteria sets regularly contain concepts some of which belong to the domain of a concept in question, others of which do not. For example, the maid's murder case involved both a bloody knife (neutral, I should judge, among conceivable domains) and a room disheveled by struggle (in the same domain as "murder"). Nonetheless, what follows from the justified assertion of a murder by way

28

of sensible questions, inferences, and actions does not follow from the collection of facts which served as criteria justifying the assertion.

A simple example using a common concept will illustrate the various points of the sketch of event and action concept use. Suppose a mother observes her child taking from a bookshelf several large volumes. He drags them to the kitchen and stacks them on the countertop. He then climbs upon the books and reaches toward the top shelf. The mother and her friends know that cookies are kept up there. The spying mother tells her gossipy neighbor, "Johnny has a plan to get cookies." The neighbor runs out to tell the old woman across the street, "Johnny planned to get some cookies." The old woman replies, "He's an ingenious lad," and "His taking of the book was part of his plan," and finally, "Such plans lead to injuries and perhaps, if unchecked, to juvenile delinquency." What a wise old soul!

Obviously, John's having a plan is quite unlike his having a wart or blue eyes. Too, there is something more to having a plan than merely the observed facts (we never did see the cookies). As Dray has correctly pointed out, however, one adds no new empirical facts to those given when one asserts that Johnny had a plan.[25] Contra-Walsh, on the other hand, the additional element does not consist in any hidden inner connection, if that inner connection consists of anything more than the convention by which one ascribes or attributes a plan to Johnny on the basis of his acts. The old woman's comments follow reasonably only from her justified assertion of the plan; they do not follow from the single acts or from the collection of acts *qua* collection. Nor are her comments deducible in any formal sense; rather, they are conventionally justified, just the sort of things one says of a child's cookie plot. Not just statements, but acts as well follow from criterial assertions. One does not spank a child for taking books from the shelf (unless taking them is in itself forbidden on other grounds), but for his plan to get cookies. Nor need one ask the child if he has such a plan. If he says no, he will likely receive a spanking for lying, too, along with a standard lecture on cutting cherry trees. In short, criterial justification may, as here, take precedence over testimony.

Just this much would have sufficed to warrant Collingwood's long and insightful tirade against "scissors and paste" history. Authority in history rests with neither memory nor eye-witness. The only authority which the historian can recognize is the facts which justify his assertions. Not only does Collingwood recognize this, as in his approval of Oakeshott's dictum that history is what the evidence obliges us to believe, but he also sees a most obvious though overlooked parallel to historical work, one which could destroy the false authority of memory and eye-witness, namely police work.[26] Moreover, the pains which corroborating tales cost ancient Thucydides tells an instructive story about the reliability of eye-witnesses. The fact that criteria other than testimony find use in justifying historical assertions, however, does not dismiss testimony *in toto*, say, in favor of a wholly relic oriented history. It only points to the variety of facts which may serve to warrant the assertions of events and actions.

The demise of scissors and paste does not necessitate Collingwood's restriction of historical interest to human action alone, at the expense of "mere" events. Thus far in this conceptualization of language, no distinction has been made between event and action concepts. To the extent that both receive warrant for use in factual assertions via the fulfillment of criteria, no distinction need be made. The distinction between event and action concepts rests not with the fact of criterial justification, but with the kinds of things which may count as criteria. Moreover, the dissimilarities between kinds of events or between kinds of actions may be greater than that between some paired action and event. Plans and plots almost invariably involve events occurring in an order, as well as an element of purpose or motive (the assertion of which may itself receive criterial justification). Temporal order becomes less relevant with historical movements; in a renaissance, a Leonardo may appear early or late. Wars and revolutions are assigned to groups, or to leaders in their stead, though sometimes to time periods (the Hundred and the Thirty Years Wars). One rarely attributes renaissances to anything smaller than nations (the Italian renaissance), and more often ascribes them to areas (Europe) or to periods (the Carolingean renaissance). Plans and plots belong to individuals or groups; movements belong to masses, classes, or nations. One may distinguish classes of criterially justified concepts on the basis of criteria types, but such classification usually occurs within a context and for the purpose of finding a solution to a particular problem.

Equally pragmatic considerations also give rise to distinguishing among the sorts of elements which might serve as a criterion within a set. Nothing apart from conventions themselves legislates that one sort of item serves as a criterion for actions, another for events, still another for mental characteristics. Objects, events, actions, conditions, and almost any other category of fact may have members fulfilling criterial roles. Indeed, any given criteria set, should one theoretically be able to complete it, would probably contain almost all possible manner of elements. Wars require soldiers (people), instruments of destruction (objects), declarations of war and peace (documents), battle plans (goals and means), attacks or defenses (actions), explosions and deaths (events), and a host of other items. Whether or not one could complete the list with respect to one sort of concept and thereby distinguish that sort from others, an enumeration of the possible sorts of concepts would not itself determine historical interests. Instead, such a project could only serve to illustrate the range of items in which a historian must interest himself if he is to do his work in terms of saying what events and actions occurred. Thus, no special status accrues to one or another kind of entity with respect to events and actions. To put it another way, no metaphysical conclusions follow from the nature of the concepts used by historians (and

30

by us all).

Conversely, events and actions display no special qualities which alone mark them out as such. They have typical, but not universal criterial features. For example, events do not stand for spatio-temporal complexes, and such complexes are not events. Events may occur within a complex, or they may mark the move from one complex to another. It is possible, for instance, to call the activity of Copernicus the discovery of the heliocentric theory or to call it the rediscovery of that theory.[27] One may also call it the writing of a book, the entertaining of heretical ideas, and so on. But a cautionary note goes with the expression "call the activity": in the present context, the expression locates a so-called spatio-temporal complex, but does not name an activity or event. Not everything in the given complex has a relevant place in each of the possible assertions, although the "materials" of the complex, the objects, actions, conditions, mores, words, *et al.*, permit each of the assertions (except, of course, for the assertion of rediscovery, which makes necessary reference outside the boundaries given).

Moreover, some kinds of events have no temporal limits. We may assert the occurrence of the revolution in France, giving it a central date (1789) or dates (1789 to 1792) without specifying limits, i.e., when it began and when it ended. One of the easiest routes to a history publication is to argue that some event "really" began before or ended after the dates usually given for memorization in freshman courses. After considerable finagling with suggested dates, someone inevitably will suggest that one cannot "really" specify a beginning and ending for events like revolutions as one can for baseball games or for space trips. The point is not that no one at the game or revolution has a good enough time piece, but that no time piece could be good enough. We lack both need and criteria for relevantly splitting the last note of the anthem from the first motion of the players. And splitting some of Adams' activities into pre- and post-Lexington/Concord would more likely hinder than help one understand a certain revolution. (One can, of course, imagine and invent occasions for profitably doing just these sorts of things.) The metaphysical wonder which prompts Paul Weiss to tell us that every event has at least two moments, that--in effect--an event is something having a beginning and end, has more place on stage than in history.[28]

The attempt to treat events as having characteristics--spatial, temporal, or both--exemplifies once more the temptation to treat events according to the canons of object language. Every historian knows the futility of seeking termini for revolutions or renaissances. We can give termini, and for a variety of reasons and purposes, but they do not constitute essential characteristics of events in general.

Events, of course, do not exist. They occur; they happen. Actions also occur, and have agents. Agents perform actions, do acts. Nothing of object-relevant terminology necessarily attaches itself to

31

such matters. One might counter that events and actions necessarily involve objects, and that they exist. However, even were the existence of objects to count as a necessary condition for the occurrence of events, that fact cannot suffice as an analysis or even a key to an analysis of event concepts. Very often, the existence of objects of the relevant sort constitutes part of the context, but not the criteria set, for an event concept whose use stands in question. And when existence becomes a germane question, only the fact of an object's existence, not the categories by which one analyzes existence assertions, have relevance to the question of an event's occurrence. Perhaps it is because one feels less uneasy over the analysis of object existence and assertion that conceptual problems with events arise. In any case, the point of noting that events do not exist (and as a corollary, do not *not exist*) is solely to call attention to the inapplicability of object categories and to point to the proper dimension for the analysis of event and action concepts.

IV. Conceptual Proposals and Labels

So far, this portrait of the use of event and action concepts has confined itself to the realm of ordinary, i.e., non-controversial concepts. Yet, not all words which historians use and which look like ordinary event and action concepts in fact are. There are two important categories of words which present special problems when contrasted to ordinary concepts. One group we may call labels or perhaps proper names; they are used to identify individual events, collections of events, eras, and the like. A second group we may call conceptual proposals, concepts whose criteria for warranted use are in question. In this section, I shall examine the relation of both groups to the position taken in the preceding section with respect to ordinary concepts.

"The Renaissance," "The Dark Ages," "The French Revolution," "The Golden Age of Greece," all may be used as labels, as conventional brands to mark out in one or another way a particular segment of history. The segment marked out and designated by the labels may be as large as an era or as small as an event. In many ways, especially with respect to the identification of what bears a label, the expressions indicated parallel the use of proper names for objects. Expressions like "The Renaissance" and "The Golden Age of Greece" are not concepts. Even though a given label strongly suggests the contents of what it demarcates, it has in fact no criteria for warranted use. Indeed, the very notion of criteria for warranted use becomes inapplicable to the extent that such expressions have singular use. As a minimal condition, a concept must be multiply usable. With the demand for more than one possible use goes the demand for criteria to supply warrant for use on each occasion. Consequently, the statement, "The French Revolution is a revolution" is not a tautology in the sense that the statement "The revolution in France is a revolution" would be a tautology. In the first, "Revolution" is part of a label; in the second, "revolution" is used as a concept in both occurrences.

Labels, however, sometimes become concepts. One does not have to turn to aspirin or other formerly brand-named objects for examples. "The Renaissance," *qua* label, typically focuses attention on Italy and other parts of western Europe from, say, 1400 onward. Nowadays, Medieval historians speak of a Carolingian renaissance,[29] whereas 15th and 16th century experts talk of the renaissance in Italy, in Spain, and in England. Minimally, one must have some idea of what sort of things to look for to justify the assertion of the occurrence of a renaissance in Charlemagne's day and realm or to justify the setting of differing dates for the English and Italian renaissances. To take another example, an antiquarian revelling in the Golden Age of Greece may be merely poetic in his label. The literary historian who refers to comparable golden ages in Greece and Rome on the grounds that the two nations exhibited parallel degrees of creativity and originality has passed well beyond labeling to the level of using concepts.[30] His work meets the required conditions that the expression "golden age" be multiply usable and that there be criteria which warrant the assertive use of the concept.

In neither the case of "renaissance" nor the case of "golden age" have the criteria used by historians reached the conventionality of non-controversial concepts. Consequently, a historical debate differing from those mentioned in the preceding section of the chapter becomes possible: to attack (or defend) the criteria proposed by a historian whose work transforms a label into a concept. Since a historian who uses a label as a concept in effect transmutes what a label suggests into criteria for using a word, he thereby introduces a conceptual proposal, one open to critical judgment by those in whose province use of the concept is likely to fall. As with debate concerning essentially contested concepts, debate over conceptual proposals occurs at a level different from that of historical facts. In other words, empirical discovery is not in question. The outcome of the debate, if any, determines what the criteria shall be for the warranted use of the concept. This determination has the consequence of delimiting the assertive use of the concept, or loosely put, it delimits what we can call a renaissance or a golden age. The debate over the criteria for the use of a concept determines, in effect, what the possible facts of history can be. For example, if the criteria for asserting the occurrence of a golden age in literature include too high a standard of creativity, then a literary historian might not be justified in asserting that there occurred a golden age of Roman literature. Should the criteria set include a lower standard of creativity, then the assertion that Rome had her golden age as well as Greece would be warranted.

The ramifications of this account of the nature of debates that occur with respect to conceptual proposals are many, but two have particular importance here. First, it is only rarely that debates with respect to concepts fall within the province of the formal scrutiny of philosophers, whatever their orientation. Instead, they are most often disputed and settled by the practitioners of a discipline within which the use of a concept is most likely to occur. Moreover, it is the active practitioners rather than the methodologists of a field who are likely to have the most influence upon the shaping of criteria for the use of concepts. Perhaps it is only an unjustifiable impression, but it does sometimes appear that methodologists often miss the arena of active conceptual debate in their fixation upon standard or traditional issues and in their inability to extract from the practice of a field those issues which are conceptual from those which are empirical.

The second ramification of the account of the nature of debates that occur with respect to conceptual proposals is that conceptual debates have factual consequences. This particular phenomenon has been noted in other connections within the general study of the philosophy of history. Danto, for example, remarks that "phenomena *as such* are not explained. It is only phenomena *as covered by a description* which are capable of explanation. . . ."[31] We have already noted earlier Fain's remark to the effect that knowing that something occurred pre-supposes often knowing what occurred.[32] In a similar vein in the be-havioral sciences, Turner holds that "facts cannot be neutral for they reflect our classificatory penchants."[33] All these remarks illumine certain factual consequences of conceptual debates. However, they all stop short of what might be termed a radical claim, namely, that concepts determine what facts are possible. Without a concept, or an appropriate combination of interrelated concepts, no fact at all is possible. The importance of settling criterial disputes thus becomes apparent, for the manner in which a dispute is settled, that is, the criteria which are determined as warranting the use of a concept, establishes what can count as a historical fact. We may have occasion to reopen a dispute, to re-establish criteria, but that fact does not alter the logical role played by the criteria for the use of a concept at any given point. At any point of investigation, what can count as a possible fact is a function of what concepts are available for use, what conventions exist at that time. What the facts are rests upon the fulfillment of the criteria for the use of those concepts in factual assertions.

Although no investigator to my knowledge at present insists upon there being such a thing as a basic level of facts with respect to events and actions, one consequence of the position which follows from the analysis of concepts presented in this study is that the notion of a basic level of facts cannot arise.[34] Speaking of levels of events and actions does make sense over a restricted range of data and pur-poses. For example, saying that the concept of "war" is a higher level concept than "battle" to the extent that battles make up (partly) wars and that one can win a battle but lose a war all makes good sense with respect to showing the interrelationship which exists between two particular concepts. However, a general case for levels which included a "lowest" level could not be made. The criteria for the use of any event or action concept or conceptual proposal can in principal be stated with respect to any question which might arise. To that extent, every event and action concept entails with respect to itself a "lower" level, that is, a set of concepts in terms of which one can state the criteria for the use of the concepts in question. This consequence does not imply that there is an unending regress of ever lower levels; rather, it suggests strongly that the notion of levels has no proper function in a general analysis since all the notion can indicate is that certain facts fulfill criteria for the warranted use of a concept in question. The notion of "criteria" thus already does the work of "level" without introducing misleading suggestions concerning the possible overall structure and interrelationship of the total body of event and action concepts.

The discussion of concept levels and the ramifications of debates with respect to conceptual proposals arose from our treatment of the transition from labels to concepts as conceptual proposals. However, not all conceptual proposals emerge from labels. Some represent direct proposals for the use of a new concept in accord with specified criteria, for example, Freud's notion of unconscious motivation.[35] Others may result from intentional or unintentional applications of metaphors and analogies, for instance in the outgrowth of the concept of institutional evolution from the notion of biological evolution. A fairly clear example of conceptual proposal occurs in the writings of Herbert Marcuse and concerns the concept of "revolution." "By revolution," writes Marcuse, "I understand the overthrow of a legally established government and constitution by a social class or movement with the aim of altering the social as well as the political structure."[36] The proposal Marcuse offers rests upon his purpose--to examine the relationship between ethics and revolution--and a consequent concern for human freedom and happiness as social conditions. He specifically assigns to "revolution" a meaning which excludes "all military coups, palace revolutions, and 'preventive counterrevolutions' (such as Fascism and Nazism) because they do not alter the basic social structure."[37] Marcuse, then, for philosophical and polemical purposes, attempts one more sort of conceptual proposal: the restructuring and precising of a common existent concept.

Moreover, not all conceptual proposals retain the application intended for them by those who introduce them. The failure of Spencerian theory and the resultant theoretical uselessness of "institutional evolution" does not prevent that concept from finding or having a perfectly good narrative application. Reference to the evolution of Parliament may genuinely inform one, regardless of Spencer.[38] More on the subject of conceptual proposals will appear in Chapter IV in connection with the subject of the historian's use of metaphors and analogies to generate unities among events. The short notes presented here perhaps suffice to confirm Fain's view that "most concepts are subject to historical erosion and transformation. . . ."[39]

Although I agree with Fain about the fact of conceptual change, it is important to note that we differ with respect to the significance for the philosophy of history of the fact of such changes. Fain views the erosion and transformation of concepts through history as constituting a primary concern of the philosophy of history. To complete the

sentence incompletely quoted above, Fain holds as an appositive to the
clause cited the following clause: "that the philosophy of history,
instead of being treated as a peripheral and esoteric philosophical
subject, ought to be brought close to the center of the philosophical
enterprise."[40] For Fain, it appears, philosophy of history deals less
in the context of justification than it does in the history of concepts.[41]

Despite this difference of outlook, of the purpose for which we
have undertaken to analyze historical concepts (the present study con-
fining itself to event and action concepts), Fain's views appear similar to those presented herein to the extent that both studies focus
upon a criterial analysis. Indeed, Fain distinguishes among several
notions of criteria: a. the "criteria for the intelligible application" of a term or the "traits" of something designated by a concept,
b. the "decision procedures" by which one tests for traits, and c.
the rule by which one formulates criteria.[42] The last notion is encompassed by the term "convention" in this study and presents no problems. However, one can ask whether there is a useful distinction to be
made with respect to philosophic analysis by referring separately to
criterial traits and to decision procedures. Fain does note that the
two senses of criteria "are of course related" and that conceptual
changes created by altering either criterial traits or decision procedures bear "a certain resemblance."[43]

In justification of the distinction between criterial traits and
decision procedures, Fain cites two examples of conceptual change, one
of which originates with changes in decision procedures, the other of
which originates with changes in criteria of intelligible application.
"Intelligence" underwent a change by virtue of the introduction of the
intelligence test, a decision procedure for the comparative judgment of
intelligence. Although now one might be inclined to say that the criterial traits of the concept "intelligence" are whatever the intelligence test measures, there was a point in time (if not the present) at
which one could say without an air of paradox that someone was intelligent but had a low I.Q. It may be that this order of change, from decision procedure to traits, typifies for Fain most conceptual changes:
"I think that most concepts are changed by the decision procedures that
capture them, that decision procedures, by poaching on criteriological
territory, redefine the concepts attached to them."[44] On the other
hand, Fain cites the changes in the concept of time which have been
wrought by the theory of relativity as an example of a conceptual
change brought about by changing the criteria of application rather
than changing the decision procedures, i.e. the means of measuring
time.[45]

I do not think the distinction Fain wishes to make between criterial and decision procedures will stand close scrutiny. First, the intelligence test example can be quite misleading insofar as it represents more a history of conceptual change than an analysis of change.
At the point in time when it appeared to be no paradox to say that one

36

had intelligence but a low I.Q., what was in conflict was a conceptual proposal and an established concept. The former had criteria in accord with certain testing procedures; the latter had broad observational criteria in terms of the ability to make a wide variety of judgments. Although the equivalence of "I.Q." and "intelligence" may be more conventional today (though certainly not universal), the older sense of the term still has perfectly good uses. One can say that we have two concepts of intelligence or that we have one concept with two (at least!) uses. Examining separable concepts or separable uses of concepts during a period in which there is considerable debate over the appropriateness of a set of proposed criteria can obscure the fact that decision procedures and traits tested by those procedures are logically interrelated so as not to be readily separable. Whatever the traits Binet and others thought they were measuring, their tests can measure only traits which are logically enabled by the form and content of the test. In short, the distinction of test and trait, while possible, is artificial with respect to the analysis of the logic of conceptual change. (This does not deny the distinction a place in the history of conceptual change.)

Although the time example appears much harder to encompass under these remarks, it too shows the inseparability of test and trait. It may be true that changes in the concept of time were not brought about by changing methods of determining time, but instead by theoretical proposals which changed the criteria of application of "time." It is difficult to see from Fain's brief remarks that this is the whole truth; what appears also to have changed are some of the implications which follow from the application of the concept "time." Nevertheless, we may, for the sake of argument, assume that Fain has the correct view, that changes in the criteria traits for "time" occurred without a corresponding antecedant change in decision procedures. Examining this view, however, will reveal that changes have also occurred in decision procedures; not changes in the activities of time measurement, but instead changes in terms of the conceptualization of the procedure of measurement. To be more dramatic than correct, what a clock is (as a time measuring instrument) is no longer a standard of physical occurrence in tune with the universe, but instead a standard of physical occurrences whose deviation in specified ways from an occurrence in question is not significant enough to destroy utility, say, in terms of synchronization, etc. In concentrating upon historical aspects of concept changes, Fain has perhaps overlooked important conceptual aspects of those changes.

In consequence of these observations, I cannot view the distinction between criterial trait and decision procedure as analytically important. The interrelationship of a test with what it can test for makes the two inseparable for analysis. Moreover, the notion of a test in a formal sense, the sense in which it applies to Fain's examples, has somewhat dubious applicability to history and even less to the use of event and action concepts in undisciplined, i.e., ordinary conversation. Many of our tests for traits or for other criterial events, ac-

37

tions, states, and conditions are matters of a loose sort of expertise
or a matter of "look and see." Granted that history, to the extent
that the discipline holds much concern for supporting what its accounts
record as fact, has many partially and some fully formalized procedures, the mere fact of formalization cannot alter the appropriateness
of expertise in the field.[46] Nor can it alter the relation of the test
to the tested.

These remarks do not in any sense constitute a refutation of
Fain's distinction. They instead amount to a treatment of the distinction which results from certain more fundamental differences which exist between Fain's approach and the one used in this study. These differences encompass in an interrelated way both the approach to the philosophy of history and the general view of what is important with respect to concepts. Fain approaches the philosophy of history in a manner which he views as in conflict with analytical philosophy of history, with its emphasis upon the sorts of problems encountered in the
philosophy of science. Such a view he finds prejudicially "ahistorical."[47] To do philosophy of history one must have a historical sense,
and in keeping with this view, he concentrates upon the history of conceptual change rather than upon the logic of the justification of conceptual changes. From these fundamentals follow Fain's views upon
concepts and their analysis.

By contrast, the present study presupposes the appropriateness of
a context of justification for studies within the philosophy of history. Consequently, not the history of concept use, but the logic by
which the use of a concept may be justified in factual historical assertions represents the primary concern. Accordingly, historical analyses of conceptual changes are less appropriate subjects for study than
the interrelationships of concept, criteria, and reasons for proposing
new criteria with respect to any concept which is at the time of analysis a conceptual proposal. To this extent, then, the present study is
consistent with the general "ahistorical" nature of analytical philosophy of history, although the proposed analysis of event and action
concepts is far removed from analyses that typify the philosophy of
science.

V. Sources of the Criterial View of Event Concepts

Although the analysis of event and action concepts proposed in
this study is non-typical with respect to the treatment of concepts in
most analytical philosophies of history, the terms of the analysis are
not particularly original. In fact, one might characterize this chapter as an attempt to apply to events and actions terms of analysis
which are already commonplace in other fields. In view of this possibility, perhaps a few remarks concerning the sources of the ideas used
in the proposed analysis of event and action concepts may be in order.

The notion of "criteria," as an appropriate concept to employ in the analysis of the use of concepts, has served as fodder for philosophic debate since Wittgenstein. In Chapter II, I shall have occasion to examine at least one interpretation of what Wittgenstein meant by the term, although that discussion arises in a context different from the present one. It is perhaps not too much of a historical distortion to suggest that only metaethical studies have made any consistent progress toward refining and applying the notion of criteria to problems of analysis. Urmson, for example, noted the close analogy between using standards in the grading of things which were of the same general variety and making ethical evaluations. The result of his work is a criterial analysis of evaluative concepts like "good,"[48] the influence of which analysis upon this study seems obvious.

What appears to me to be a necessary adjunct to criterial analysis appears in the work of Hare: his treatment of the so-called descriptive meaning of "good" precludes the need for having a single meaning applicable to all possible uses of the concept. Instead, the descriptive meaning of the concept must be common to all applications with respect to items of the same kind, but could vary as one moved from one kind of item to another.[49] The variation of meaning from one kind of item to another seems to me to represent a precising of the notion of "context," and in that role, Hare's analysis is not only consistent with Urmson's, but also is a necessary condition for Nowell-Smith's notion of "contextual implication." With the notion of "contextual implication," Nowell-Smith discards formality with respect to implication and approaches the notion which in this study goes under the name of "convention." His particular formulation, "a statement p contextually implies q if anyone who knew the normal conventions of language would be entitled to infer q from p in the context in which they occur," is not completely adequate.[50] It suffers a redundancy with respect to "being entitled" and "inferring," unless the entire phrase "would be entitled to infer" equates with "would be justified in asserting." One is entitled to q in the same sense that one can (loosely) infer q, namely, the sense in which one can warrantably assert q on the basis of p. The warrant specified by the term "entitled" goes to q, not to some particular person who makes the statement q. Moreover, with respect to the sorts of concepts studied herein, entitlement is perhaps best rephrased in terms of warrant or justification, and inference disappears altogether to avoid any confusion between the relation of criteria to concept on the one hand and on the other the sorts of relations the term "inference" traditionally designates. Consequently, the form in which Nowell-Smith's fundamental point finds expression in this study is that the criterial facts (p in the Nowell-Smith formulation) warrant or justify the assertion of the occurrence of an event or action (q in the Nowell-Smith formulation) according to the conventions of language and the context of the assertion.

Although it is necessary to reject the word "infer" to designate the conventional relationship between q and p in Nowell-Smith's account, one should note the initial and intuitive plausibility with which the word seems to describe the relation. The conventionality of the relation makes the move from p to q immediate, and this fact suffices to suggest inference. However, one must also note the disparateness of p and q (which cannot in any ordinary sense be said to be analytically related). Interpreted with respect to the class of concepts under study herein, the disparateness becomes marked: except by virtue of convention there seems to be no relationship between the facts which fulfill criteria and the fact which is asserted by the use of the concept whose criteria the facts fulfill. Toulmin appears to have noted a similar point with respect to the criteria for the use of evaluative concepts: the criteria resemble more reasons given for a judgment than they do premises of an argument. Criteria neither contain nor equal the evaluative concept.[51] The same claim can be made with respect to events and actions, that is, the criteria for the use of an event or action concept do not contain or equal the concept itself, and for this reason cannot be said to define it.

The use of event and action concepts bears a resemblance to the "ascription" of evaluative concepts, in the sense of ascription which Hart employed to distinguish between evaluation and description so as to prevent the reduction of the former to the latter. For example, one ascribes responsibility for an action (in a moral or legal context), that is, an individual is not responsible until judged so, and judgments are to be grounded in facts.[52] To the extent that Hart holds some evaluative assertions to gain their warrant from guided fiat, his model is of dubious accuracy, although the absence of precise formulations may give conventions an air of arbitrariness. Moreover, the notion of ascription itself has limited application. It demands the existence of something (as indicated by prior assertion) to which an evaluation, feature, trait, or property can be ascribed. Events and actions are, instead, asserted to have occurred. Nonetheless, the features of the relation between the ascriptive concept and the facts which warrant its use carry over in a general way to the relation between event and action concepts and the criteria which warrant their use.

That the suggestive notions which arose in metaethical studies, when stripped of the special considerations of the subject matter which engendered them, should carry over into other realms of concept use seems plausible enough to invite study. However, little effort seems to have been given to the direction in analysis. Achenstein has recently attempted something of a criterial analysis of concepts in the physical sciences, though his particular aims limit the utility of his work for the present subject.[53] Fain's use of criteria in the study of historical concepts has also been noted, along with the reasons for holding a conception in some ways different from his. In any event, it does appear to be worth the while to trace out in a consistent manner the implications of a criterial view of event and action concepts for problems in the philosophy of history, and upon the results which accrue from accomplishing such a project the merits of the analysis may be judged.

The criterial analysis used in this study does bear terminological similarities to the work of Dewey in his *Logic: The Theory of Inquiry*, and therein lies a potential source of confusion which the following remarks hope to eliminate. One might construe Dewey's notion of "warranted assertibility" as having more than terminological similarity to the idea of the warranted or justified use of event or action concepts in factual assertions. Genetically, I cannot accurately estimate the debt which the present idea owes to Dewey. Logically, however, I can draw attention to important distinctions. First, Dewey attempts to develop a theory encompassing the entire range of epistemic concerns, a theory he summarizes in these words: "all logical forms (with their characteristic properties) arise within the operation of inquiry and are concerned with control of inquiry so that it may yield warranted assertions."[54] His further remarks equating "warranted assertibility" with certain senses of "belief" and "knowledge" make clear the scope of his work.[55] That scope far surpasses the work of this study, which confines itself to the justification of event and action assertions and its implications for the philosophy of history.

Second, Dewey views the object of his study as constituting, in part if not in whole, a process in which "patterns" or "logical forms" function as "means" or "agencies" which "provide" or by which one "obtains" warrantably assertible conclusions.[56] As a consequence, "all knowledge as grounded assertion involves mediation," that is, an inferential function of one or another order in the process of generating the grounded assertion.[57] The view on which this study rests differs from Dewey's to the extent that its subject matter consists of the logical form of a certain sort of justification, one applicable to event and action assertions. The process of justification makes use of the form, but the process itself is not of central concern. Thus, no claims arise in this study as to the nature of "historical thinking." For Dewey, concern for process forces great attention to genetic considerations, as, for example, in the detailed explanation of his propositions "(1) that logical theory is the systematic formulation of controlled inquiry, and (2) that logical forms accrue in and because of control that yields conclusions which are warrantably assertible."[58] For this study, which operates within a context of justification, genetic concerns are for the most part irrelevant.

Despite these important, if not crucial, distinctions, Dewey's work holds considerable suggestive power for the formulation of any adequate criterial conception of event and action assertions. For example, Dewey's discussion of evaluation, and especially his note that "we evaluate only when a value . . . has become problematic," proves useful in understanding that the justification of assertions ordinarily occurs in situations of demand, and that demand may arise from a situation or from persons who examine a set of assertions.[59] What is true of evaluation for Dewey also holds true for event and action assertions made in the course of writing history, as earlier sections of this chapter have tried to show.

41

For another example, Dewey notes a certain relativity of terminology. Material relevant to inquiry requires double designation: when undergoing inquiry, Dewey terms it "subject-matter" (or in another context, "content"); when it comprises the outcome of inquiry, that is, "produced and ordered in settled form by means of inquiry," Dewey terms it "object."[60] A parallel relativity exists within the terminology describing the justification of event and action assertions. An event or action assertion which has a proper justification is a fact. The event or action asserted to have occurred, along with others, may fulfill criteria which justify the assertion of another event or action. Whether one treats what is justifiably asserted as a fact or as a criterion-fulfilling event or action depends upon what role that which was asserted plays within a given context. However, since criteria-fulfilling events and actions are asserted via statements and since their use can be to justify another event or action assertion, one may also say that facts (event or action assertions whose justification is not in question) fulfill criteria in justifying the use of event or action concepts.

The relationship of fact to fact does not conflict with earlier remarks to the effect that, without a concept having criteria for justified use, no fact at all is possible. Such remarks elicit a necessary condition for their being facts, but they do not describe the interrelationship of concepts and facts. The criterial relationship describes one of many possible relationships. In a developed language of events and actions, facts play roles in the justification of other facts, and the kind of role having interest for this study is criterial. One may also have occasion to say, without error or necessary enigma, that events and actions may justify the assertion of other events or actions. The situation described here parallels Dewey's own note on the use of the term "objects" in contexts where they are means within an inquiry to "attaining knowledge of something else." Strictly, in this context, they function as "part of the *contents* of inquiry," but retrospectively can be viewed as objects "in virtue of prior inquiries which warrant their assertibility."[61] In either case, Dewey's or my own, one can only hope that context will make clear the appropriate use.

The criterial analysis of event and action concepts has yielded a set of considerations which may be summarized as follows. First, the logic of event and action concepts use may be expressed by the statement that events, actions, states, conditions, traits, characteristics, and objects fulfill criteria for the warranted or justified use of event and action concepts. Second, the relation between a concept and its criteria is conventional. Third, warranted or justified use may be construed as the use of a concept in an assertive or factual statement; that is, the warranted or justified use of an event or action concept asserts as fact the occurrence of the appropriate event or action. Assertions of events or actions may be put to further uses, for example, in explanations, in warnings, in predictions and forecasts, etc., but insofar as each of these uses presupposes the assertion of the occurrence of an event or action, the fundamental use of event and action concepts to assert facts will constitute the central topic of this study. Fourth, event and action concepts have been distinguished from singular event and action terms (labels or proper names) and from conceptual proposals, both of which involve factors of justification which vary from those which are applicable to ordinary event and action concepts. Fifth, the dual nature of possible debates concerning event and action concepts--at once both conceptual and factual--has been established.

Sixth, the relation between the criteria to be fulfilled and the concept use to be justified has been called "criterial." The supposition behind the label has been that the relation designated by it is primitive in the sense that the label is not either a new name for a well known relation designated by another term or a name for a relation derived from some one or more other well known relations. Before attempting to apply the analysis of event and action concepts to problems in the philosophy of history, it would be wise, I think, to investigate the propriety of this supposition, and such an investigation forms the purpose of the next chapter.

Finally, one should note that the conception of event and action language presented in this chapter amounts to a sketch rather than to a completed portrait. Were the subject of this study a formal theory, the portrait could achieve a relevant level of completion by following out deductive consequences of the initial assumptions. The analysis of this study, however, arose because of the existence of certain problems in the philosophy of history, and it has sense and utility only with respect to the problems which gave rise to it. Consequently, the preliminary analysis and language conception presented in this chapter can only acquire their relevant completion by viewing the implications of them on the problems of the philosophy of history which rest upon an account of events and actions. The completion of the sketch thus becomes the subject of chapters three through six.

NOTES

[1] Herodotus, *The Histories*, trans. Aubrey de Selincourt (Baltimore: Penguin Books, 1965), p. 503.

[2] *Ibid.*, p. 525.

[3] See for example, Michael Oakeshott, *Experience and Its Modes* (Cambridge: At the University Press, 1933), pp. 108-109, and R. G. Collingwood, *The Idea of History* (New York: Oxford University Press, 1956), pp. 249 ff.

[4] Oakeshott, *Experience and Its Modes*, p. 108 and all of Chapter III, for example.

[5] E.g., Carl Becker, "What Are Historical Facts?" *The Philosophy of History in Our Time*, ed. Hans Meyerhoff (Garden City: Doubleday and

Co., Inc., 1959), pp. 120-37.

[6] See, for instance, John Passmore, "The Objectivity of History," *Philosophical Analysis and History*, ed. William H. Dray (New York: Harper and Row, Publishers, 1966), pp. 75-94.

[7] For example, William H. Dray, *Philosophy of History* (Englewood Cliffs, New Jersey: Prentice-Hall, Inc., 1964), pp. 21-40.

[8] As one of many examples, see William H. Dray, "On the Nature and Role of Narrative in Historiography," *History and Theory*, 10 (1971), pp. 153-171.

[9] Ernest Nagel, "Some Issues in the Logic of Historical Analysis," *Theories of History*, ed. Patrick Gardiner (New York: The Free Press, 1959), pp. 375-76; cf. Heinrich Rickert, *Die Grenzen der naturwissenschaftlichen Begriffsbildung* (Tubingen: J. C. B. Mohr, 1921), p. 281.

[10] W. H. Walsh, "The Intelligibility of History," *Philosophy*, 17 (April, 1942), pp. 130-33; cf. *An Introduction to Philosophy of History* (London: Hutchinson University Library, 1958), pp. 60, 62.

[11] William H. Dray, "'Explaining What' in History," *Theories of History*, pp. 403-404, 406.

[12] Ramsey Muir, *A Short History of the British Empire*, II (London: George Philip and Son, Ltd., 1922), p. 123; cited by Dray, "'Explaining What' in History," p. 403.

[13] Dray, *Philosophy of History*, p. 20, and "'Explaining What' in History," p. 407.

[14] Dray, "'Explaining What' in History," pp. 403, 407.

[15] Danto, *Analytical Philosophy of History*, pp. 218-27.

[16] *Ibid.*, p. 218. For a similar position handled in a different manner, see Robert C. Stover, *The Nature of Historical Thinking* (Chapel Hill: University of North Carolina Press, 1967), pp. 7-8, on "Occurrences." The clearly parallel treatment of occurrences and objects, both of whose "essential particularity" is said to rest upon "a certain discriminable kind of trait," reflects an orientation inclined toward the position that there is an event E which one then describes in terms of traits.

[17] Haskell Fain, *Between Philosophy and History* (Princeton: Princeton University Press, 1970), p. 121; cf. pp. 249, 253 in which Fain applies this notion to the subject of explanation.

[18] Dray, "'Explaining What' in History," p. 406.

[19] Becker, "What Are Historical Facts?" p. 122.

[20] The example is taken, with modifications, from Walsh, *An Introduction to Philosophy of History*, p. 49.

[21] A. J. P. Taylor, *The Origins of the Second World War*, 2nd Ed. (New York: Fawcett Publications, 1961), pp. 279 ff. esp. 281.

[22]William Alston, *Philosophy of Language* (Englewood Cliffs, New Jersey: Prentice-Hall, Inc., 1964), p. 42. Alston does recognize, though from a quite different point of view, the difficulty of achieving complete analysis.

[23]W. B. Gallie, *Philosophy and the Historical Understanding* (New York: Schocken Books, 1964), all of Chapter V, but esp. p. 161.

[24]See Danto's analysis of Mandelbaum's treatment of social concepts, *Analytical Philosophy of History*, pp. 270-75.

[25]Dray, "'Explaining What' in History," pp. 403-404.

[26]Collingwood, *The Idea of History*, pp. 154, 155, 159, 266 ff.

[27]The example is taken from Danto, *Analytical Philosophy of History*, pp. 156-57.

[28]Paul Weiss, *Modes of Being* (Carbondale: Southern Illinois University Press, 1958), pp. 246-51 (propositions 3.67-3.74).

[29]For example, Karl Stephenson and Bryce Lyon, *Medieval History*, 4th Ed. (New York: Harper and Row, 1962), pp. 163 ff.

[30]The example is from Buckner B. Trawick, *World Literature*, II (New York: Barnes and Noble, Inc., 1953), pp. 129-30.

[31]Danto, *Analytical Philosophy of History*, p. 218.

[32]Fain, *Between Philosophy and History*, p. 121.

[33]Merle B. Turner, *Philosophy and the Science of Behavior* (New York: Appleton-Century-Crofts, 1967), p. 194. It should be noted that none of the three sources of remarks concerning the role of concepts with respect to possible facts seems willing to go as far as I am willing to go. Danto and Fain both speak of the role of concepts with respect to the possibility of explanation, while Turner wishes to distinguish "facts" from something he calls "raw data" (which seems to be something nameable and hence already involved in the use of concepts). The position of this study is that the possibility of facts rests in part upon the existence of concepts at any level of concern, including what would count as the "lowest" level with respect to any particular theory, whether that level includes raw data, sense perceptions, or other facts which are then ordered by further uses of concepts.

[34]See J. L. Austin, *Sense and Sensibilia*, ed. G. J. Warnock (New York: Oxford University Press, 1964), esp. Chapter X (pp. 104 ff.) for similar conclusions with respect to perception and material object statements (where in some cases the former were considered a "lower level" than the latter).

[35]According to the treatment of A. C. MacIntyre, *The Unconscious* (London: Routledge and Kegan Paul, 1958), pp. 44 ff.

[36]Herbert Marcuse, "Ethics and Revolution," *Ethics and Society* ed. Richard T. DeGeorge (Garden City: Doubleday and Company, Inc., 1966), p. 134.

[37] *Ibid.*, p. 135.

[38] The example is originally Dray's, "'Explaining What' in History," p. 407.

[39] Fain, *Between Philosophy and History*, p. 194.

[40] *Ibid.*

[41] *Ibid.*, pp. 206, 216.

[42] *Ibid.*, pp. 200, 49-50.

[43] *Ibid.*, pp. 49, 300-201. The resemblance of changes involves for Fain changes in criterial traits and "historical forces little understood but certainly beyond the control of the innovators," (p. 201).

[44] *Ibid.*, pp. 194-201, quotation from p. 194.

[45] *Ibid.*, p. 200.

[46] See for example the remarks of J. H. Hexter, *Doing History* (Bloomington, Ill.: Indiana University Press, 1971), pp. 5 ff.

[47] Fain, *Between Philosophy and History*, p. 206.

[48] J. O. Urmson, "On Grading," *Mind*, n.s., 59 (April, 1950), pp. 145-69.

[49] R. M. Hare, *The Language of Morals* (New York: Clarendon Press, 1964), pp. 112-18, 132-33.

[50] P. H. Nowell-Smith, *Ethics* (Baltimore: Penguin Books, 1954), p. 72.

[51] Stephen Toulmin, *The Place of Reason in Ethics* (Cambridge: At the University Press, 1950), p. 28.

[52] H. L. A. Hart, "The Ascription of Responsibility and Rights," *Essays on Language and Logic*, ed. Antony Flew (New York: Philosophical Library, 1951), pp. 145-47.

[53] Peter Achenstein, *Concepts in Science* (Baltimore: The Johns Hopkins Press, 1968), esp. Chapters I and II.

[54] John Dewey, *Logic: The Theory of Inquiry* (New York: Henry Holt and Company, 1938), pp. 3-4.

[55] *Ibid.*, pp. 7-9.

[56] *Ibid.*, pp. 11, 104.

[57] *Ibid.*, p. 139.

[58] *Ibid.*, p. 22.

[59] *Ibid.*, pp. 172-73.

[60] *Ibid.*, pp. 118-19.

[61] *Ibid.*, p. 119.

CHAPTER TWO

Criteria and Contending Conceptions

The sketch of the criterial view of the use of event
and action concepts presented in the first chapter presumes
that the relation between a concept and its criteria cannot
be reduced to or adequately analyzed in terms of some other
relation. Since the presumption is central to the treatment
of issues in terms of the criterial conception of event and
action language, this chapter examines the possibilities for
analyzing the criterial relation such that one may substitute
for it a more traditional relation. After separating the
questions of meaning and use for the purposes of this study,
the chapter examines the following candidates for substitution: 1. definition, 2. reference and description, 3.
classification, 4. wholes and parts, 5. sufficient conditions, 6. necessary conditions, 7. probability and induction, 8. hypothesis and evidence, 9. normic connection.
In each case, the proposed analysans is found wanting in one
or more respects. Nonetheless, the discussion proves useful
insofar as the contrasts it elicits between the criterial
relation and the various candidates for substitution informally precise and circumscribe the notion of conceptual
criteria.

In the two decades of its popular unpopularity, the notion of criteria, with respect to conceptual analyses and theory, has created more
difficulties than its introduction was supposed to solve. The following questions stand out as typical of the sorts implicit in and raised
by various analyses. (1) Does a criterial analysis of concepts supply
a viable notion of meaning or meaningfulness? If so, how? (2) Precisely what relation does the label "criteria" specify? (3) How can
one distinguish the criterial relation from others which have already
received detailed and fruitful analysis.

Ultimately, only the third question opens the way to productive
study.

Theorists have asked and answered the first question without a
concomitant ability to convince or a willingness to be convinced. The
famous but fuzzily translated Note #43 of Wittgenstein's *Investigations*
provides solid root for both the question and the quandry: "For a
large class of cases--though not for all--in which we employ the word
"meaning" it can be explained thus: the meaning of a word is its use
in the language."[1] (There seems no good reason for translators to render "*erklaren*" as "define" in this sentence and as "explain" in the one

47

following.) "Criteria" and "use" go together in talk of concepts quite as conventionally and naturally as to "definition" and "meaning." To the extent that one takes #43 seriously, one cannot evade the association of "meaning" with "use," and consequently with "criteria."

The attempt to precise the terms of the association has engaged many writers. Danto, for example, argues that criteria of application presuppose the meaningfulness of a concept.[2] For certainly, we could never find (perhaps outside of nonsense verse and the like) an application or criteria for a meaningless term. Such a position and similar ones endure, despite the existence of alternatives, because meaning and meaningfulness have traditionally interlocked with theories of definition, analyticity, and synonymy, key elements in accounts which set out the means for explicating a word's meaning. Although volumes are fast filling up with the troubles which beset such concepts, confidence remains high that one day a full analysis shall emerge to give clear sense to "meaning" in just these terms. This confidence underlies, I think, the unwillingness of analysts to accept or encourage any proposed conception of language which seeks to change or challenge the meaning of "meaning." Thus, few, if any, seem prepared to entertain seriously the alternative that use does not presuppose meaningfulness, that to have criteria and use is to be meaningful. Few would accept that the analyst's task is not to find a general definition, an account of a term's meaning, but instead to see in what way a particular and troublesome concept is meaningful through the examination and explication of its criteria and range of use.

Such a radical departure from tradition may well be unnecessary. It is possible to accept--or at least to live with--the dictum that use presupposes meaningfulness, and then to go on to establish an account of use. For the mere fact of presupposing the meaningfulness of a concept in no way commits one to a particular theory of meaning. Nor does one have to choose among the many theories of meaningfulness. To "go on" in the conversation or speech activity, to be able to define terms, to be able to select or identify referents: all these and more may (or may not) be parts of meaningfulness. Accounts of use under the present concession to accept the dictum require that a term or class of terms analyzed have a meaningful use. (The expression "meaningful use" may itself be interpreted as fitting the dictum that criteria presuppose meaningfulness or as fitting the alternative that to have criteria and use is to be meaningful.) Such accounts do not require or entail a full analysis of "meaningfulness." This fact permits one to separate the questions of meaning-meaningfulness and of use at least to the extent of permitting an initially independent investigation of the latter.

Separating the questions of meaning and use side steps question (1). Question (2), the specification of what relation "criteria" designates, arises next, and in a sense, this study seeks to examine the candidates which one may offer as answers to it. So there can be no side stepping here.

48

Prior to analysis, however, there remains one possibility not yet mentioned: perhaps the criterial relation cannot be explained in terms of other relations, i.e., the label "criteria" does not specify some relation already well understood. (Of course, to have a relation at all one must be able to say what counts for relata and how to tell if one has the relevant relation.) Should this be the case, then exploring possible answers to question (2) will at the same time produce answers to question (3). For part of showing why a relation fails to be the critical relation must include showing how the two differ.

Therefore, if an answer to question (3) makes the criterial relation indistinguishable from some other relation, one may drop the whole notion of criteria from accounts of language use. If not, then one may be forced to admit the relation as something like an ordinary language analog to the formal notion of a primitive relation, i.e., its use is explicable but not reducible. While such a result does not entail primitiveness, even barring serious omissions from the list of candidates, it would provide good reason to treat the criterial relation as if it were primitive.

I. Definition

The most naive temptation wrought by the need to explicate the relation of a concept to a particular criteria set draws one into treating the criteria set as a definition. If x, y, and z warrant the assertive use of Q, then there seems no immediate reason for not defining Q as x, y, and z. Perhaps this natural tendency comes to Dray's mind when he, in effect, rejects it by noting that, in explaining what events amounted to, Q amounts to something more than just x, y, and z.[3] He goes on to note that the something more could not include new empirical information. The definitional irreducibility of criterial terms with respect especially to human and social concepts also informs Comte's over-simple hierarchy of science in which he claims that each succeeding level of complexity also contains a new element, one which prevents complete reduction. Thus, while few philosophers have sought to define event, action, and like concepts in terms of their criteria, the urge to do so has sufficient importance to justify an exploration into why that direction proves fruitless. Hopefully, any such account can avoid the vague mysteries of expressions like "something more."

The investigation of definition and criteria needs a restriction. The claim that criteria cannot count as the definition of a concept of the relevant order cannot apply to all possible senses of "definition." Obviously, a dictionary, all of whose entries may go under the name "definition," may routinely give criteria of use for a given context rather than other sorts of entries. For the purposes of this study, the relevant form of definition consists of one in which a concept is definitionally equated with something else, *viz.*,

$$Q = df \ x, \ y, \ z.$$

49

Most commonly, the definiens contains reference to a genus. However, to the extent that the genus can itself stand definition, i.e., reduction to terms consistent with the others on the x, y, z side of the equation, such a procedure has no effect on the relevant considerations.

Moreover, for the problem at hand, it makes no difference whether or not such definitions give the meaning of the expressions defined. For the crucial element in definitions which distinguishes them from criterial conventions is the equation itself. In all cases, and rhetorical considerations aside, one may substitute the definiens for the definiendum without loss or gain, without alteration. To put the point another way, whatever follows from the use of a concept also follows from the use of its definition.

If x, y, and z constitute criteria, then they do not comprise a substitute for a concept Q whose use they warrant. In the alternative expression, what follows the assertion of Q does not follow from the assertion--singly, disparately, or collectively--of the set of criteria. For example, following the warranted assertion of a revolution, one may ask whether there occurred a subsequent counter-revolution. Such a question would have no basis should one simply assert those events, acts, conditions, etc., which would justify the assertion of a revolution. A change of governmental form, violent removal of a ruling class or party, an ideological contest, all may constitute the grounds upon which one warrants the assertion of a revolution, but without the assertion itself, the following question loses the justification of its sensibleness. Of course, as a rhetorical possibility of narrative, one may leave the assertion of revolution implicit. In such cases, nonetheless, the citation of the mentioned facts in the narrative has its ground in the implicit assertion, i.e., the facts are treated as criteria. Thus, any question of a counter-revolution does not rest for warrant on the collection of facts, nor does it rest on them as a criterial collection. Rather, it rests on the concept whose factual use they warrant.

Although a criteria set, x, y, and z, in a given context may warrant the use of more than one concept, the two concepts warranted are not necessarily logically equivalent or synonymous. A man who boasts before strangers may be said to be vain. The same boasting in the same circumstances also warrants the assertion of self-seekingness. That the two concepts used correctly in this case do not equal each other follows from certain features of criteria sets. Explicated criteria sets, as noted earlier, rarely contain all elements which may count as criteria. Instead, they contain those elements which one may or does question regarding a given assertion. Consequently, elements relegated to the status of context, i.e., omitted from consideration under the rubric "in cases like this," also count as part of the complete criteria set. Whether one speaks of moving to a new context or of using a different criteria set depends on pragmatic considerations concerning what sort of question one is asking about a concept's use. A woman who primps for hours before a mirror may also be vain, though her self-less devotion of time and energy to worthy causes may preclude the ascription of selfishness. There are even cases in which the terms may totally cross each other, as when Hoffer remarks, "The vanity of the self-less, even those who practice utmost humility, is boundless."[4] Obviously, there are uses of concepts (here vanity) in which one may also use other concepts on the same relevant grounds and cases where one may not. Part of the explanation lies in criteria themselves. If a different set of criteria is used, then the second concept may not be warranted.

Since, however, the concepts in question receive relevant but not full explication, one cannot say to the satisfaction of theoretical rigor that the same grounds warrant both. Although the grounds of relevant questions include x, y, and z, but not all the grounds for asserting either of two concepts, Q or R, no rigor attaches to any attempt to equate Q and R on the basis of x, y, and z. Muir, then, in asserting that the events of late 18th century England amounted to not just an economic revolution, but as well to a social revolution, did not assert an analytically true statement.[5] Likewise, the boasting man is vain and self-seeking non-tautologically. There are contexts where boasting may be vain but not self-seeking or self-seeking but not vain. From the fact that no contextual element bears immunity from treatment as a criterion, it follows that no given criteria set can suffice as a definition.

This last conclusion only serves to distinguish the function of soliciting criteria sets from functions usually assigned to definitions. It remains for the earlier cited fact, that criteria do not equal the concept whose use they warrant, to close off the theoretical possibility of completing a criteria set and calling it a definition. A completed criteria set would still lack the required equivalency to the concept for which it was a criteria set. Whether there exist complete and adequate definitions of any terms whatever falls outside the range and need of this study. That certain kinds of theory make them a relevant possibility sufficed to necessitate the distinctions made here.

II. Reference and Description

Definitions, like the notions of reference and description, owe their present theoretical dimensions to considerations originally brought up in connection with object concepts. Consequently, some of the commitments which follow from the use of certain expressions containing nouns or substantives require considerable revision when event, action, and similar concepts fill the noun slot.

For example, the expression "this x" has constituted a fundamental element in metaphysical studies in recent years.[6] One way of treating the expression, in the rough, is to let "x" denote the object identi-

fied by the expression "this x," where some method of ostensive location or some time-space referential framework provides whatever else
the idea of successful use in communication requires. Alternatively,
one may argue that the expression "this x" supposes the expansion of
"x" into "x of sort P" such that not the referential framework or method of location, but the species P comprises the fundamental feature of
identification.[7]

What both alternatives entail is a locatable "x" which counts as
an "x" by virtue of a certain conceptualization. In the "x of sort P"
alternative, "this x" immediately entails that "x" is A or B or C or
. . . , where A, B, C, etc., represent species words, concepts. A similar condition also follows from the "blank x" alternative, albeit
somewhat less directly. Although identification may be accomplished
prior to subsumption under species concepts, identification still requires some minimal notion. In an analysis by Strawson it requires the
notion of a material body.[8] However, to say "x" is a material body entails that it be a body of sort "P," i.e., that it is either an A, or a
B or a C, etc. Thus, regardless of the basic demands of identification, subsumption of "x" under one or another species remains a necessary feature of object language.

Whatever the outcome of these issues for object concepts, such
conditions do not apply to events and actions, nor to ascriptive concepts. The relation of X, y, and z to Q is in no way a case of subsum-
ing "x" under "P" above. If Q is used on the basis of x, y, and z,
which comprise its criteria, then denying Q has quite different results
from those of denying that x is an A. In the object case, one may say
that, if x is not A, then it is B or C or . . . . With events, denial
of Q does not commit one to R or S or . . . . Rather, denial of Q may
leave one only with the x, y, and z that formerly one thought to have
fulfilled the criteria for asserting Q, assuming that the argument over
Q did not initially rest on denying the fulfillment of criteria. Of
course, the lack of entailment does not preclude a historian from opting for one of two or more concepts, as when Schlesinger writes, "The
fight against depression was, to be sure, the heart of the New Deal,
but it has not been the central issue of traditional American reform. . . ."[9]

Where the argument originates from a debate over the fulfillment
of criteria, the point that no alternative substantive of the same
level as Q necessarily follows becomes all the more obvious. Without
denying that sometimes the denial of Q involves the assertion of Q's
contradictory, the point still holds that the denial of Q may resolve
itself into the denial of warrant for Q's assertion or use. From this
latter sort of case, nothing by way of an alternative assertion follows. Nor does the failure of Q in such cases hold any implications of
notion of species and, hence, of identification via species become irrelevant to events unless one drains those notions of any content other
than the multiple use factor common to all concepts. Such a tack would

make the word "species" effectively only a synonym for "concept."

One cannot evade these consequences by opting for a more Strawsonian version of identification. First, ostention as a method of location would have no application with events (regardless of its role or lack of one with objects). Second, time and place do not suffice as conditions of identification for events. If, in fact, time and place mark out objects, then they cannot also mark out events without leaving us with no means of distinguishing the two. As noted earlier, time and place may constitute elements by the use of which we note certain aspects of events for certain purposes, but they do not alone either count as events or enable one to locate events.

The contrast between "x is a A" and "x, y, and z amount to (or warrant the use of) Q" finds reinforcement in an examination of seemingly parallel expressions. "Something happened (occurred, was done, etc.)" to all appearances forms an event analog to the object expression "something exists." In the latter case the assertion commits one (apart from the question of identification) to an x of sort P, and the next question becomes which P. The former contains no such commitment insofar as Q and all alternatives are deniable without denying the assertion that something happened. That is, to deny all possible disjuncts of P, i.e., A or B or C, etc., for objects entails the denial of the existence of x for any account in which reference to x implies either directly or indirectly that x is of sort P. To deny all disjuncts of Q or R or S, etc., for events is to deny the warranted applicability of a concept of a certain order, that is, to deny that an event of that order occurred. But it does not entail a denial that any event occurred. For x, y, and z of the formulation "x, y, and z amount to a Q" do not serve the same function as the "x" of "x is an A." X, y, and z themselves represent events, objects, conditions, actions and other phenomena as may serve criterially and therefore stand conceptualized. Just this factor enables historians to argue in all propriety against each other's conclusions with no compulsion to replace the damned with any, let alone more saintly, counter-conclusions. Unlike A. J. P. Taylor, we may even deny that Hitler planned to conquer Europe without also saying that he expected the war.[10]

"What is it?" and "What happened?" also appear analogous to each other. However, the former question presupposes a referential use of "it." Consequently, the object relevant question amounts to asking, "In which P do we drop 'it'?" "What happened?" on the other hand, may or may not be a request for the name of an event. Given that an event occurred, the question does request the assertive use of an event concept. Equally, it may amount to a general request to tell a story, a factual one, without commitment to either a sort Q or the denial of x, y, and/or z. In other words, unlike the move from "x" to "A," a move which one can roughly put as going from object to concept, the move from x, y, and z to Q goes from concept to concept or fact to fact, depending upon whether one is examining the concept used or the use to which one puts the concept.

53

III. Classification

One might object to the preceding analyses on the grounds that the notion of species has received the short end of the stick. Events have been allowed to display a hierarchy of sorts, i.e., while event Q was denied, events x, y, and z were not. Instead of paralleling that hierarchy with the classificatory hierarchy of objects, the account stressed on the object side the relation between entity and concept. There are, however, good reasons for beginning at that point. More than one school of philosophical tradition has bequeathed to object studies the attempt to count nouns as conceptual labels. One relevant consequence for the present study is the view, whether implicit or explicit in a given theory, that objects exist independently of their assigned species words at any level of consideration. Thus, levels play no role in the object side of the distinction made above.

Events, however, have not suffered the fate of objects, perhaps because so little attention has been focused on them. The meagre attempts to formalize event language founder on identity conditions, as the discussion of criteria sets suggests they might. Consequently, no temptation to consider event language as a veneer on the world has yet produced an event-oriented Aristotle. Without the temptation and tradition, one can turn directly to the question of the grounds wherein event assertions find their justification, and those grounds turn out to include, along with everything else, other events. Thus, any explication of the criterial relation must distinguish those events which fulfill criteria from those which are asserted on the basis of fulfilled criteria. The term "level" occurs quite naturally in such connections, but carries no implications regarding the size, importance, or ontological status of events. It only functions to distinguish criteria from concepts when both involve events.

Nonetheless, the notion of classification, either parallel or analogous to the species-genus relations possible in object language, has long infected discussions of events. The relation between event concepts and the conditions, states, actions, and other events which warrant their use or which may in some way be encompassed by them has often been expressed in terms taken from the vocabulary of classification and genus-species relations. Nagel rightly holds that Rickert's grounds for thinking historical event concepts to be individual is based on the idea that, contra-conventionally, event concepts increase mutually in extension and intension.[11] Dray, again, treats colligation or "explaining what" as a kind of classification, or synthesis, an explanation by means of a general concept, although his emphases on conceptual proposals and their roots in metaphors and analogies suggest that he does not want an Aristotelian notion of classification.[12] How seriously we should take the notion of classification precisely constitutes the present question.

Of course, there is the sense in which any application of a concept counts as a case of classification. Even apart from particular linguistic theories, the use of a concept carries consequences beyond the assertion at hand: it precludes the use of other concepts; what follows from the use of one concept does not follow from the use of others; the potential species-genus structure resulting from one concept does not necessarily result from another. All these effects of concept use warrant the serious use of the word "classification" in connection with any concept use. Yet, since these facts apply to all concepts and catalog what follows concept use, they do not touch the question of whether the criterial relation is a form of classification or something else. If the criterial relation is a form of classification, it is a form of some other sense of classification.

Among other kinds of classification, class formation by the enumeration of membership has obviously no relevance. Classes formed by reference to common characteristics also miss the point. It is possible to form such classes, e.g., to class revolution with war because both involve violent activity. Since "violent activity" counts as a criterion for both concepts (that is its "involvement"), this type of class formation cannot establish the nature of the criterial relation.

The most likely candidate seems to be the species-genus relation which arises in systems of definitions. To say that a cow is a mammal is analytic to the extent that "mammal" comprises a satisfactory genus for the species "cow." One can make similar assertions of events, e.g., of the relation of political revolutions to revolutions. Such cases even avoid difficulties inherent in the cow-mammal case, because the appearance of the word "revolution" in both event concepts obviates the need for definition. The cow-mammal case depends for its justification upon definitions of an order such that all the elements in the definition of "mammal" also occur explicitly or implicitly in the definition of "cow." Whether or not one can or cares to generate an extensive or all-encompassing hierarchy of concepts, these elements of the species-genus relation hold for every minor or major instance of its occurrence.

The criterial relation differs in several important respects from the genus-species relation sketched above. A partial sentence from Claude Bowers, *The Tragic Era*, may illustrate the differences. Writes Bowers, ". . . the Radicals intrigued and fought to mould the policy of Johnson," referring, of course, to the events immediately following the death of Lincoln. In support of his claim of intrigue, Bowers cites the following events: Julian's diary records a meeting of radicals, held within eight hours of Lincoln's death, in which the attendants agreed to urge Johnson "to get rid of the last vestige of Lincolnism;" Radical leaders met with Johnson to express faith in him and were pleased with his declarations; Sumner, Stanton, and "a few Radicals" met to discuss reconstruction plans for Virginia; and members of the Radicals made speeches and demands, all aimed at harsh reconstruction measures.[13] These events and actions (together with others omitted for brevity) justify Bower's assertion that a certain group intrigued in order to establish a certain goal. The relation between the events

55

narrated and the assertion is criterial to the extent that such things conventionally justify the assertive use of "intrigue." The relation, however, is not one of species to genus.

First, nowhere between the concept "intrigue" and the concepts used in expressing the criterial conditions--e.g., "meeting," "discussion," "speeches,"--whether taken singly or together, need there exist any common definitional or explicatory elements. If one could claim that concepts like "intrigue" have no definitions of the sort examined earlier, then the entire question of genus and species would necessarily disappear. Short of that claim, however, one may still note that on the basis of criteria alone, event and action concepts clearly accept judgments of correctness. Altering the events with respect either to their nature or to their timing might well remove warrant from Bower's assertion. Had the meetings and speeches occurred before Lincoln's death, warrant might exist for a concerted effort to mold national policy, but not perhaps for an intrigue to mold Johnson's. Thus, criteria and concept sustain a close relation despite the absence of the common element or elements required by species-genus.

Second, the very disparateness of criterial elements which warrant the use of a concept displays something other than a species to genus relation. The given criterial factors have nothing necessarily in common with each other and thus do not constitute species of any one genus. (It is an accident of the example that all the cited events involved speech acts: had it occurred, a silent act--say, the preparation of documents--would have equally been countable within the justification of Bower's assertion.) Moreover, the meetings, discussions, and speeches do not become steps or parts of the intrigue and fight until after the assertion of intrigue. (The point has to do with a logical priority, not a temporal sequence.) Just as each of a flight of stairsteps may differ, so too the steps of an intrigue may have nothing more in common than their occurrence in pursuit of a goal (to call acts and events "steps" presupposes a goal).

Finally, the concept does not summate the criteria or collect them in the manner in which a genus collects species. The genus class collects by repetition of a portion of a definition or description of the species. The event concept need not repeat its criteria or even a portion of them. To the extent that what follows from a concept's use may not follow on the assertion of the criterially used events alone, the use of the concept opens assertion possibilities which a genus cannot open with respect to its species. Thus, event and action concepts do not summarize in any sense the concepts used to express their criteria. For reasons which will appear with regard to the suggestion that criteria count as parts of the conceptual whole, it is preferable to say the concepts do not summarize rather than to say that they add something more or go beyond summary. In fact, the criterial relation differs significantly from summation and especially from the conception of summation relevant to the species-genus relation.

56

IV. Wholes and Parts

Nagel's rejection of Rickert's claim that historical concepts are
individualistic raised a number of questions in the early stages of
this study, questions which, as noted, gave rise in part to the present
conception of event and action concepts. The present point seems appropriate to examine Nagel's remarks and perhaps to lay some of those
questions to rest while examining another possible confusion with the
criterial relation. Nagel argues that larger phenomena--like the
French Enlightenment--may encompass other phenomena--like the life of
Voltaire--but "the *extension* of the term 'French Enlightenment' does
not include the *extension* of the term 'the life of Voltaire'." More
than a classificatory relation, the situation here reminds Nagel of a
whole-part arrangement.[14]

One might be able to interpret Nagel's remarks in such a way as to
make the whole-part relation a candidate for being an analysis of the
criterial relation. The quotation concerning the French Enlightenment
gives this line of thought an initial plausibility. Unfortunately,
Nagel chose an ambiguous example. The term "French Enlightenment"
might lay equal claim to the status of a proper name or to that of a
specific instance of a concept. As a proper name, and with a specification of what one is naming, the whole-part suggestion gains plausibility. If we name a period of time and a place the French Enlightenment, then Voltaire's life, as a time span within that of the Enlightenment, becomes a part of what is named. But, on this alternative, the
French Enlightenment and the life of Voltaire do not count as phenomena. Rather, they function as names for (pardon the expression)
spatio-temporal complexes. One might even refine this account by restricting what "French Enlightenment" names to a certain collection of
events (and perhaps objects). In such a case, only certain events in
Voltaire's life become part of the Enlightenment. This interpretation
does justice to Nagel's remarks on extension. However, not only does
the extension of the term "French Enlightenment" not include the extension of "the life of Voltaire," the collection itself does not include
Voltaire's life. Instead, it includes only certain events (or objects)
related to Voltaire while he lived. Thus, the life of Voltaire fails
to be a part of the given whole.

If the French Enlightenment is a phenomenon, namely, a particular
enlightenment, then aspects of Voltaire's life fulfill criteria for the
assertion of an enlightenment. In this role, these aspects are not
parts of the Enlightenment, for the Enlightenment--as asserted in this
case--is not the sort of "thing" to have parts. It is an event, not a
spatio-temporal complex. Voltaire's life is not part of the event, but
only some things that he did which, along with the acts of others, justify our assertion that an enlightenment occurred. Although this interpretation also adheres to Nagel's injunction concerning extensions,
it differs from treating the Enlightenment as a collection of events.
For what follows from asserting a phenomenon does not necessarily follow from asserting a collection. For example, phenomena lead to

things, like changes in ideas and attitudes of the French intellectuals and people, whereas collections *per se* lead to no such thing. Thus, one cannot take both options at once in order to have an event with its concept and a whole with its parts.

In order to keep these points straight when examining cases of use, one must attend closely to the purpose for which a given historian uses the term "Enlightenment." Were Voltaire's life in general a part of the time-place segment labeled Enlightenment, then one could cite indiscriminantly both his writing and his eating beef as relevant facts. The fact of eating beef becomes irrelevant to "Enlightenment" as either the name of a collection or as an event concept, but for different reasons. In the collection case, one must have grounds of inclusion or exclusion relative to the collection, and Voltaire's writing meets the test. Such grounds exist independently of Voltaire's writing. If we are just beginning our study, his writing may give a clue or suggest that there is a class of events to be labeled, but that fact fails to count as the justification of inclusion. As a concept, "Enlightenment" rests on Voltaire's writing for justified assertion, but does not rest on his eating beef any more than it does on the French peasants tilling soil in the manner of their fathers. For the concept use of "Enlightenment," Voltaire's writing becomes a test (one of many tests, i.e., fulfillments of criteria), not the tested. In narrative, of course, authors shift from one use to another without self-consciousness. Quite naturally, one moves from Voltaire's love life to his writings, to the effects of the greater phenomenon, all under the rubric of the Enlightenment.

To shift the example, Hurlbut's division was not part of the Battle of Shiloh, but was part of the army under Grant and took part in the battle. What it did--fight, fall back, fight again--might be said to have been part of the Battle, i.e., part of the Battle action. Too, Shiloh was part of the Civil War. But so were bravery, incompetence, victory, defeat, slaughter, singing, and Private Bruce Edwards. Even this small hint of the possible meanderings through uses of event concepts suggests that the notion of a whole-part relation, when in contact with events, loses any simple clarity it may (or may not) carry around in connection with objects. One may argue that applications of the whole-part relation to events depend upon and derive from prior applications of it to objects, but that would solve nothing. For what may be inferred about objects from the application of the relation would not necessarily carry over to events. The fact of dependency may be a point in logic, but the manner of dependency appears to be merely genetic.

Whatever the precise uses of "whole-part" with respect to events, this relation still fails to capture the essential elements of the relation between an event concept and the criterial events, actions, entities, and conditions which justify its use. This criterial relation, however, has the strange effect of partially warranting Rickert's observation of a concomitant increase in both scope and richness of event

58

concepts, so long as one does not take his claim to include an "intension-extension" thesis (the terms become inapplicable with criteria) or an interpretation of richness along the lines of valuation or definition. Certainly an expression like "Lee's plan to invade the North" does "cover" more than just the northward march of an army, and more follows from the invasion plan than the northward march. To boot, because plans are the sorts of "things" to have parts, the northward march (disrupted, along with the plan, in the vicinity of Gettysburg, Pennsylvania) was part of the plan.

A study of wholes and parts, as possible ascribed attributes of events and actions, would fill volumes. The following samples the range to show its variegation. Small scale events—window breakings, volcanic eruptions, and the like—tend not to be spoken of in terms of parts. Neither do many kinds of individual acts of people or groups, such as walking, talking, reading, and writing. Larger historical events, like wars, often have parts, although the parts may not add up to a whole. E.g., the sum of battles do not make a war; nor do the wartime divisions of responsibility such as combat, intelligence, administration, and logistics. A baseball game has its object parts (men, bats, gloves), its event parts (singles, put outs, stolen bases), its actions (chasing flies, bunting, striking out), its rules, and some hard to classify items like team spirit. Plans and plots have steps or temporally ordered parts, like the manufacture of complex items. Movements, like the Italian Renaissance in the arts show temporal development, but very often neither a goal nor distinct parts. In such phenomena, the last man or event of the movement may also be the first of a new movement (if one follows). Beginnings and endings count as parts only if one relevantly speaks of a beginning, or ending, event or action, as when the President begins the baseball season by throwing out the first ball. Merely dating the start and end removes the termini as parts. As Ryle has noted, occurrences like winning or seeing represent achievement, not temporally stretched events, actions, or processes; winning can have no parts or termini. Yet, we have criteria to warrant their assertion. The very unsystematic collage of applications of the concept "whole-part" itself precludes the use of that relation as a model for criterial justification of concept use.

V. Sufficient Conditions

The explication of the criterial relation given in the preceding chapter argues that the fulfillment of criteria provides *sufficient grounds* for the assertion of an event. To the extent that the phrase "sufficient conditions" is similar to the phrase "sufficient grounds" and usually receives interpretation in terms of implication, one may easily conclude that the criterial relation falls under the many-faceted notion of implication. Informally, one would probably not create any serious difficulties by using such terminology. However, the formal notion of implication as a truth-functional concept does not in fact coincide with the notion of criteria. The differences lie in several areas.

Let x, y, and z be criteria for asserting Q. If the criteria are held to imply Q, then

(x and y and z) implies Q.

This, of course, is equivalent to saying either of the following:

not (x and y and z) or Q;

not [(x and y and z) and not Q].

Treating criteria as implying the concept whose use they warrant commits us to saying that it is not the case that we have the criteria fulfilled and we do not have a Q. Such a statement commits us to far too much. First, the formulae make no reference to context. The point is vital, for without reference to context, the implication formulae are simply false. It is quite possible to have cases of violence, changes of governmental ideologies and institutions, and concomitant changes in social and economic structures and not have a revolution. The American Civil War might well stand as one example: but for the circumstances which led to secession by southern states, the course of events in the middle years of the nineteenth century might be called a union revolution instead of a confederate rebellion.[15]

What has changed in the example is not an entire domain of discourse, but only one or two elements in the context. Thus, one is not in the position of setting boundary conditions for a term's use. Rather, contexts become relevant to the extent and in those aspects which permit one to decide the warrant for a particular assertion. The easy way amounts to including the context among the criteria, e.g.,

[(x and y and z) and C] implies Q,

where C summarizes the context. In advance, however, one cannot analyze C. Nothing in principle counts against anything's being included in C. The only possible limit for the number of elements conjoined under C is the number of sensible, but non-relevant questions one might ask about the situation of Q's use. Not only do the questions include reference to the general situation of use, but insofar as x, y, or z may be criterially justified and thus subject to justification, their criteria and context fall under C. The C thus loses its potential for coherent meaning and analysis.

An appropriate counter to this point might be that C's non-analysis is a matter of fact rather than one of principle. While C presents innumerable practical problems, it presents none to theory. Were this study dealing with or offering a formal theory, such a response would be appealing. However, the conception of event and action concepts outlined in this study does not extend to formal theory and is not de-

signed for its purposes. Rather, the present conception intends to
serve only those issues arising from historical and related practices.
For that reason, the non-analysis of C represents a strong reason for
rejecting its introduction. Since the notion of criteria was generated
to cover the feature of language practice in which justification occurs
on demand, the treatment of C as meaningful would be inconsistent with
the relevancy requirement of any demand.

Second, the lack of principle by which to specify what C may include leaves only the useless utterance that potentially anything may
be included. This fact will have considerable importance in evaluating
certain explanations of historical inference offered by Collingwood.
Here it has the function of eliminating C as meaningful to the so-
called implication of Q. Since there also exist no principles by which
to set the boundary conditions for a context or situation, introduction
of C amounts to saying that Q is implied by everything. But then, so
is everything else. The formal and, hence, artificial closure of C
would be inconsistent with the pragmatic dimension of the request for
justification and of the consequent pragmatic practical closure of context.

Moreover, introduction of the formal notion of implication makes a
mystery of the fact that more follows from Q than from x, y, and z (assuming C can be closed). Originally, the notion of "following from Q"
was not treated formally with respect to criterial justification; which
is to say, it was not claimed that Q implied anything. Nonetheless, if
C is not present in a proposed implication formula, then Q can imply no
more than x, y, and z, and what more may follow from Q takes on the air
of either a contradiction or a miracle. Introducing C, in the absence
of closure principles, merely enters a catch-all into the formula, one
which permits a sign of formal relief but leaves explication to take up
the anxiety. What serves as a catch-all usually turns into a waste
basket.

Besides formal difficulties, the notion of implication presents a
problem of interpretation. One may reasonably ask in what sense criteria imply a concept. From the discussion of definition it becomes
apparent that implication does not work as it would in the case of asserting that being a brother implies being a male sibling, or vice ver-
sa. Partial definitions are implied by the concept but do not imply
it. Empirical implications, e.g., where by constant conjunction and
association one comes to say with covering law theorists,

$$(C_1, C_2, C_3, \ldots C_n) \text{ implies E,}$$

has no application. Such a formula presupposes the independent assertion of the events and conditions represented by E and the C's, a feature precisely lacking with criterially justified concepts and their
criteria. Nowell-Smith's notion of "contextual implication" also fails
as an interpretation. If p contextually implies q for "anyone who knew
the normal conventions of language," then besides problems noted ear-

lier, the formula suffers an ambiguity.[16] One cannot distinguish cases in which "p" and "q" represent separable assertable items, which one might conventionally rather than scientifically associate, from cases in which "p" expands into criteria for using the concept "q." The former alternative differs genetically but not formally from empirical implication, while the latter alternative simply restates the explicated formulation of the criterial relation.

Attempts have been made to permit the use of the words "imply" and "entail" and to shift the irregularity of the criterial relation to a different point in the explanation. Albritton, in trying to explicate Wittgenstein's use of the term "criterion," opts for an entailment relation. Using toothaches and behavior of "a certain manner, under certain circumstances," Albritton concludes that the behavior "can entail that anyone who is aware that the man is behaving in this manner, under these circumstances, is *justified in saying* that the man has a toothache, in the absence of any special reasons to say something more guarded. . . ."[17] So much is correct, but merely a lengthy alternative expression of the criterial relation. Criteria justify assertion, from which it follows that the fulfillment of criteria entail that an assertion is justified (notice that Albritton has not said that *fulfillment* entails either a situation or an assertion), from which it further follows that the fulfillment of criteria entails that he who knows of the fulfillment is justified in asserting whatever is in question. This formulation in no way translates criterial justification into an entailment.

In the following sentence, however, Albritton moves the word "entails" and recoils in horror, not from the shift, but from the entire notion of criteria. "That a man behaves in a certain manner, under certain circumstances, can entail that he *almost certainly* has a toothache."[18] Quite rightly Albritton notes that "this way of putting it may be very misleading," but not as he supposes, i.e., not because "almost certain" allows us to act and speak as if we were certain. What misleads is Albritton's having allowed the behavior, the fulfillment of criteria, to entail a situation. The connection gives the appearance of an induction: that something is almost certain amounts to its having so high a probability that one can be quite confident. This in turn leaves the mystery of how the probability is entailed. However, criteria do not entail or warrant situations; they warrant assertions. And Albritton (for the wrong reason) rightly doubts that there are criteria "of having a toothache." Unproblematically, there are criteria for saying justifiably that someone has a toothache.

VI. Necessary Conditions

The rejection of implication as the relation named by calling the conventional fact-to-concept link criterial entails the rejection of the notion of necessary and sufficient conditions as a candidate. For the only clear interpretation of necessary and sufficient conditions involves the notion of implication. To say that x, y, and z are sufficient conditions for Q is to say that x, y, and z entail Q. Such an analysis again suffers precisely the objections raised in the preceding section. The failure of sufficient conditions, on the counts of both formal considerations and interpretation, suffices to falsify the attempt to analyze the criterial relation as both necessary and sufficient conditions.

Nevertheless, analysis of certain concepts, especially those vaguely cataloged as "mental," in terms of necessary and sufficient conditions remains popular. Hempel, for one, has suggested such an analysis of these "cluster" concepts in terms of Carnap's ordered sentence pairs.[19] Although a full analysis of this suggestion falls outside the scope of this study, one or two enticing features of the program have particular relevance to the attempt to supplant criteria. In Hempel's view, both necessary and sufficient conditions occur in clusters such that at an advanced stage of analysis, i.e., the production of several ordered pairs, the fulfillment of any set of sufficient conditions entails the feature predicated, which in turn entails all the necessary conditions. By the freshmen's friend, hypothetical syllogism, the predicate itself drops out, allowing the direct relation of sufficient to necessary conditions.[20]

$$(S_1 \text{ or } S_2 \text{or } \ldots S_n) \text{ implies } (N_1 \text{ and } N_2 \text{ and } \ldots N_n),$$

where S is any set of sufficient conditions and N is any set of necessary conditions.

Besides succumbing to the objections raised earlier, Hempel's account clearly assumed that context provides no barriers between uses of the relevant class of concepts. The entailment of the conjunction of all necessary conditions presupposes that all uses are consistent, compatible, and sensible in all contexts. Recognition that context does comprise some sort of barrier which precludes such easy universalization has resulted in alternative analyses of necessary conditions with respect to concepts. Ryle, for example, argues that the use of certain "dispositional" concepts entails any number of heterogeneous forms of behavior which "unpack" the meaning of the concept in question. Ryle attempts no analysis of the conditions of assertion, but describes that matter as being inductive, or something like induction.[21] This much of Ryle's account needs attention here: since the so-called heterogeneous forms of behavior would in this study be treated in the category of criteria, one may ask if a necessary condition analysis suffices to subsume the criterial relation.

Unlike Hempel, but like Scriven,[22] Ryle's analysis suggests that a concept does not entail every condition set, but rather only one or more of a disjunction of condition sets:

$$Q \text{ implies } (N_1 \text{ or } N_2 \text{ or } \ldots N_n),$$

63

where N_1, N_2, etc., are sets of conditions or behaviors. Such an analysis preserves contextual barriers while seemingly accounting for the fact that the vague concepts in question--events, actions, mental predicates--yield only partial or open-ended definitions.

The plausibility of notions like partial meaning and their seeming compatibility with the notion of criteria derives largely from the multiple uses of "meaning." In the present instance, the meaning of a concept is what the concept entails. But a concept does not entail all the criteria which justify its use, even within a given context. One may recognize that certain analytic relations do hold among event, action, and mental concepts, and that these do give rise to necessary condition statements. Murder is one form of killing, which, in turn, is one way of inducing death. Thus, it is analytic in a straightforward way that there must be a death in order for there to be a murder, or at least one death is a necessary condition for the assertion of murder.

However, similar reasoning cannot be applied to all criteria for "murder." There can be murders without a knife, without a corpse, without a messy room. In short, the absence of no single item in a given criteria set counts as a sufficient condition of a non-murder. Sometimes, even the absence of most items fails to remove warrant from an assertion. Jacques Ellul writes, for example, that "we are inclined to recognize [the Commune of 1871] as a revolution. Yet it had few of the characteristics of revolution."[23]

The most that the absence of criterial conditions warrants is the claim that one is not justified in asserting an event or action. Since several criteria sets may be relevant to an assertion in a given context, especially in the broad contexts over which historians spread their work, the task of showing a lack of justification may be as long or longer than the original justification. Neither accident nor verbosity inform Taylor's book-long attempt to remove warrant from the claim that Hitler had a certain plan or Schlesinger's denial that the fight against depression was the central issue of traditional American reform.

The discussion of sufficient conditions allowed the claim that, if criteria supply sufficient grounds for assertion, then the fulfillment of those criteria implied that the assertion warranted by the criteria was justified. A similar claim holds with respect to necessary conditions and must be distinguished from a claim about criteria themselves. One who shows there was no death has also shown there was no murder. However, one who shows there is no fulfilled criteria set relative to the assertion of murder in a given context has not shown that there was no murder, but only that the assertion of murder was not justified. In many cases, the distinction is crucial. Given a certain course of events and actions, the assertion that there was no plan *may* imply that there was something else, perhaps a set of accidents or an unplanned but directional movement. If nothing else is required here, it is at least necessary to so categorize the course of events as to remove the need for explanations in terms of plans. In other cases, the removal of justification from an assertion *need* entail, suggest, or insinuate nothing beyond itself. This point will take on considerable import in the discussion of historical evidence and inference.

The notion of "necessary conditions," then, has little or no use with regard to the conceptual criteria. Insofar as the removal of warrant consists in either showing the non-fulfillment of all applicable criteria sets or in showing no set to be applicable, no criterion nor set becomes necessary in the requisite manner. A justified assertion entails the fulfillment of at least one relevant criteria set, just as above, the fulfillment of a criteria set entails that a certain assertion is justified. Both claims are true, but trivially, since "fulfillment of criteria" and "justification" are equivalent expressions in this context. Extracting either implication from a tautological equivalence contributes nothing to the attempt to subsume the criterial relation under some other concept.

The very fact that in both necessary condition and sufficient condition analyses attention turned from the criteria themselves to the various sets of criteria suggests that a misdirection has occurred. For no analyst working outside the realm of objects has suggested a formula to the effect,

Q implies (x or y or z) or

Q implies (x and y and z),

where Q is the concept and x, y, and z are the criteria of a given set. Yet, it is the relation of the criterial items to the concept used and not the relation of criteria sets to a concept which has remained the underlying problem confronting all analyses over the relevant classes of concepts.

"Sufficient grounds" seems adequate at this point to portray the relation between criteria and concept, and that only to preserve the conventionality of the relation while stressing the role of justification. Convention and justification by themselves do not necessitate the confinement of attention to wholly linguistic considerations. In the course of studies devoted to non-object concepts, analyses have exhibited empirical strains, tendencies, and motives which deserve some comment. From the British Empiricists on, the relation of empirical data to the use of concepts has never sunk far below the surface of epistemic debate, and even in the present study of portions of history's activities, the fact-finding and fact-making enterprises form a close alliance with the logic of concept use.

That the assertion of an event or action should lend itself, at least initially, to empirical analysis proves tempting. Historians and others dealing in event and action assertions which call for justification often, and perhaps habitually, speak of the "evidence" for their conclusions. While the subject of historical evidence receives more detailed inspection farther on, at this point, common sense may be blamed for temptation: since ordinarily and unreflectively one associates the use of evidence with statements of fact, and since historians in particular deal in facts, their assertions should be treated as empirical conclusions based on the evidence. To an easily under-estimated degree, common sense leads in the proper direction: nothing counts against calling the historian's work empirical to the extent that he makes factual assertions which rest upon other facts.

Characterizing the historian's assertions as empirical is not, however, tantamount to rejecting the conception of language presented in the preceding chapter. The claim in fact says very little, if any, more than one could say in calling his assertions factual. And factually assertive uses of event and action concepts (or the factual assertion of events and actions) comprise this endeavor's central concern. Moreover, to ascertain the fulfillment of criteria is an empirical or fact-finding task. Consequently, the essential question does not concern whether this or that particular portion of the historian's work is empirical or a matter of fact-finding. The pertinent question is this: can the relevant class of assertions be subsumed under an analyses of fact-finding? If a knife, a corpse, and a disheveled room amount to murder, perhaps they do so in some empirical way. If Lee marches north with his Army, crosses into Pennsylvania, and so on, perhaps one hypothesizes that he has a plan or reaches the conclusion that he is making an invasion on the basis of some empirical generalization. In short, it may be that the criterial conventions are not wholly linguistic and that some empirical relation captures what has heretofore been termed criterial.

VII. Probability and Induction

As a candidate for the criterial relation, probability almost suggests itself. Actually, the grounds for the suggestion come from several sources. Albritton's statement that someone's behavior "can entail that he *almost certainly*" has a certain trait lies open, as one example, to probability treatment. Similarly, one might argue, the criteria make very probable the occurrence of the event whose assertion they warrant. Such an analysis would coincide with certain tendencies in phenomenalism, where the failure of perception to guarantee or to be guaranteed by the existence of an object leads to the conclusion that perception and object have a contingent relation.[24] Perceptions thus yield a high probability that something exists, usually a probability so high that our actions and speech with respect to the object can ignore the minute logical gap.

One might claim that the murder case is analogous to the phenomenalist's existence case: what the maid saw warrants her assertion, since it provides a high probability of murder. However, the more

sophisticated techniques of the police may well overrule her, in effect, by lowering the probability. A case more explicitly relevant to
historical writing, but parallel to the preceding artificial example,
can be found in Hexter's reexamination of the middle class in Tudor
England. By noting the elevation of merchants to positions of public
trust, the measures designed to encourage commerce and industry, the
grants of privileges to commercial groups, and the direct assertions
relating commonwealth welfare to trade, past historians could "make a
strong case for the theory that the Tudors especially favored the middle class. . . ." The strength of that case Hexter deflates. He shows
that some of the elements of the case do not in general lend support to
the conclusion (e.g., the political rhetoric), that others suffer too
many counterexamples (e.g., grants of privileges), and that still
others might be deemed misinterpretations of fact. When rightly viewed
and set with other particulars, the support provided by the facts
"either dwindles to insignificance or loses its shape in a mist of ambiguity."[25] The hypothesis or "theory" loses most of its probability
of being correct. Even Collingwood entertained this mode for analyzing
the reasoning apropos to historical inference and assertion. Although
he rejects it, his grounds for doing so do not rest upon an examination
of the relevant relations, but lean almost wholly upon a desire to
claim for history the ability to reach "certain" rather than merely
"permissive" conclusions.[26]

Probability theory currently suffers a multiplicity of interpretations. Fortunately, distinguishing among them does not form a prerequisite to seeing what ails the present suggestion. The correlative
function of probability brings together two events, features, or other
items and assigns to them a measure, whether or not the measure has
numerical expression. "Given a, what is the probability of b?" is the
general question of probability, answers to which comprise a numerical
ratio or degree of confidence or some other less-then-perfect, better-
than-nothing measure. In the examples given, behavior, perception,
what the maid saw, and Tudor actions and assertions stand in for a,
while the toothache, existence, murder, and Tudor favor of the middle
class substitute for b.

However, the correlating function of probability presupposes that
a and b are independently assertable. The phenomenalists' failure to
relate existence to perception by way of entailment suffices for him to
declare their logical independence and to see them related probabilis-
tically. Likewise, a partial motive behind declaring behavior to make
almost, but not quite certain the fact of a toothache seems to have
been an intuitive understanding of the two as logically separate or
separable. In general, to insure that a particular correlation has no
analytic but only empirical grounds requires that the elements correla-
ted be independent of each other.

The requisite independence of events does not characterize the
criterial relation. The assertion of a Q, i.e., the assertive use of
the concept Q, rests on the criteria, which is to say that an assertion

of Q cannot be justified without reference to the relevant x, y, and z. X, y, and z, of course, may be asserted without reference to Q. The maid's assertion of murder is criterial; so too is the "theory" or "hypothesis" of Tudor favor to the middle class. Hexter undercuts this claim, not by giving the conclusion a lower probability, but by showing Tudor actions do not warrant or justify a claim of favor to a middle class. Middle class favor thus cannot justifiably be asserted independently of the fulfillment of criteria, and the requisite independence of elements to a and b in probability formulae is not present. Yet, as noted earlier, the relation is not one of implication, either. To this extent, the alternatives of implication and probability are not exclusive. (This much alone would suffice to make the phenomenalist's inability to link perception and existence via entailment an inadequate reason for urging a probabilistic relation. The two might well be related criterially.[27])

Yet, genuine cases of probability (and none of the cited cases seems genuine) bear enough similarity to criterial cases that one must wonder whether they have a substantial kinship. Whatever kinship there is resides more in etymology than in logic. Since the criterial relation explicates informal conventions rather than formal rules, correlative connections between formerly independently asserted events, actions, and the like may in time become conventional and dependent. One may treat conceptual proposals, at least for some purposes, as attempts to speed up for one or another reason a process that goes on naturally in the course of the use of language. Regardless of the ultimate transition of correlative to criterial relations, the fact of change does not alter the respective requirements of the two relations. At worst (or best), it muddies up the status of use for certain concepts caught by analysis in the midst of metamorphosis.

The requirement that elements in an empirical probability correlation be independently assertable has the effect of also ruling out another probability relation as a candidate to capture criteria. The old notion of inductive analogy appears on the surface to describe certain aspects of the criteria-to-concept relation. Because every swan we have seen in the past has been white, we can expect the next swan we see also to be white. In a parallel way, because every (or nearly every) case of knife-corpse-messy room in the past has been a murder, the maid's case expectably will be one also. Moreover, both cases may be taught through generalizations rather than demanding actual observations. Hence, the parallel extends beyond the mere fact that one can express the two cases in sentences of like grammar.

Whatever the similarity, the cases differ with respect to the relation among the concepts involved. In order for the swan case to permit genuine expectation based upon inductive analogy, "swan" and "white" must have separable grounds for assertion (for this context, since in contexts of non-expectation the grounds may overlap). In other words, being white is not a criterion for being a swan, nor is being a swan a criterion for being white. Otherwise, not being white

68

would count as a reason (whether or not sufficient in itself) for denying that one had encountered a swan. The precisely required independence demanded by inductive analogy does not exist with the murder or any other criterial case. Neither parallel grammar nor teachability via generalization suffice to liken the cases; they only suggest that we can assert both linguistic and empirical generalizations. That very possibility again suggests that a historical or genetic connection may sometimes exist, a connection which enables one to move from using whiteness as an accident of swans to counting it as a criterion. Nevertheless, the two uses do not occur simultaneously within the justification of a single assertion, and that suffices to keep the cases distinguishable and distinguished.

Straight-forward inductive generalization, another empirical candidate to encompass criteria, begets an analysis similar to that given probability and inductive analogy. Roughly speaking, one observes that each case of A, A_1 through A_n, exhibits some feature x, x_1 through x_n. On that basis, one generalizes that all A's have x, even though one has not observed all cases of A, namely those designatable A_{n+1} through A_{n+m}. In this account, the general assertion rests upon x_1 through x_n, though x is assertable independently of A.

The decisive differences between this form of inductive generalization and event assertions can be reduced perhaps to three. First, an event assertion based on criteria does not relate two items, but asserts in the singular, i.e., the occurrence of an event or an action. The inductive generalization related logically separable A's and x's. Secondly, the generalization that all A's have x takes its justification from the collection of observationally justified singular assertions A_1 has x_1, A_2 has x_2, etc. In contrast, the singular assertion of an event or action takes its justification from the general convention (the two terms are redundant insofar as to call something a convention is to assert its generality). To turn the A case around so as to justify as assertion that A_{n+1} has x_{n+1} on the basis of the generalization that all A's have x is to return consideration to inductive analogy. Third, the x's, x_1 through x_n, which justify the generalization do not parallel the criteria, x, y, and z insofar as the latter dissimilar elements are not instances of some single generally applicable concept. These differences suffice to differentiate empirical generalization from the criterial relation. Like all the other inductive candidates, however, nothing precludes the generalization process from playing a genetic role in x's becoming a criterion for the assertion of A.

The entire discussion of empirical and criterial relations cannot help but remind one of the now sterile debates over whether scientific "laws" (why was it always Boyle's Law?) describe or define. Perhaps the most useful fact to emerge from the skirmishes was that empirically derived generalizations do not necessarily retain that status. Indeed, their status does not depend on their form, their source, or their means of confirmation. Rather, it depends on how one uses them in making various kinds of possible assertions. In this regard, it becomes otiose, if not anachronistic, to speak of Boyle's Law as a Law. We may question its confirmation as a generalization, or question its use to include or exclude some new "stuff" as a gas, or . . . . In particular realms of discourse, e.g., physical theory, history, *et al.*, some questions become more serious than others, and some uses become more questionable than others. The balance of seriousness and questionableness may change with time. Even with simple event or action assertions, where criteria have yet to fix themselves firmly, facts may come in for various treatment, and all the debates suggested as possible in the preceding chapter may arise in full fury. Though the questions involve facts, to the extent that debate aims to establish the criteria for the use of a given concept, the concerns become conceptual.

VIII. Hypothesis and Evidence

Many candidates which one might propose as capturing the criterial relation fail to do so because the parallels between candidate and criteria break down after only a narrow range of correspondence. Others fail because they cover the criterial relation too well. One such case would be the attempt to subsume the criterial relation under the heading of hypothesis and evidence. Although rarely given credit for it by the social scientists working in history, the idealists actually engender the possibility of such a view. Oakeshott argues that history is "what the evidence obliges us to believe," or more modernly, to assert.[28] Collingwood characterizes history as an inferential activity, neither deductive nor inductive, which answers questions, i.e., which presents hypotheses and supports them with evidence.[29] Such language should not offend (except perhaps for the anti-induction remark) even the most rigorous of the pro-scientists. It stresses history's fact finding activities as fundamental to the discipline.

Moreover, the sorts of assertions mentioned thus far in examples seem amenable to hypothesis-evidence treatment. (a) The assertion of a revolution may be taken as a hypothesis which the historian supports by citing relevant evidence, i.e., the facts of a violent change of government, a new ruling class or party, etc. (b) The maid, in effect, if not consciously, hypothesizes murder on the grounds of what she saw in the room, on the grounds of the evidence available to her. The police, more scientific in their ways, have both stricter standards and more subtle means for evaluating evidence. (c) Concerning the historical claim that "of princely concern for the welfare of the middle class and favor to its members the evidence is abundant," Hexter replies, "If we undertake a reasonably careful examination of the evidence that purports to demonstrate Tudor favor to the middle class, that evidence either dwindles to insignificance or loses its shape in a mist of ambiguity."[30] (d) John's combing his hair at every opportunity and for excessive periods of time evinces his vanity. None of these examples represents an unusual way to talk under certain circumstances.

In order to catch the relevant parallels and divergences, consider these cases. (A) An appropriate examination of samples of all known gases is taken as evidence for the hypothesis that the pressure of a gas varies with the temperature and inversely with the volume of the gas. (B) The flash of lightning and the general association of thunder with lightning are evidence for the hypothesis that one will soon hear thunder. (C) A significant chi square value for course evaluation responses comparing upper and lower classmen becomes evidence against a null hypothesis that "there is no difference in ratings made by students of different classes in school."[31] (D) Mind, argues a hypothetical philosopher, is a hypothetical entity, and by so classifying it as a logical construction, he removes from relevance the very notion of evidence for its existence. (E) Courts speak of evidence for both crimes and guilt, but not for hypotheses. Hypothetical cases have a different function.

Now the question arises as to whether the evidence in cases (a) through (d) is the same sort of thing and bears the same relation to the hypotheses as the evidence in cases (A) through (E). This question has no possible answer until one can first say with assurance that every case in (A) through (E) has the same nature and relation. Cases (D) and (E), each of which carries but one of the two terms "evidence" and "hypothesis," must have special status. Neglecting them as extraordinary, one has only to contend with (A) through (C). (A) represents a case of inductive generalization (and does not pretend to say how in fact we came by Boyle's Law). (B) shows an ordinary deduction of the sort covering law theorists would have us do or suppose as doable. The case (C) displays elements of a common technique used in statistical studies, and is especially notable for the fact that researchers who employ it ordinarily do not expect or want the evidence to favor the null hypothesis; they set up the null case precisely because they expect otherwise. Establishing a positive hypothesis would demand a positive level of expected result in order to make the chi square test work. In the absence of either theory or prior investigation, they have no means of setting up a level of expectation, but only the expectation itself.

Even the brief characterization of (A) through (C) shows a lack of means for identifying the evidence-hypotheses relations with each other. (A) is inductive but not statistical; (C) is inductive and statistical; (B) is neither. Nor do we have grounds for saying that the evidence in (A) through (C) is relevantly similar, let alone identical. The sorts of things used in the three cases differ with no more a common connection than the title "evidence." Moreover, the particular relation sought in each of the cases determines in part what kinds of items will count as evidence. (A) and (C) require samples; (B) does not. (B) requires a particular instance of a certain kind of event; (A) and (C) do not. (A) demands a continuously variable measure (three, in fact), (C) requires only counts. Which one shall one say that (a) through (d) are like?

71

The answer is none of them. To the extent that the criterial relations in (a) through (d) are in no clear sense inductive, as shown in
the preceding section, or deductive, as explored under the notions of
implication and of necessary or sufficient conditions, the relation
does not coincide with any of those in (A) through (C). To the extent
that the examples in (a) through (d) do not readily drop one of the two
terms "evidence" and "hypothesis" without also dropping the other, they
do not coincide with either (D) or (E). Consequently, one can gain
nothing by calling the criterial relation an evidence-to-hypothesis relation, if one's intent is to capture the former and reject its terminology as redundant of presently operative categories. The only gain
could be misconception. For the practice of calling criteria evidence
may well bring to mind a favorite or familiar member of the set (A)
through (E), one which imposes upon the criterial relation an inappro-
priate model.

Apart from that danger, however, nothing improper accrues to the
motiveless practice of calling criteria fulfilling events the evidence
for the event or action asserted by the use of the relevant concept.
With respect to history especially, and only slightly less so to other
areas using event assertions, the rubric of evidence and hypothesis is
common. The Hexter example shows this most clearly. What the present
inquiry suggests is not that the criterial relation fails to involve
evidence and hypothesis, but rather that "evidence" and "hypothesis" do
not name a relation. They name the relata. How they stand related in
particular kinds of cases comprises a separable and separate investigation. Consequently, evidence and hypothesis do not comprise the criterial relation. A succeeding portion of this study will explore to
what extent the reverse holds true, that is, to what extent the historian's talk of evidence and hypothesis constitutes talk of criterial
relations.

Although incidental to the present study, the remarks concerning
the possibility of evidence-hypothesis relations being criterial and
conceptual forces one to re-think certain aspects of the case regarding
(E). If evidence and hypothesis intend to capture criteria, the absence of the term "hypothesis" in legal cases of the relevant sort suffices to preclude identification with criterial cases. However, if
criterial contexts constitute instances in which it makes sense to
refer to evidence, then (E) may itself count as a special set of cases
wherein one justifies assertions, e.g., of acts or guilt, on the basis
of fulfilled criteria. The events, actions, conditions, objects, and
other items which fulfill criteria comprise legal evidence, for which
the court has rules. A detailed exploration of this analytic tack and
its implications would go, even in its initial stages, far outside the
bounds of this study. In its own milieu, however, such a study might
prove interesting.

IX. Normic Connection

One final suggestion for the analysis of criterial relations concludes this quest. In the late fifties, Scriven introduced a notion which sought to overcome many of the difficulties engendered by too rough and ready an adherence to the traditional distinction between analyticity and syntheticity. Initially, he introduced the "normic generalization," a loose heading for a patchwork of generalizations which supply justification for the historian's singular explanations. Neither so universal as general laws nor so loosely connected to individuals as statistical laws, this collection of truisms, definitions, and other "guarded generalizations" arises by non-scientific means. Moreover, each member remains immune to counterexample.[32] Shortly after his first immersion into normics, Scriven attempted to explicate the "logic of criteria" using the notion of a "normic connection." The aim of this divergent application of the normic was to subsume criterial relations under the form of necessary and sufficient conditions analyses, while not allowing the connection between criteria and concept to become synthetic. The entire thrust of Scriven's normic blade, however, turns out to rest on a failure to distinguish concepts and statements from their use and justification. Insisting on the relevant distinctions, in turn, obviates the need for the special normic connection.

Using the example of lemons, Scriven begins his account of concepts by distinguishing between indicators and criteria: the former relate to concepts synthetically, the latter normically. Indicators do not yield necessary conditions, since by virtue of their synthetic relation to an object, their denial does not result in a denial of the applicability of a concept in question. A normic criterion, however, does not thereby gain the status of analyticity, i.e., of being either "a logically necessary or sufficient condition." A criterion becomes normic if it is a member of a disjunction which (a) is as a whole analytically necessary and (b) loses its analytic necessity by dropping any disjunct. To draw a clearer line between indicators and normic criteria, Scriven introduces the notion of "characteristic," as in "Ripe lemons are characteristically yellow." Being characteristic connects an attribute to its object more strongly than synthetically owing to the relation's immunity to counter-examples. Yet, the connection does not achieve analyticity, since it can be falsified under certain conditions. Nevertheless, "characteristic statements" do manage "jointly [to] encapsulate the meaning of the term to which they refer," even if they fail to yield sufficient condition statements which would "guarantee applicability of the term." Such guarantees Scriven leaves to an unexplored analysis of statements having the form "if C_j and C_k . . ., then probably x," where "probably" takes on a "normic sense."[33]

Scriven's analysis holds several advantages which one should not overlook. It accounts for the clustering of the descriptive feature sets which mark multiuse concepts. It attempts to come up with an

73

analysis amenable to the use of ordinary logical categories, an aim
clearly desireable if there appears any chance of success. Though the
analysis does not get beyond lemons, it does suggest that criterial
analysis does have applications in the range of object concepts which
formerly had vainly clung to one definitional scheme after another.
Finally, in concert with Ryle's unpacking of dispositions and other
necessary condition analysis, it does reconstitute the concept of
"meaning."

Beginning, as this study does, with event and action concepts
holds one advantage over an analysis of objects: it reins in one's
tendencies to over-extend the reach of one's claims. Scriven's account
presents many a problem the moment one goes past lemons into events and
actions, and the problems refuse to rest comfortably under the rubric
of cluster concepts and characteristicalness. What gave rise to the
notion of "characteristic" was the practical inability to complete the
necessary condition set of disjuncts. The term "characteristic" substitutes for that set. However, both notions--cluster concept and
characteristicalness--suffer some misunderstanding of the role of the
clustered or characteristic criteria.

As noted earlier, for a given context, only one (or a small number) of the total possible sets of criteria has any relevance to the
use of a concept. Consequently, and apart from the oddity and incor-
rectness of saying that a concept entails those things which stand as
criteria *for* it, the disjunction of criteria sets *in toto* has no relevance to the explication of a concept as used. This very point becomes clearer when one looks beyond the work Scriven would like "char-
actistic" to do and examines what the use of that term commits one to.
Just as being yellow is characteristic of ripe lemons, so too significant changes in social-economic-political systems may be said to be
characteristic of revolutions, like those of France or Russia. In the
event example, however, such an analysis of the concept can be misleading. Significant systemic change may have criterial relevance to some,
even to many, contexts in which one appropriately asserts a revolution,
but its relevance clearly does not extend to all, or perhaps even most
contexts. (Just this fact makes necessary Brinton's lengthy section on
"Changes in Institutions and Ideas" in his *Anatomy of Revolution*.
While trying to find significant changes, Brinton also finds himself
forced to admit that "Our revolutions seem in many ways to have changed
men's minds more completely than they changed men's habits."[34]) Similar considerations hold true of Scriven's lemon, except that being yellow does have relevance (perhaps) to most contexts occasioning talk
about a ripe lemon. The extension of "some" to "many" to "most," however, does not warrant the notion of "normic criteria" if by that notion one wishes to avoid reference to context. For to claim that being
yellow is a normic criterion, a characteristic of ripe lemons, is only
to say that in many, if not most, contexts yellow stands as a criterion
for the assertion. Insofar as any particular assertion still depends
for its justification upon a context dependent criteria set, and since
the incomplete disjunction of criteria sets and the terms "characteris-

74

tic" equally imply context dependency, the necessary condition analysis loses both its justification and relevance.

What counts as being characteristic may change with time and place. Although this fact hardly shows with lemons, it appears with a shocking obviousness in connection with events. Bullet wounds may (artificially, to the extent that anything is characteristic of a kind of event) be characteristic of assassinations now, but in 700 B. C. they could not. To say that bullet wounds could not *possibly* have counted then is not to remark on what assassination entails, but only to say that contexts which arise now would not have arisen then. Although the absence or presence of a context has conceptual implications, the occurrence of the context remains dependent upon a state of affairs. It was not logical necessity that withheld bullets from the ancients. Consequently, even though one may say that criteria bear a conceptual relation to the assertions they justify, what count as characteristic criteria is not wholly a conceptual consideration, since the term "characteristic" makes implicit reference to context and hence to states of affairs. Calling what is characteristic a normic criterion thus does not introduce a new or intermediate category between the analytic and the synthetic. That appearance is plausible only so long as one suppresses the implicit contextual reference in the term "characteristic." At most, the so-called normic criterion introduces a concatenation of conceptual and factual considerations.

Much of Scriven's need to distinguish normics from the analytic and the synthetic disappears if one keeps in mind two points: (a) concepts do not themselves require explication, but only concepts as used (or to be used); (b) requests for justification and explication arise sensibly in a context of use (or proposed use) and in terms of that context. Scriven's analysis, however, aims to explicate a concept apart from any particular use; for that reason, it remains incomplete whether he chooses disjunctions of necessary conditions or characteristic properties as the terms of analysis. Within contexts, the unfulfillable desire for a necessary condition statement and the occasion to mention the disjunction or normic connections never arises. Moreover, they cannot arise, since they involve a cut across contextual frontiers, or leaps from one context to another. Held within bounds, the request for conditions, the absence of which would remove warrant from the use of the concept in question, does not result in mere characteristic properties or in an endless disjunction of properties. Rather it results in precisely those conditions relevant to the question. Thus, the consideration which made problematic the fuzzy realm between analytic and synthetic—namely, that many concepts rest in use on features which are not present in all situations but which hold a non-empirical relation to the concepts—simply does not occur in practice.

None of this denies the possibility of generalizing upon the uses of a concept, e.g., that in some, many, most, or all uses, x, y, and z are criteria for Q's use. Such generalizations, however, in no way specify (or even help to specify) in what the criterial relation consists. Any claim that Q entails (characteristically or not) x, y, and z is ambiguous. It may amount to a claim that x, y, and z are always (or almost so) the criteria of Q, a claim which leaves the term "criteria" unexplicated. Or it may amount to the claim that for every (or almost every) context, Q entails its criteria x, y, and z, a claim which does not analyze "criteria," but only presupposes without warrant that to be a criterion is to be entailed by the concept. Both alternatives evade the problem at hand, one by talking about something else, the other by prejudicial predecision.

The failure to distinguish a concept from a concept as used shows its parallel in Scriven's other use of the notion of "normic." Normic generalizations, immune to counter-example but neither universal nor statistical, depend upon a failure to distinguish a statement from its use. This failure, and not something peculiar to their form or content, keeps one from being able to pin them down to one or another of the usual categories (though, of course, new useful categories may yet appear). "Rhombi are four-sided" may be analytically true if used to define "rhombi" for one wanting to know what they are. The assertion may be descriptive of a set of rhombi for someone who is asked, apart from any geometric definition, to look at the set and describe what the members have in common. This is a common grade school teaching technique, and a child who answers is not *eo ipso* defining "rhombi" by his reply. The assertion may also be used as a universal, say in a syllogism. Even Scriven's own example, "Rhombi means the same as equilateral parallelogram," has many uses--as a definition, a report on usage, etc.--but in each, the status of the assertion remains clear. Equal treatment goes to others of Scriven's generalizations, e.g., "Strict Orthodox Jews fast on the day of Atonement" or "A rise in tariffs characteristically produces a decline in the value of imports."[35] The last, supposedly usable as a general economic "law," suffers from the vague word "characteristically" such that any purported deduction from it and the premise "Here is a case of a rise in tariffs" must either omit the word or include another premise to the effect that the present case is characteristic. In short, the presence of the word "characteristic" does not change the assertion's status (from synthetic generalization to normic), but instead changes its content and possible uses. To the extent, finally, that each use is analyzable without reference to its normic-ness, nothing accrues from calling the sentences normic, except to say that they have many uses.

Moreover, the sentences do not of themselves comprise guarded generalizations. Warrantably to title them so, one must be able to say in what the guardedness consists via a general account, examples (caveats, conditions of defeat, etc.), or other appropriate means. Even this feature applies not to the statements in general, but to uses of them. To say that "Strict Orthodox Jews fast on the day of Atonement" amounts to a casual observation which is generally but not exceptionlessly true, is to speak of the assertion as a generalization needing justification, but not to speak of it as a canon of behavior which expresses

how certain people should act nor to treat it as a covering law universal which allows deduction of a singular assertion. To construct a
syllogism using the same assertion as its universal is not to speak to
the question of how the universal is to be justified, but to fulfill
the requirements of a logical form. One may also ask for justification, but that question is as separable from the question of which universal will allow deduction of a certain conclusion as are the questions of factualness and validity. Whatever the direction, whatever
the example, Scriven's normic category disappears in a puff of attention to use.

Oddly enough, the most promising direction in Scriven's analysis
turns out to be the loose end on which he gives a promissory note:
sufficient condition analysis will take the form "if C_j and C_k . . . . ,
then probably X." Without the word "probably," the form fits under the
analysis of sufficient conditions given early in this chapter. With
"probably" taken seriously, it fits the analysis of probability and induction. With a special "normic sense" applied to "probably," one can
only wonder. Assuming the best--an attention to use--it might yield
the notion of sufficient grounds. Given the problems of "normic" noted
in this section, assuming the best may be assuming too much.

The problem, many alternatives back, was to examine the question
of precisely what relation the label "criteria" specifies and how to
distinguish that conceptual relation from others (questions (2) and
(3)). The task of exploring the most plausible alternatives has distinguished the criterial relation from others with which one might confuse it. The analytic safari has not satisfied the question of specification, if one interprets "satisfaction" so as to entail finding a
substitute for the criterial relation. Instead, it has elicited a number of considerations which precise and circumscribe the notion of conceptual criteria. And though the list of candidates for substitution
cannot achieve exhaustion (without condemning the future inventiveness
of analysts), the rejection of so many does supply a strong motive to
move on. For the aim all along has been to employ the conception in
tackling certain overaged issues whose static morbidity seems to demand
a different conception of event and action concepts in order to break
present impasses.

NOTES

[1]Ludwig Wittgenstein, *Philosophical Investigations* (New York: The
Macmillan Company, 1953), #43, pp. 20e-21e.

[2]A. C. Danto, *Analytical Philosophy of History* (Cambridge: At the
University Press, 1965), p. 108.

[3]William H. Dray, "'Explaining What' in History," *Theories of
History*, ed. Patrick Gardiner (New York: The Free Press, 1959), p.
407, where the something more is an "intelligible pattern." Cf.
William Whewell, *The Philosophy of the Inductive Sciences Founded Upon*

Their History (London: John W. Parker, 1840), pp. 168-72, from which Walsh and Dray draw the notion of colligation.

[4]The example of vanity is taken with much modification from Gilbert Ryle, *The Concept of Mind* (New York: Barnes and Noble, 1949), p. 89. The quotation is from Eric Hoffer, *The True Believer* (New York: Harper and Row, Publishers, 1951), p. 23.

[5]Ramsey Muir, *A Short History of the British Empire*, II (London: George Philip and Son, Ltd., 1922), p. 123.

[6]See P. F. Strawson, *Individuals* (Garden City: Doubleday and Company, Inc., 1953), esp. Chapter I, for an example of this sort of view.

[7]I owe this side of the debate to Michael Durrant, whose own detailed position I do not pretend to have stated accurately or with justice.

[8]Strawson, *Individuals*, esp. pp. 23-24, 49.

[9]Arthur M. Schlesinger, Jr., "The Sources of the New Deal," *Paths of American Thought*, ed. Arthur M. Schlesinger, Jr. and Morton White (Boston: Houghton Mifflin Company, 1963), p. 373.

[10]A. J. P. Taylor, *The Origins of the Second World War*, 2nd Ed. (New York: Fawcett Publications, 1961), p. 281.

[11]Ernest Nagel, "Some Issues in the Logic of Historical Analysis," *Theories of History*, pp. 375-76.

[12]Dray, "'Explaining What' in History," p. 407.

[13]Claude G. Bowers, *The Tragic Era* (Boston: Houghton Mifflin Company, 1962), pp. 6-9, quoted sentence from p. 9.

[14]Nagel, "Some Issues in the Logic of Historical Analysis," pp. 375-76.

[15]There are, incidentally, remarkably close parallels between, on the one hand, the course of events and kinds of personages met in the Civil War and, on the other, the patterns found to exist in most revolutions and mass movement by writers such as Crane Brinton, *The Anatomy of Revolution* (revised and expanded ed.) (New York: Vintage Books, 1965) and Eric Hoffer, *The True Believer*.

[16]P. H. Nowell-Smith, *Ethics* (Baltimore: Penguin Books, 1954), p. 72.

[17]Rogers Albritton, "On Wittgenstein's Use of the Term 'Criterion'," *The Journal of Philosophy*, 56 (October 22, 1959), p. 856.

[18]*Ibid.*; the italics are Albritton's.

[19]Carl Hempel, "Explanations in Science and History," *Philosophical Analysis and History*, ed. William H. Dray (New York: Harper and Row, Publishers, 1966), pp. 119-20; Rudolf Carnap, "Testability and Meaning," *Readings in the Philosophy of Science*, ed. Herbert Feigl and May Brodbeck (New York: Appleton-Century-Crofts, Inc., 1953), pp. 53 ff.

[20]Hempel, "Explanations in Science and in History," p. 120.

[21]Ryle, *The Concept of Mind*, p. 90. For a fuller analysis of both Ryle's and Hempel's formulations, see my "Dispositions," *Systematics*, 7 (March, 1970), 329-46.

[22]Michael Scriven, "The Logic of Criteria," *The Journal of Philosophy*, 56 (October 22, 1959), p. 865.

[23]Jacques Ellul, *Autopsy of Revolution* (New York: Alfred A. Knopf, 1971), p. 102, n. 20.

[24]E.g., A. J. Ayer, *The Foundations of Empirical Knowledge* (London: St. Martin's Press, Inc., 1958), pp. 239-41.

[25]J. H. Hexter, "The Myth of the middle Class in Tudor England," *Reappraisals in History* (New York: Harper and Row, Publishers, 1961), p. 99 (for the quoted lines) and pp. 99-105 (for the examination of the supporting materials). Specifically omitted is Hexter's use of the word "evidence" which will appear in the next section. The use of Hexter's writings does not commit their author to the given analysis.

[26]R. G. Collingwood, *The Idea of History* (New York: Oxford University Press, 1956), p. 261.

[27]See, for example, J. L. Austin's treatment of phenomenalism in *Sense and Sensibilia*, ed. G. J. Warnock (New York: Oxford University Press, 1964), pp. 123-24.

[28]Michael Oakeshott, *Experience and Its Modes* (Cambridge: At the University Press, 1933), p. 108.

[29]Collingwood, *The Idea of History*, pp. 9-10, 252, 261.

[30]Hexter, "The Myth of the Middle Class in Tudor England," p. 99.

[31]The example is from Dwight L. Freshley and Don Richardson, "Student Evaluation of Basic Speech Courses," *The Southern Speech Journal*, 34 (Winter, 1968), p. 86.

[32]Michael Scriven, "Truisms as the Grounds for Historical Explanations," *Theories of History*, pp. 463-67.

[33]Scriven, "The Logic of Criteria," p. 862 ff.

[34]Brinton, *The Anatomy of Revolution*, p. 247.

[35]Scriven, "Truisms as the Grounds for Historical Explanations," p. 465.

CHAPTER THREE

Facts, Evidence, and Truth

The most immediate application of the proposed
criterial conception of event and action concepts ranges
over certain uses in history of the notions of "evidence,"
"inference," and "truth." Because Collingwood's position
on evidence and inference replicates within a different
terminological framework the implications for these topics
of a criterial view of language, his views can serve as a
starting point for the explication. Besides noting agreements between Collingwood's position and the one proposed
herein, the chapter also notes divergences, e.g., on the
notion of re-enactment. Specifically, the first section
explicates Collingwood's view of history as an evidential
and inferential activity. The second examines the relation
between evidence and facts inferred from evidence:
Collingwood views the relation as essentially pragmatic,
i.e. based upon an interrelationship between questions and
the evidence which permits answers to them. In the third
section, Collingwood's departure from his analysis of
evidence and inference in order to embrace the theory of
re-enactment is sketched in terms of three factors: a.
his conception of history as a whole, continuous process,
b. his theory of historical imagination by which one
interpolates between known events to produce the whole,
and c. his separation of what happened in the past within
the special category of thought and what historians infer
to have happened. Avoiding the theory of re-enactment,
section four explores the coincidence (over a relevant
class of cases) between the evidence-inferred event relation and the criteria-concept relation for events and
actions. The following section goes on to show that the
realm of thought that Collingwood had held to be distinct
may be treated in the same manner as the realm of events
and actions, thus allowing one to dispense with re-enactment
altogether. In this regard, two examples of Collingwood's
re-thinking are re-analyzed as cases of "conceptual expectation" (to distinguish such cases from other forms of
expectation). Collingwood's distinction between "certain"
and "permissive" conclusions, noted briefly in the first
section, opens the question of truth with respect to historical inferences. Section six outlines the implications
of a criterial view of language for the conditions of truth
of event and action assertions. One major consequence is
that truth and falsity with respect to event and action
assertions do not adhere to the principle of the excluded

middle. The final section deals with the sense in
which one can say that an entire history is true,
specifically contrasting Collingwood's conception of
history as a coherent whole with the application of
the concept "plausibility" to historical writing.

The criterial conception of event language has lain around for
many a year, as the attempts to engulf it with other rhetoric readily
attest. Just the attempts to add rigor to the notion by introducing
into it elements of formal logic (not to mention philosophic theory)
have prevented analysts from examining the implications of a criterial
conception for endeavors, like history, which depend on event and action concepts. One purpose of this study, however, is to do just that.

A worthy place to begin is with the concept of evidence. In dis-
allowing the possibility of simply ditching "criteria" and embracing
the name "evidence," the preceding chapter noted the wide range of uses
for the term "evidence." Most of them the historian has some occasion
to employ. Where applicable, he cites legal evidence, or makes a syllogism, or reaches a statistical conclusion. Generally, however, these
occasions add up to only a portion of his work. The historian, nonetheless, continues to refer to many of the remaining activities and results as inferential and evidential. At least one important part of
the remainder occupies center stage in this chapter. Because Collingwood has said much on the matter of evidence, he makes a proper subject for the spotlight of examination. However, one must keep in mind
that the topic for discussion herein is not evidence and inference in
general, but only one of many logically distinct types. The conclusions apply solely to the sorts of activities noted in the discussion.
They do not constitute a criticism, either explicit or implicit, of
theories which cover other forms of evidence and inference.

Collingwood, Croce, and Oakeshott seem agreed on at least one
point: history deals in "what the evidence obliges us to believe."[1]
In addition, Collingwood sustained the troublesome thesis that history
takes for its object "actions of human beings that have been done in
the past" (IH, 109). From this point he moves through the conception
of creative "historical imagination" to the doctrine of the "re-enactment," "re-creation," or "re-thinking" of past thought lying behind
actions.[2] Today, we inform practically no one when we record that the
doctrine of re-enactment makes little if any sense. After criticizing
traditional intuitive interpretations, even Collingwood's most recent
editor, Debbins, can do no more than to leave re-thinking and related
ideas as views "incompletely worked out by Collingwood."[3] This rather
dissatisfying result wills to us Collingwood's conception of evidence,
a shaky notion of imagination, and a *prima facie* unwanted theory of re-
creation. With these elements we must do something.

I will venture that, should we drop the notion of re-thinking as
simply wrong, take "imagination" with a grain of salt, and concentrate

effort on "evidence," we stand some chance of breaking the impasse which keeps the assertion and explanation of past human actions in a muddle. Most of Collingwood's statements about evidence and those which immediately follow turn out to be correct as they stand, though they need better underpinning than their author gave them. Collingwood's concept of evidence in history will, in fact, coincide largely with the earlier explicated notion of criteria. The coincidence preserves some of Collingwood's best, for example, his meritorious attack on "scissors-and-paste," while avoiding the worst, that is, the idealism, subjectivity, and re-thinking.

What keeps critical readers of Collingwood pinned to the idea of re-enactment, I think, is this. The author expends great effort from the beginning of his *Idea of History* to confine history to the study of "*res gestae*: actions of human beings that have been done in the past" (IH, 9). Moreover, "history is 'for' human self-knowledge" (IH, 10). Immediately, we suspect that something non-specific, non-objective will have to follow in order to get us from the spectator's "outside" of an event to the human "inside" (IH, 213). Whether or not we favor dualisms, typical interpretations of Collingwood begin with the outside-inside distinction.[4]

Yet, of the four elements in his provisional definition of history, the "human" orientation necessarily affects only two, the second and fourth (IH, 9-10). The first asserts that "history is a kind of research or inquiry. . . . generically it belongs to what we call the sciences: that is, the forms of thought whereby we ask questions and try to answer them." The third statement concerns the method by which the historian "can get answers to the questions he asks about past events," namely, "by the interpretation of evidence." Now if we are ever to get clear of re-enactment without overlooking some of the genuine worth Collingwood has, we must shift our starting point to the notions of inference and evidence. When we return to the consideration of action, nothing will remain which requires re-enactment.

I. Collingwood on Historical Evidence and Inference

Collingwood once judged that Oakeshott's great contribution to philosophy of history was his demonstration of historians' "indefeasible right and [their] peremptory duty, to play their game according to its own rules" (IH, 159). Elsewhere, Collingwood expands the metaphor of games, paying especial attention to the idea of rules. "One rule--the first--runs thus: 'You must not say anything, however true, for which you cannot produce evidence'" (LHK, E, 97). When he explicates the metaphor, Collingwood equates the rules of the game with the "definition of historical thinking," i.e., "interpreting the evidence with the maximum degree of critical skill" (LHK, E, 98-99).

The notion of a game, as Collingwood uses it, suggests many of his other views, in particular, the assertion that history is not an obser-

vational, but an inferential activity. He rejects the tacit view of
the Greeks that eyewitness reports form the backbone of history. Instead, the business of history "is to study events not accessible to
our observation, and to study these events inferentially, arguing from
something else which is accessible to our observation, and which the
historian calls 'evidence' for the events in which he is interested"
(IH, 251-52, cf. IH, 25-28). Collingwood refuses to opt for either of
the narrowly defined inference procedures called deduction and induction. The historian's demonstration consists (broadly) in "justifying
his claim by exhibiting . . . the grounds on which it is based," and
these do not necessarily fit either the deductive or the inductive mold
(IH, 252). Between historical assertions and evidence stands a "peculiar relation" (IH, 246).

Foremost among Collingwood's concerns about historical inference
is that the qualified may judge its results as true or false. "In history," he argues, "we demand certainty," the certainty which characterizes inference in the natural sciences wherein "nobody can affirm the
premises without being obliged to affirm the conclusion also" (IH, 270,
261). He rejects inductive argument with its merely "permissive" conclusions: in the negative it "absolutely forbids the thinker from affirming what he wishes to affirm," while in the positive, the most it
gives him is a *nihil obstat*" (IH, 261). Document study, Collingwood
holds, produces no more than this latter sort of result, e.g., that one
has no reason to think the document faulty. It follows that critical
document study cannot alone produce the sort of history Collingwood
seeks. The historian's conclusions must "follow inevitably from the
evidence," though not necessarily in a formal deductive sense.

Collingwood already asks too much of inference. A number of reasons, some of which appear farther on, suggest that the maximum that
many types of historical accounts seek is the most *plausible* account in
view of the given evidence. Without precising Collingwood's notions of
inference and evidence, one may still note that, in general, the thin-
ner the evidence, the greater are the number of events and reasons or
causes for their occurrence which may be plausible. The 19th century
German scholars and the 20th century British philologians wrote very
different accounts of Socrates (to cite just two species with an indef-
inite number of subspecies), whereas biographies of Napoleon scarcely
differ at all.[5] The greater the mass of evidence and agreement as to
how it should be used, the less room for variations in historical conclusions. The gradual accretion of evidence and ways of using it suggests an equally gradual narrowing of what is "permitted."

Investigators such as Dray have arrived at similar conclusions.
His "how-possibly" form of explanation rebuts presumptions against a
proferred account, showing that, "appearances to the contrary, [the
event] is not an impossible one after all."[6] Examples of explanatory
techniques like this one suggest that Collingwood either simply erred
or that he had something besides evidence and inference in mind when he
wrote. His long-standing feud with historical scepticism supplies one

impetus for overreaching the mark. He flatly rejected the sceptic's claim that "the past as such is unknowable" in favor of his own view that "the past as such can be known and is known by history" (LHK, E, 100). The historian's quest for the past confines itself to issues surrounding the evidence at hand and has nothing to do with the purely epistemic possibility of new evidence and new rules of interpretation. "If there once happened an event concerning which no shred of evidence now survives, that event is not part of any historian's knowledge" (LHK, E, 99). Such possibilities have no relevance to the historian's present work; his task consists in interpreting present evidence and reaching conclusions obliged by present evidence. "He must argue from the evidence he has, or stop arguing" (A, 139).

In sum, as Collingwood's juxtaposition of his game metaphor and his rejection of scepticism suggest, he seeks to guarantee the authenticity of the historian's product. Perhaps his idealistic and rationalistic tendencies make him hesitate to grant authenticity to eliminative or permissive conclusions and thus to demand the "inevitable." In any event, merely separating the historian's possibilities from the philosopher's neither justifies nor validates the assertion that historical conclusions are certain. Whatever the outcome of this issue, it does not affect the remainder of Collingwood's remarks on evidence.

In his blast against scissors-and-paste history, Collingwood notes that not until the 17th century did historians systematically examine authorities via principles of credulity or make use of "non-literary" sources (i.e., artifacts) to broaden the base of historical study (IH, 258). The effect was to transform what historians had previously treated as fixed data into mere evidence to be treated as any other kind. Documents or artifacts, the historian's "business is to discover what the past was which left these relics behind it" (IH, 282). Moreover, not only were there no longer any fixed data, but as well no longer any fixed principles of evidence. "The enlargement of knowledge comes about mainly through finding how to use as evidence this or that kind of perceived fact which historians have hitherto thought useless to them" (IH, 247). Indeed, "no competent historian who reflects on the progress of his own thought can overlook the way in which that progress was created ["created, not discovered, because evidence is not evidence until it makes something evident"] by masses of evidence bearing on questions concerning which there was once no evidence whatever" (NAPH, E, 52). Collingwood holds the "principles of evidence" to be logically inseparable from evidence itself: "Evidence is only evidence so far as it is used as evidence, that is to say, interpreted on critical principles; and principles are only principles so far as they are put into practice in the work of interpreting evidence" (IH, 203).

II. The Relation of Facts and Evidence

Collingwood's remarks give the notion of evidence a pragmatic dimension. When he urges that "the principles by which this evidence is interpreted change, too," he calls upon the influence of the entire range of growing human knowledge--historical, scientific, mathematical, philosophic--and "mental habits and possessions of every kind" to justify the assertion and its consequence: "Every new historian, not content with giving new answers to old questions, must revise the questions themselves" (IH, 248). However, changes in what shall count as evidence do not emerge from whimsy, subjective factors, or even cultural changes. If the historian "can find a new piece--quote a hitherto unexploited source of information--," he does not thereby win his game by virtue of the novelty of his finding; "he must begin a new game, after putting [the piece] on the table for his opponent to use as well as himself" (LHK, E, 98). The opponent may use the evidence, criticize the use made of it, or criticize the principle by which it was used, in his own effort to bring from it and his other evidence answers to the questions asked.

The role of questions and answers reinforces the pragmatic nature of evidence. "Every actual inquiry," wrote Collingwood, "starts from a certain problem, and the purpose of the inquiry is to solve that problem; the plan of the discovery, therefore, is already known and formulated by saying that, whatever the discovery may be, it must be such as to satisfy the terms of the problem" (IH, 312). To illustrate this "logic of question and answer," Collingwood uses--in *The Idea of History*--the fable of solving John Doe's murder (IH, 266, 270 ff). The discovery of the murderer depends not merely on the collection of utterances and items after the fact at the constable's disposal. He depends as well upon his having mastered the techniques of interpreting evidence. "Every step of the argument depends on asking a question," not necessarily to someone, but about some aspect of what happened (IH, 273-74). Collingwood uses this point to dispel the idea of "potential evidence": "the idea . . . disappears; or, if we like to put the same fact in these other words, everything in the world is potential evidence for any subject whatever." In fact, "anything is evidence which is used as evidence, and no one can know what is going to be useful as evidence until he has occasion to use it." Principles of evidence arise from the questions we ask. "Questions and evidence are correlative. Anything is evidence which enables you to answer your question-- the question you are asking now." As a corollary, "A sensible question . . . is a question which you think you have or are going to have evidence for answering" (IH, 280-81).

Collingwood's case for the interrelation of question and evidence in no way contradicts his assertion in another place that "the historian does not just think of a problem and then search for evidence bearing on it; it is his possession of evidence bearing on a problem that alone makes the problem a real one" (LHK, E, 102). What the sum of Collingwood's remarks deny is that it makes any sense to look for an absolute starting point in the train of historical thought. We have "relics" which raise questions and logically exclude questions. Collingwood illustrates the point in a footnote on numismatics wherein he suggests that a beginner might well see "that certain alternatives are tacitly ruled out, without knowing why. . . . One might suppose that the logic of an historical argument could be judged by one ignorant of its subject matter; that is not the case" (LHK, E, 103). Questions of fact determine what can count as answers within the limits of the situation in which they arise, i.e., they determine what the evidence *can* be. To ask about the dates of certain old coins suggests both an analysis of the metal (for comparison with other specimens of known age and with established facts on the state of metallurgy in various places and times) and an interpretation of inscriptions. The relic coins, as evidence, in turn modify the question, for example, if the inscription is too worn to read.

In light of Collingwood's *Essay on Metaphysics*, scholars have largely spent their efforts in connecting the logic of question and answer with his thoughts on presuppositions, relative and absolute, and with other aspects of his more speculative ideas.[7] The notion of a relative presupposition appears implicitly in the numismatics example insofar as the questions arising about the coins presuppose some knowledge of coins. An absolute presupposition is something which goes unverified, unquestioned, undiscovered; "it is a thing we must take for granted" (EM, 31). Donagan takes as part of Collingwood's meaning that any series of questions would be "logically impossible" except for absolute presuppositions. Interpreting "logical impossibility" in terms of its use in deductive logic, Donagan denies sense to the idea of an absolute presupposition. "No presupposition can be self-evidently a necessary truth or a contradiction," and thus, "any presupposition can be converted into a relative one."[8] Ritchie argues similarly that Collingwood introduced absolute presuppositions to avoid "those fabulous monsters the Vicious Circle and the infinite regress," i.e., to avoid pitfalls common to epistemological systems.[9] Although the rarified atmosphere of the *Essay* permits such maneuvers, making them obscures the point of Collingwood's notions for historical study: the pragmatic nature of evidence.

"No two propositions," asserted Collingwood, "can contradict one another unless they are answers to the same question." Herein lies a reply to both Donagan and Ritchie. As an obscure aphorist once put it, explanations must come to an end somewhere. One might counter the aphorism with the reply: no, they do not, since we may question the presuppositions. And then might come the Collingwoodian rejoinder: one cannot question indefinitely, if one is ever to answer his first and quite practical question. To question the presuppositions of knowledge in history is, to a certain extent, to question historical knowledge, as for example in questioning the techniques of comparative metallurgy in determining the dates of faceless coins. To this extent, the inquiry resembles that made by the constable about the rector's daughter's confession in Collingwood's murder mystery: it showed not the face value fact of her guilt, but rather that she suspected "her young man" of having done the job (IH, 270). Beyond a certain point, however, the questions asked do not contribute to a solution to the given problem. They attack instead the foundations from which one's ques-

tions and answers become possible. To ask whether the yellowish disc
with the faint markings is "really" in one's hand or whether John Doe
(the slain) is really dead since for sure some cells still live and
subdivide is, in each case, to change the subject, to change the question and the problem to be solved. These crude "presuppositions" serve
to show that Collingwood's point in introducing absolute presuppositions is less to avoid circularity or regress in the ancient philosophic senses, and more to define the nature of historical problems.
Granted, one may convert absolute presuppositions into relative ones,
that is, count the former as part of the problem to be solved. The
conversion, however, is not always nor under all circumstances justified. Einstein, in setting the speed of light as a constant, questioned relevantly Newton's absolute presuppositions. Boyle, in solving
the relation among pressure, volume, and temperature for gases, did not
do so and did not need to; indeed, he could not have done so and still
have solved his problem.

While discussing the historian's use of the concept "causation,"
Waters asserted that "in the ordinary sense of the word 'cause,' its
distinction from mere conditions is, unless pragmatic, purely Pickwick-
ian. But its being a pragmatic distinction does not entail that it is
a distinction arbitrarily arrived at. It is a distinction which shifts
with a change of contexts."[10] If we read "evidence" for "cause" and
Collingwood's word "relics" or even "observed facts" for "conditions,"
we are left with a relevant, correct, and quite Collingwoodian position. Collingwood himself covers this ground when he discusses the
"right" answer to questions: "By 'right' I do not mean 'true.' The
'right' answer is the answer which enables us to get ahead with the
process of questioning and answering" (A, 37). A true proposition,
suggests Collingwood, is a "'right' answer" to a "sensible or intelligible question" arising in the "question and answer complex" which constitutes a legitimate historical problem or inquiry (A, 38). What constitutes evidence making a case for an answer also depends upon the
"complex" or problem and the particular question; to both the particular and the overall problems, the evidentially used relic contributes
in terms of the argument given to the answer and settle them.

Any number of examples might illustrate Collingwood's point. In
asking why George VI had a personality so vastly different from that of
Edward VIII, we may rule out the influence of the duchess-to-be of
Windsor as coming too late to be effective in character formation. For
the question at hand, our knowledge of Miss Simpson is relic or non-
evidential only (although it may help to illustrate a difference). On
the other hand, knowledge of the differing states of childhood health
and the consequent divergent childhood and adolescent activities would
could as highly usable evidence in arriving at an answer of a particular sort. The example, of course, does not preclude other approaches
(e.g., the psychoanalytic), even new ones. A change in method, say a
new analysis which identifies character formants by the nature of one's
adult friends, or a change in fact, say a discovery that the abdicator
and his wife-to-be were secretly raised together, may equally convert

relic information into evidence.

However, if one were to demand a complete list of what can count
as evidence, the only appropriate reply seems to be this: think of all
the possible questions you may ask about past actions and events, and
all the possible ways of answering them, and then all the possible assertions that may count toward supporting those answers. Then one will
have an idea of what potentially may be evidence, although again, the
question does not arise for the historian.[11] His quest for evidence
emerges from the context of the particular (meaning neither large nor
small) problem he seeks to solve. "In practice, the common difficulty
for the historian is to identify the problem," i.e., the question to be
asked, without which "he has no criterion to judge the success of his
work" (IH, 313). To identify the problem, to say that a particular
question arises, is to say "that it has a logical connection with our
previous thought, that we have a reason for asking it and are not moved
by capricious curiosity" (PH, E, 137). Question and evidence are
"pragmatic" concepts, but neither arbitrary nor whimsical.

III. Re-enactment

Collingwood did not concern himself with all possible kinds of
evidence, for he set a limit to what he would count as history, namely,
human actions. How Collingwood came to define the object of history as
human affairs, from what scattered premises he began, comprises a
first-rate jigsaw puzzle well beyond the reach of this study.[12] In the
Autobiography, he summed up his conception of history: histories "were
narratives of purposive activity, and the evidence for them consisted
of relics they had left behind (books or potsherds, the principle was
the same) which became evidence precisely to the extent to which the
historian conceived them in terms of purpose, that is, understood what
they were for" (A, 109). Here, as elsewhere, human purposive activity
is central to the conception of history. Part of the urge to restrict
historical study to purposive activity arose from the necessity Collingwood felt to distinguish events from actions as part of a broader
distinction between natural science (including "pseudo-history," e.g.,
paleontology) and history. The former studies events, occurrences
which have only an "outside" and thus suit only spectators. The latter
studies actions, occurrences which have an outside of movement, and an
"inside" of thought, and both sides in unity (IH, 213-14). "The processes of nature can therefore be properly described as sequences of
mere events, but those of history cannot. They are not processes of
mere events but processes of action, which have an inner side, consis-
ting of processes of thought, and what the historian is looking for is
these processes of thought." There follows Collingwood's famous aphorism: "All history is the history of thought" (IH, 215). Collingwood
distinguishes thought from subjective feeling: the former alone is a
reflective act. "Reflective acts may be roughly described as those we
do on purpose, and these are the only acts which can become the sub-

89

ject matter of history" (IH, 308-09).

Understanding a historical event, an action, consists of being able to answer "how" and "why" questions about the event in terms of purpose and the means for carrying out purpose. "Nothing is added to our understanding of that process by the statement (however true) that similar things have happened elsewhere" (IH, 223). All of which, to interpret Collingwood's assertion, amounts to circumscribing the use of the words "how" and "why" so as to exclude scientific-mechanical explanations and the associated notions of regularity and law. Relics, literary and otherwise, become evidence in answer to "how" and "why" questions to the extent that one can discover from them, or find a place for them, in purposive activity. "Whenever you find any object you must ask, 'What was it for?' and, arising out of that question, 'Was it good or bad for it? i.e., was the purpose embodied in it successfully embodied in it?'" These questions do not serve as grain for a mill of speculation. "These questions being historical questions, must be answered . . . on historical evidence; anyone who answers them must be able to show that his answer is the answer which the evidence demands" (A, 128).

The foregoing account I have adduced mainly to point out the continued close connection Collingwood exacts between historical assertion and evidence, even when he has narrowed history to the quest for the thought or purpose underlying actions. Nevertheless, the now infamous theory of re-enactment leads Collingwood directly away from the satisfaction of his demands, satisfaction which might well have come by way of the theoretical paths of evidence he had already prepared.

Three factors of importance contribute simultaneously to Collingwood's untenable notion of re-thinking. The first is his conception of history as a whole, a continuous process in significant ways analogous to natural processes. The second is Collingwood's introduction of the theory of historical imagination by which one interpolates between known facts to produce the whole continuous process. The third is a consequence of leaning upon the notion of imagination with ever more weight and dependence: Collingwood comes to cast aside his earlier position and to treat as separate entities what happened in the past (in terms of thought) and what historians conclude happened, about both of which the historian supposedly can say much. The following is a sketch of the influence of these factors.

The task of differentiating natural science and history Collingwood inherited from philosophers like Dilthey, Rickert, Croce, and Oakeshott. Making the distinction led Collingwood to designate natural science and history as inquiries into logically separate processes, but processes nevertheless (IH, 225H). Both were continuous, the historical by way of the "incapsulation" of residues of former processes in present ones (A, 140-43). Elsewhere, Collingwood stresses history as a narrative; "it is a story with a plot, the intelligible story of the doings of intelligent people" (PP, E, 111). The continuity of both process and tale reflects in the role Collingwood assigns to another continuity, the notion of history as a whole. "Take away the conception of a universal history in which every special history finds its place and justification," he had early written, "and you have committed the first and deepest sin against history" (SM, 235). Though less the naive idealist, the later Collingwood continues to conceive history as a continuum, in this respect very like the continuous stories told by such a "pseudo-history" as paleontology. History and "pseudo-history" differ in principles of study by only as much as their objects of study differ.

Collingwood stresses continuity until it comes to constitute one, if not the, criterion for the use of evidence. Perhaps Bradley's view that the historian's use of evidence denotes "a foregone conclusion" or entails "a preconception" leads Collingwood to link historical fact to the whole of history.[13] In any event, although Collingwood's analyses of evidence and question had established an interrelationship of considerable extent, at this point he turns to the view that the historian discovers and corrects falsifications "by considering whether the picture of the past to which the evidence leads is a coherent and continuous picture, one which makes sense" (IH, 245). The evidence immediately justifies only particular assertions, for example, "that one day Caesar was in Rome and on a later day in Gaul." "With a perfectly good conscience," the historian legitimately "interpolates" Caesar'e journey, not in order to invent "fanciful" detail, but as a "construction" which "involves nothing that is not necessitated by the evidence" and "without which there can be no history at all" (IH, 240-41). Collingwood never considers that the interpolation in his example is purely conceptual--a "journey" is what we call a human's getting from one place to a second distant place. (Less mysteriously, Danto has termed such exercises as assertions based on "conceptual evidence" rather than material evidence.[14]) Collingwood also fails to explain in what way the evidence necessitates the construction, whether logically or materially, or as evidence under the onus of the overriding principle of continuity. The last seems most likely, since Collingwood does tell us that the "web of imaginative construction," which makes a continuous story out of a collection of well-evidenced assertions, constitutes the core of "historical thinking."

Collingwood viewed his notion of re-enactment as fundamentally an extension of creative or imaginative reconstruction. To accomplish the extension, he had to contend with two of his own tenets, the evidential basis of historical assertions and the unity of thought and action. The answer to *why* Napoleon ascended to power in France is given, on Collingwood's account, in finding his purpose (or purposes, both ultimately and along the way) and how he carried it out, i.e., what he did. To the extent that there are cases of "purely theoretical thinking," however, thought becomes separable from action (IH, 311). Thus, a person's actions are "the expression of his thoughts" (IH, 216), but need not include all thoughts. Faced with both the expression and the thought expressed, the historian must look through actions in order to achieve his goal to "discern the thought within them" (IH, 214). Evidence for an action serves the historian who knows how to use it as evidence for the thought expressed.

The unity of action and thought, which had undergone a slight shift in rhetoric under the terms "expression of thought" and "thought expressed," now suffers a major shift. Thinking itself is an activity (IH, 288-89), a process with continuity, and therefore is susceptible to the same treatment as action. We can have "evidence of what . . . men thought" (IH, 296). We can interpolate or imaginatively reconstruct the course of thought. Just as "we find ourselves obliged to imagine [a ship] as having occupied intermediate positions" between times we look at it (IH, 241), so we are obliged to "envisage the situation in which a personage stood" (say Caesar or Theodosius) and "the possible ways of dealing with it" (IH, 215, 283). Moreover, we "must envisage it as that [person] envisaged it," (IH, 283). Just here lies the shift which ends the analogous treatment of thought and action. The notion of re-enactment in part could simply designate the form of imaginative reconstruction appropriate to thought, *viz*. a conceptualization in terms of means and ends, as opposed to that appropriate to objects (e.g., the ship's motion in time and space). Such a view would in all ways be consistent with the treatment of evidence, insofar as any relic might find use under alternative but not exclusive conceptualizations as evidence for an event, an action, and a thought. A charred sandal may help date a Vesuvian eruption, locate a running individual, and reveal a person's suddenly developed escape plan.

However, Collingwood has altered his stance, and perhaps the more radical position begins with the rhetoric of action expressing thought, as if it were a veneer upon thought to be penetrated by the historian. Wherever the first seed, the historian must now enter the inner side of an act so as "to re-enact the past in his own mind" (IH, 282). Thus, *besides* meeting the canons of evidence and continuity, the historian must do something which parallels and is vitally like what happened in the past. The notion of re-enactment, as its grammatical form suggests, discards Collingwood's earlier refusal to grant separate ontological statuses to the past and to what historians adduce.

Criticism of Collingwood's "re-enactment" has largely rejected only one of two essential parts of the theory. Walsh, for example, argues that the theory rests on intuition, on "penetration [behind the phenomena] by an intuitive act." He would replace intuition by "experience" expressed in a form which makes "at least implicit reference to general truths."[15] This critical revision rejects re-enactment as the means by which one arrives at past thought, but it does not attack Collingwood's tacit postulation of thought in the past as distinct from the historian's reconstruction of past thought. Despite Collingwood's lengthy declamations on the vacuity of the distinction between what "really" happened and what historians justifiably assert on the basis of evidence, the theory of re-enactment rests on just such a distinction. Replacing intuition with experience analogies or even general truths only substitutes one special tool for another in an attempt to bridge two worlds. The sceptic against whom Collingwood inveighed has only to refute the utility of each of the tools in order to re-make his case for a history distinct from the historian's product and categorically unknowable. Given the fundamental soundness of his arguments against scepticism, Collingwood's discourse on the identity of past and present thought (e.g., IH, 283–301), insofar as it presupposes thoughts to exist apart from any historical establishment of them, approaches the level of self-contradiction. Indeed, the historian *qua* historian does not re-enact either thought or action; he establishes what was thought and done as a prerequisite to re-enactment, either by ingenious actors, patriotic citizens, or overzealous school children.

Collingwood himself hinted at a way out of this dilemma. Without attending to the implications of his remark, he asserted that we do have evidence of what men thought. He also provided clues for interpretation when he argued that "the historian is not interested in the fact that men eat and sleep and make love and thus satisfy their natural appetites; but he is interested in the social customs which they create by their thoughts as a framework within which their appetites find satisfaction in ways sanctioned by convention and morality" (IH, 216). This tribute leads elsewhere to a discussion of action "without rules" and the importance of the historian's recognition of actions that occur in opposition to or apart from sanction (A, 102 ff). Social customs thus supply the context of action and a key to its interpretation. To detach actions from their contexts, he later wrote, robs the ability to say in what connection and for what purpose one acted or to recognize the act *contra* convention. Detachment changes experience into "an objective spectacle" (IH, 299). Although one may see how Collingwood might have used these remarks to lead into an analysis of using evidence to determine someone's purpose or motive, of ascertaining what sort of calculation one performed, or of seeing what plan one carried out step by step, he in fact employs them only to support the abstract conceptions of mind and mental acts on which re-enactment as a theory rests. Re-enactment has lost touch with evidence and thereby with history itself.

This brief sketch will suffice, perhaps, for many have covered the failure of re-enactment properly to relate historical evidence to historical fact and truth.[16] It is less important, I think, to see that Collingwood botched the job of relating evidence to fact with respect to human thought than to see that he provided the means by which to establish the relationship correctly. It is to this task, and to the job of making use of the materials supplied in earlier chapters of this study, that we next turn.

IV. Evidence-Inference and Criteria-Concept Relations

If one omits reference to re-enactment, one must still decide what to do with Collingwood's extensive case for the nature of historical evidence and the inferential nature of historical procedure. As Collingwood presented them, the scattered remarks comprise less an argument than a description of the historian's activities. This situation leaves open the question of why--if the account has any accuracy--historical evidence and inference should be this way. Collingwood himself appears to have left the basis for his account to a supposedly truistic understanding of the obvious nature of history and its object. To the extent that we approach the notions of historical inference and evidence from the viewpoint of historical objects and working historians, perhaps we must reach such a conclusion. Or perhaps not. In any event, an alternative viewpoint exists from which to examine inferential activities, a viewpoint which may supply further justification for Collingwood's remarks and which may at the same time vindicate in part the adoption of the viewpoint.

Quite evidently, inference and evidence relate to the making of statements or assertions. Evidence allows us to infer the assertion that such and such is the case. Inferences from the evidence justify our statements to such and such effect. Perhaps by seeing what conceptual elements are involved in Collingwood's analysis of evidence we can find some further basis for it. Oversimplified but typical historical assertions include these: (a) Caesar crossed the Rubicon; (b) the Nazis planned to conquer Europe; (c) between 1789 and 1793, a revolution occurred in France. The first example asserts that someone performed a certain act, the second that someone (or ones) had a certain plan or intention with a particular goal, the third that a certain event occurred.

In terms of Collingwood's analysis, examples (a) and (c) would constitute straight-forward historical conclusions--assuming them for the moment not already so well established as in fact they are. Their justification would consist in a marshalling of facts. In the case of Caesar fording the river, we should probably rely upon assertions in his memoirs, some eyewitness reports, and other evidences of his having been in Gaul and later in Rome. For the assertion of a French Revolution, we would well note the overthrow of the royal government and rule, the formation of a new assembly, the writing of a new constitution, along with certain special events like the storming of the Bastille and the guillotining of Louis and Marie. In question-answer terms, evidence enables one to answer the question, "What did Caesar do?" specifically at a certain time, and evidence also makes possible a reply to the query, "What was going on in France in those years?" The questions, as do the answers, admit of considerable variation, even within the desired range of simplicity. Changing the questions may well change the relevant evidence. The evidence would change, say in the case of revolutions, if we shift the time to 1920 and the place to Mexico. What counts for evidence for a revolution, then, varies also with the context.

That Caesar's crossing the Rubicon is an act while the revolution in France is an event fails to warrant any difference in handling at this point. What differs is the evidence, not that we assert both acts and events evidentially. Should we change the context, e.g., substitute Patton for Caesar and the Loire for the Rubicon, the evidence relevant to asserting a river crossing will change (Patton dressed as though he liked to ride horses; he--unlike Caesar--did not have to). What counts for evidence for an act also changes with context. (a) and (c) thus show, from the standpoint of evidence, relevant similarities in their justifications and in the possible variations of their justifications.

There are, for both sorts of cases, limits to the variation. Only so much alteration can occur before someone objects that we can no longer justifiably call what happened a revolution. The objection claims, to put it one way, that the evidence does not justify or allow us to infer the conclusion. Alternatively put, it claims that one cannot in this case use the concept "revolution," because the facts do not fulfill the criteria for so using that concept. In brief, the notions of conceptual criteria and historical evidence, with respect to the relevant class of cases, are not merely inextricably linked; they amount to two perspectives or formulations of the same activity. Most of Collingwood's remarks concerning evidence have corresponding observations about concept use, and most of the latter appeared in the conception of language presented in the first chapter. For example, pointing out that criteria vary with the context and purpose of use repeats Collingwood's remarks on the pragmatic nature of evidence, e.g., that it varies with the question asked and the context of asking. The comments on the development of techniques for interpreting evidence, and especially the public examinability of what one proposes as a new piece of evidence, echo the notes on conceptual proposals, i.e., proposals of new sets of criteria for using a concept, along with reasons for supporting them. Perhaps the only failure of coincidence appears between Collingwood's desire for "certain" conclusions and the conceptual notion that a given criteria set justifying a concept's use comprises sufficient grounds, but not sufficient (or necessary) conditions. The latter idea resembles more closely the "permissive" conclusions which Collingwood discarded.

Holding this one topic in abeyance momentarily, one cannot fail to note the remaining overall correspondence. Given the question, "What happened in France in those years?" the historian's evidence is precisely that which justifies the assertion that a revolution occurred. Should another historian argue that, although there arose a new assembly and constitution, the royal government did not lose its power to rule, he would (if successful) have "disproven" the conclusion that a revolution occurred to the extent of removing the "*nihil obstat*." In other terms, he would have shown the use of the concept "revolution" to lack justification in this particular case. All this supposes that the objecting historian could show that the royal government did not lose power, a supposition which illustrates the way in which one justification, one evidential inference, may rest on others.

If the two notions, historical evidence and conceptual criteria
(again, with respect to the relevant class of cases), are in fact coincident one may relevantly inquire into the grounds for choosing to refer to the justification of facts as evidential rather than conceptually criterial. In narrative practice, there exists no hard and fast
boundary between evidential and non-evidential assertions of events,
although there are desiderata which occasion one term or the other. To
the extent that all event or action concept uses involve (for factual
assertions) the fulfillment of criteria and since the fulfillment
amounts to having at hand justifying facts, all such uses may take in
the abstract the name "evidential." Likewise, since every use of evidence for making event and action claims presupposes some standard by
which we judge a fact as evidence and as evidence for the particular
claim, those assertions may take, again in the abstract, the name "criterial." Insofar as what is in question is the use of a particular
concept to make a factual claim, the criteria become conceptual.

In practice as opposed to in the abstract, calling an activity
evidential is as pragmatic a consideration as choosing between facts so
as to call one evidence and the other mere relic. When events are far
enough past or far enough distant, we move from speaking of criteria
(or not speaking at all in view of "obvious" justification) to speaking
of evidence for the event's occurrence. We have, however, no rule, nor
even a rule of thumb for saying how far is far enough. Before stadiums
ran direct lines from broadcasting booths to radio stations, baseball
games were indirectly broadcast, the studio announcer being fed a tele-
graphed running account. Reese at third, Robinson bunts. Without examining the tape further, the announcer across country hollers, "It's
a squeeze play!" It makes no difference whether Reese is still sliding
or already back in the dugout. Nor does it matter that the announcer
in New York is broadcasting a game in St. Louis. The announcer has
correctly called the play. To speak of evidence (without some further
good reason) borders on the trivial, despite the fact that the broad-
caster has drawn his conclusion from the document at his disposal, much
as historians are called upon to do.

Not only distance or space, but import, or the crucialness of deciding whether something happened (or existed or had a purpose, etc.),
counts as a desideratum occasioning mention of evidence. The more important the case (and cases are important for reason, not for mere subjectivity, taste, or whimsy), the more one wishes to evaluate formally
the justification for an assertion. Evidence is something which can be
evaluated, and the more formal the procedure, the more explicit the
standards, the most self-conscious the method, then the greater the
occasion for speaking of evidence. When events are remote in time or
place, and criteria fulfilling information concomitantly scarce, one is
also inclined to speak of the available information as evidence. It is
all one has on the basis of which to reach whatever conclusions and to
make whatever assertions one can and will. The seriousness of assertions which contain an element of justificational risk also occasions
reference to evidence rather than merely to the criteria for the use of

a concept.

These factors (and perhaps others as well) do not always act in
concert. There are cases where evidence is clear cut and overwhelming,
and cases, too, of evidence for trivial matters. Evidential evaluation
is not always formal and overt. That calling a fact a piece of evidence presupposes a standard does not entail that one can produce and
explicate the standard any more than the situation that a concept's use
supposes criteria for that use entails an ability to spell out the criteria. The point of raising these matters is only to loosen a prejudice from event concepts and assertions: there is nothing logically
special about cases to which one ordinarily applies the term "evidence"
just because one has occasion to apply it. If anything is "special,"
it is the notion of evidence as applied to event assertions in contradistinction from other relations bearing the title "evidence." Parts
of history, law, criminology, and other fields have special techniques
of evidence evaluation, special methodologies, but these are concerned
(mostly) with special criteria and special requirements for their fulfillment. Often their development and use produce alternative criteria, i.e., new uses for event assertions or restricted uses for narrow
and not generally encountered contexts. Nonetheless, even this facet
of the subject of evidence techniques neither speaks to nor alters the
fundamental critical justification of event and action concepts.

Viewing a piece of written history as a series of justified assertions (among other things) has certain advantages over talk about the
historian's contemplation and reconstruction of events, however much
the latter may lean on the word "evidence." First, it does not *prima
facie* legislate a chasm between some artificially sustained pseudo-
entities called events on the one hand and actions on the other. One
may truistically assert that the historian seeks a narrative centering
upon "human affairs" without in any way prescribing or proscribing an
interest in and relevance to events which are not actions. A historian
may discourse lengthily (and necessarily with respect to certain aims)
in geologic terminology about the mechanics of Vesuvius' eruption without guilt of neglecting humans and hence his craft. Second, the present view allows one to distinguish special technical studies and their
jargon from ordinary narratives, and to distinguish technically used
from non-technically used concepts within a single narrative, all without forcing history to commit itself (and without committing history in
spite of itself) to being either a purely technical or a purely "ordinary" discipline. In the same vein, a historian need have no mental
idea of the whole of history in order to justify his criticism of
sources or what others have used as evidence. It remains an epistemological possibility that the "then and then and then" course of a narrative has no philosophically warranted termini. For the practicing
historian, a study (insofar as we call it a study in distinction from
others) always has termini, whether in time, space, subject, or any
combination of the three.

Moreover, the point that any fact formerly accepted may stand under the hot lights of a critical third degree does not suggest that a
history has no fixed points, i.e., a body of reliable data. Had Collingwood remembered his own dictum, "To ask any question . . . , we
must already possess information" (SM, 79),[17] it is unlikely he would
have felt the need to treat the absence of absolutely fixed data as a
call to justify all histories by reference to a version of idealistic
rationalism (IH, 243-47). The absence of absolute data does not affect
the equally correct point that, given a context of inquiry, it makes no
sense for the historian to question the bulk of his data. Just as a
fact becomes evidence only when used as such, it also becomes doubtful
only when a sensible question about it arises. Such an observation in
part accounts for the fact that most historical narratives proceed un-
troubled by detailed presentations of evidence. Too, historical mono-
graphs and theses which do not use a narrative form present the evidence for their main conclusions, but they do not trouble that evidence
itself (except where new or questionable) with the minutiae of justification. A few footnotes suffice to indicate the sources, and the absence of comment in effect proclaims the want of any reason to question
them. Again, this precisely coincides with the earlier expression of
the general absence of explicit criteria sets for the use of most non-
technical concepts. Criteria become important only in cases of justification, and justification does not occur in a vacuum. It arises in
answer to relevant objections and inquiries.

The conceptual view of historical evidence also sheds some light
on Collingwood's quandry over permissive vs. inevitable, inductively-
derived vs. deductively-derived, conclusions. The issue becomes a
false one to the extent that the justification of event assertions
holds no direct analogy to either induction or deduction in their formal senses. Collingwood, then, rightly preferred neither, although he
wrongly opted for the certainty of deductive conclusions. (Either mode
of reasoning, of course, may have relevance to the justification of
particular assertions which a historian might make, but such cases fall
outside the range of those under consideration here.) The term "permissive" perhaps better fits conceptual justification than it does
probabilistic or statistical induction, wherein the conclusion itself
follows certainly from the premises, but contains a probability factor
which fails to guarantee application to the individual. Moreover, the
term "permissive" may capture some of what analysts like Scriven and
Albritton tried to portray when they inserted the word "probably" or
"almost certainly" between the criteria and the phenomenon without com-
miting themselves to any formal sense of probability.[18] Sufficient
grounds for an assertion provide Collingwood's *nihil obstat*; nothing
prevents the assertion. Not even a contrary assertion arrived at on
separate grounds, i.e., grounds which do not involve the falsification
of any fact used to fulfill criteria which justify the original assertion. Failure to satisfy the relevant criteria removes warrant from an
assertion, thereby blocking its justified use, but it does not thereby
warrant the negative of the assertion.

In consequence of these features of concept use, there exists the possibility for several sorts of opposition between or among historians. Collingwood himself notes the sort of case wherein answers to unrelated or non-conflicting questions produced an apparent opposition. This possibility resolves itself into the situation in which, because of differences in context or purpose, non-conflicting criteria sets become relevant to the justification of each assertion. However opposed in appearance, both assertions may have warrant in such a case, and out of such cases clever writers often try to make paradoxes.

In some cases, a historian may treat weak evidence as a good reason for shifting the ground of a question. Hexter, for example, takes Tawney and Trevor-Roper to task for deficiencies in their support of economic explanations of the role of the "gentry" in the Great Rebellion. At the same time, Hexter suggests that their role is better understood in terms of a "power vacuum in England" into which "poured the country gentry."[19] The power vacuum case is not merely an alternative explanation; it is a reformulation of the question. Working within economic frameworks of social history, both Tawney and Trevor-Roper had formulated "the problem of the gentry" in terms which demanded economic evidence and answers. Self-consciously, Hexter redefines the problem in such non-economic terms as "effective leadership," "royal policy," and "the burden of leading that opposition."[20] He does not thus refute Tawney and Trevor-Roper by showing them to have failed to answer his question. Rather, Hexter takes the weakness of economic evidence to support (two different) answers to economic questions to be an appropriate reason to reformulate the historical question in terms of political power. That his conclusion does not directly conflict with those of Tawney and Trevor-Roper can be seen also to follow from the fact that no two of the three historians agree as to exactly what criteria justify inclusion in the class "gentry."

Another sort of conflict which does not break down into simple affirmative-negative questions sometimes results from following the questions permitted by one concept but not by another. Suppose an attempt to oust a party from power by violence, with the avowed purpose of setting up a new government, fails. Suppose also that the attempt leads to radical reforms by the party, reforms which fulfill the demands and ideals of the unsuccessful insurgents. Do we have a revolution or a mere rebellion? The facts available for making both assertions are the same, but the relation between criteria and concept, evidence and assertion is not one of entailment. Hence, as noted in previous chapters, what follows, i.e., the next set of questions and answers, is not identical for both assertions. The decision here taken may thus have consequences leading to later assertions which oppose each other. For example, and trivially, "The rebels won" vs. "The rebels lost." To call historical conclusions "permissive" (the facts permit both assertions but necessitate neither) or even "verbal" (since what was at stake was the choice of a word: "rebellion" or "revolution) does not reduce them in importance; nor do these characterizations preclude settlement. Since the dispute did not arise over the truth or falsity of

the initial facts, however, but over which of more than one warranted
assertion to use, the settlement of the win-lose opposition will not
proceed by falsifying one option. "The revolutionaries lost the battle
for political power and won the war of ideas," might be a typical settling statement. It responds to the old saw, "before we can reach
agreement we must define our terms," a saying whose rhetoric obscures
its content. It asks less for definition than for sense, the senses of
"revolution" and "rebellion" in which one can speak of winning and los-
ing. Thereby it differentiates relevant criteria sets. The example,
besides smoothing the emotionally choppy waters of scholarly debate,
also manages to delineate the contextual and purposive elements of the
originally opaque assertions of revolutions and rebellion, and in so
doing, it defines (or refines) the criteria set pertinent to each.

Some issues are in fact not settled. Historians can unsettle previously justified conclusions with the twist of a fact or two, as
Hexter did with his reappraisal of the Tudor middle class.[21] The possibility for such maneuvers arises from the nature of the assertion
procedure, however, and not from special epistemological or metaphysical considerations. The possibility of such questions in itself suffices to account for the possibility of rewriting history, although
this kind of possibility does not exhaust the phenomena which may give
rise to rewriting history. Collingwood's introduction of a general
purpose for history, i.e., self-knowledge, sought as part of its function to explain the rewriting of history. A changing self supposedly
demands a changing history. To the extent, however, that the re-writ-
ing of history can be accounted for on the basis of elements within the
set of activities in which historians engage, the introduction of added
elements to history, such as a general purpose, seems otiose.

With respect to unsettled cases, there are, as Fain has noted, at
least two senses ". . . in which a question is unanswerable or undecid-
able: (1) the decision procedure (or procedures) ordinarily used to
resolve similar questions fails to resolve it in the particular case;
(2) the decision procedure ordinarily used to resolve such questions
is itself put into question for all cases to which it is normally applicable."[22] Although the two senses proposed by Fain appear to be
distinct, they are in practice closely related. A question, which cannot be decided because evidence which would meet a current set of rules
or (to use Fain's term) a current decision procedure is lacking, may
give rise to a quest for a new procedure, a new set of rules. The new
set of rules may then supplant the old set (or sets), and thus apply to
all cases to which the old set was formerly applicable. This kind of
possibility casts a shadow of doubt on the importance Fain places on
distinguishing between "simple matter-of-fact questions" and "their so
called philosophical counterparts." While it is true that "any transformation of a matter-of-fact question into its philosophical counterpart challenges the decision procedure to which the question is normally attached," thereby dismissing the question's "original point and
direction," a challenge to a decision procedure, to a criteria set to
be used in justifying the assertion of events, may arise from the level

of matter-of-fact questions.[23] The possibilities are related to the
Collingwood distinction between relative and absolute presuppositions:
the change in coin dating procedure, the change in the criteria relevant to asserting that a coin originates at such and such a date, coincides with changes in decision procedures which arise from questioning
matters of fact; the question of whether coins are certain yellow discs
coincides apparently with Fain's philosophical counterpart. Not every
challenge to a decision procedure is philosophical.

V. Thoughts, Re-thinking, and Conceptual Expectation

By restricting the cases so far considered to actions and events,
I hope to have cleared away enough predilections so that the analysis
of statements like (b) "The Nazis planned to conquer Europe" will
evoke no surprise. In principle, it differs not at all from the earlier analysis. The evidence or elements which fulfill criteria for
asserting that one (person or group) had a purpose, plan, intention,
motive, etc., in no case include hidden mental entities or other things
which are not susceptible to relics. Thus, they demand no special
technique, such as re-thinking or sympathetic understanding. In general the same collection of relics which allow one to assert the occurrence of an event or action provides sufficient data for ascribing to
the actors the appropriate "thought." The records of Hitler's build-up
of armed and naval forces, his diplomatic-military maneuvers in Austria
and Czechoslovakia, his *blitzkrieg* in Poland, and his writings comprise
some of the data on the basis of which historians ascribe to Hitler a
plan of conquest. Having evidence that warrants the assertion of action, the historian does not require additional philosophic justification to seek reasons, goals, influences, or motives, any more than giv-
en an auto crash, bridge collapse, or volcanic eruption, one needs
special dispensation to request the cause or causes. Testimony in memoirs and eye-witness reports which directly assert a person's or
group's pretensions or aims may serve as authoritative sources, but
such reports stand open to the same critical scrutiny as the evidence
for the occurrence of events. One is, in effect, committed neither to
a Rylian behaviorism nor to scissors-and-paste in this matter. A person's actions *may* give good reason to doubt his own account of his motives. Luther's later support of the princes rather than the people
led some historians to doubt the sincerity of his motives. Such criterial use of action is not peculiar to history. Courts of law have
long established motives for crime despite the silence of the accused.
Every week for several years Perry Mason "found" the motive for a crime
and thus uncovered the "real" guilty party.

Important to the ascription or attribution of intensions, motives,
plans, *et al.*, as Collingwood noted, is the framework of social customs
and institutions within which men act and "find satisfaction in ways
sanctioned by convention" (IH, 216). Customs and institutions contribute to the criteria by which it makes sense to attribute or to doubt a
motive for an act, to ascribe untaken alternative courses of action

101

(which in turn may serve to narrow the possible motives or goals), to
assert a violation, intentional or not, of the "normal" modes of behavior and the reasons for it. In Reformation England, with its well-
documented long list of capital crimes and major punishments for lesser
offenses, one could not sensibly attribute any abnormal motive of cru-
elty to a judge who meted out the death sentence for counterfeiting,[24]
although one would have an inclination to search out available data for
evidence of just such a motive should a 20th century judge attempt to
levy such a penalty for an equal crime.

These same social customs and institutions also lend eminent sense
to ascriptions of "feeling" to historical figures. The criteria of
justified attribution of emotions, feelings, attitudes, *et al.* do not
differ in kind from those relevant to "thought;" rather they differ in
detail. *Contra* Collingwood, we may indeed "know how Nietzsche felt the
wind in his hair as he walked on the mountains, [or] the triumph of
Archimedes or the bitterness of Marius" (IH, 296), even though we cannot re-enact the feelings and emotions. We may know if, first of all,
they tell us (ir if someone in a position to know tells us) in such a
manner as not to arouse suspicions of untrustworthiness, or if, second,
they provide sufficient clues by their actions and the objects they
leave behind. Given the more or less unlikely tale from Vipruvius that
Archimedes, having discovered the principle of displacement at the public baths, ran through the street toward home, *sans* clothing, shouting
all the while, "Eureka!", one can scarcely raise an eyebrow to the historian who notes that Archimedes felt great triumph and exultation.
(Did not the word "eureka" come to us as an expression of exultation or
triumph while the story still had some currency?) To attribute reliab-
ly feelings as well as thoughts and actions, needless to say, demands
more than passing acquaintance with the society and culture, the civilization and age in which they occur. The acquaintance may not be wholly explicable in terms of behavior or objects, just as one's acquaintance with his own mores may not be in terms of explicit rules. Nevertheless, one can master the ability to isolate the appropriate criteria
of assertion with respect to feelings and emotions. Nothing mysterious
or covert counts in the historian's attributions. The historian who
lays out his evidence thereby reveals the criteria by which he justifies the assertive use of the concepts which he employs. If one cannot
see the justification, and often historians do not present all the evidence, one can always ask how a judgment was reached.

Moreover, when the historian sets out his evidence and (usually)
some genetic account of his argument, he does not always show thereby
the logical relation between evidence and assertion. A pair of examples from Collingwood may serve to make this point.

In Collingwood's brief account of his work on "the Roman Wall," he
first notes that features of it precluded its use as a fortification,
but that it might have served as a sentry-walk. He then writes as if
he had reached a conclusion having other ramifications: "A question
answered causes others to arise. If the Wall was a sentry-walk, ele-

102

vated . . . and provided . . . with a parapet to protect the sentries against sniping, the same sentry-walk must have continued down the Cumberland coast . . . to keep watch on vessels moving in the estuary. . . . But here the sentry-walk need not be elevated. . . . There ought, therefore, to be a chain of towers . . . otherwise resembling those on the wall. . . . The question was, did such towers exist" (A, 129)? What one may miss in Collingwood's account is that he has yet to settle the question of whether he is justified in applying the concept "sentry-walk" to the wall. One condition for asserting the existence of a sentry-walk is, roughly, that it be a wall-like structure with places for lookouts (this much he has in fact, i.e., in evidence). Another condition is that the structure must stretch over an expanse that people in the Roman situation would guard (this he does not have). Failure to fulfill the latter condition would remove warrant from calling the wall a sentry-walk insofar as no guarding function could be asserted for a wall which spanned only a short distance. Until the latter condition is fulfilled--in the form of towers, owing to the lay of the land--Collingwood can only provisionally suggest that the wall may be a sentry-walk. He becomes justified in his assertion of a sentry-walk, in his use of the term in other assertions about the place, era, and people, when "old archeological publications" in fact fulfill the criteria for using the concept in the relevant context.

Collingwood's expectation of finding towers ("There ought, therefore, to be a chain of towers . . .") is based on his provisional use of the concept "sentry-walk." The conclusion that there ought to be towers does not emerge from an inductive argument (of any of the sorts noted in the preceding chapter); nor does it come from a deductive argument which has among its premises an empirical generalization. Instead, the argument appears to take this form: if "sentry-walk" can be used justifiably, then the criteria for the concept's use will be fulfilled and one could expect to find towers. Therefore, in order to complete the fulfillment of the criteria, one ought to *look for* towers. We may call cases like this, in which the argument tells us what to expect if a concept's use were justified and what to look for in order to justify that use, cases of "conceptual expectation" (to distinguish them from cases of prediction and other forms of expectation).

Note also that what follows upon the warranted assertion of a sentry-walk in terms of the Roman mission in Britain (in answer to questions such as "for what were they on the lookout?") does not follow from the assertion of the facts which fulfill the criterial conditions, i.e., from just a parapeted wall-like structure stretching over a guardable extent of land and sea coast. Moreover, the assertion of the wall's purpose (or the purpose of its builders and users) depends only upon the evidence justifying the assertion. If this is re-thinking, then re-thinking is both harmless and without need of Collingwood's special explanation.

The second example follows immediately upon the first in Collingwood's autobiography and runs straight-forwardly against the grain of his special explanation of re-enactment. Caesar says nothing of his intent and purpose in invading Britain, nor does anyone else who was in a position to know. In answer to the question of what was the goal of the incursion, Collingwood has three contending possibly applicable concepts: a "mere punitive expedition," a "demonstration of force," or a "complete conquest of the country." The candidates arise in view of the fact that Caesar's own silence in his memoirs justifies (apparently) the assertion that he failed in his aim. The decisive criterion for excluding the first two candidates is the size of the army: a large force, comparable to that later sent by Claudius, could warrant only the assertion of an army of conquest. In matching criterion to datum, Collingwood finds that there was a large army, and hence the assertion of the goal, conquest, is warranted.

Perhaps even more important in this example than the complete absence of re-enactment as a mental process is the melting away of the so-called distinction between "what" and "why" questions. To say what the Roman force was is also to say why it was, i.e., what it was for. In its resemblance to Dray's explanation of "what" in history and Walsh's notion of "colligation," this example, and the preceding one as well, emphasizes the narrative, interpretive, and classificatory functions of historical accounts without forcing us to draw artificially sharp lines between "kinds" of accounts.[25] It is often a matter of indifference as to how among several ways we frame a question, so long as we receive a relevant (and correct) answer, i.e., one "which enables us to get ahead with the process of questioning and answering" (A, 37). For example, settling the purpose of Caesar's invasion helps one to discover what conditions made possible his defeat. Not that all historical questions are "what" questions, for that term has as many and varied uses as "why" and "how." We are not inclined in history and elsewhere to classify events and objects--for one instance--under a single head, even though both answer to "what?"

Moreover, "what" and "why" questions coincide only under certain conditions. Where "why" has the force of "what for," the answer to such a question may be the same as an answer to the question of what happened. To ask why "Little Phil" Sheridan "hammered up the Pike, his flat hat waving in his hand, his bull voice bellowing," and to ask what he was doing may receive the same reply: he was rallying his men after Early's initial success in the last major battle in the Shenandoah Valley.[26] The coincidence of "why" and "what" questions extends only to those cases where the answer can be expressed in the form of an assertion of the occurrence of a single event, action, or happening. The event about which one asks "why?" serves as a criterion for the assertion of the event, action, or happening which answers to the question, and therefore the reply also amounts to a justified assertion of what happened.

If the answer to the "why" question requires the assertion of an event which does not stand in such a relation to the event questioned, if the event which answers to "why?" is independently assertable, then

"what" and "why" are logically distinct questions. To say that the
road washed out because of the heavy rains is to presuppose the occurrence of two events (each independently assertable) and to assert that
they bear a certain relation to each other. We may obscure the independent assertability of the washout and rain by formulating our assertion thusly: "The rains washed out the roads." The form suggests that
one has merely said *what* happened. If the suggestion is accepted, it
precludes one from saying in the same breath *why* the roads washed out.
"Why" would here ask about the cause of rains washing out a road, not
the cause of the wash out. If the suggestion is not accepted, that is,
if one insists that the "why" questions the wash out, the "what happened" is restricted to the wash out. That which answers to "why" refers in this interpretation to the rain and its relation to the wash
out. Indeed, in such cases as this, if "what" and "why" coincided, a
causal assertion would be unnecessary, for the relation between the
events would be conventional and linguistic, thereby eliminating the
need for an additional relation. Consequently, the present thesis concerning the coincidence between evidence for events and criteria for
the use of concepts does not speak directly to causal and other rela-
tional assertions in history; it applies only to the class of cases involving the assertion of single events (without restriction to size,
richness, and other such matters).

The inseparable entwinement of evidence for events and criteria
for the use of concepts may initially be somewhat startling. Surprise
disappears, however, when one understands that no change of fact, but
only of perspective, is required to reformulate the historian's task of
finding out what happened to seeing what one can justifiably say happened. The job of history becomes no less important. Nor does it become a mere matter of language. Its conceptual foundations simply become a mite clearer. The benefits of the present perspective show up
perhaps most clearly when one tries to get beneath the surface of Collingwood's vaguely translucent remarks on rightness and truth and to
square them away, if possible, with the idea that historical assertions
have a "permissive" rather than a "certain" air about them.

VI.   Criteria and the Truth of Event Assertions

When Collingwood defined a "true" proposition as a right answer to
a sensible question which arose in the question and answer complex of a
legitimate historical inquiry, and further specified a "right" answer
as one enabling us to get ahead in the question-answer process, he left
nothing very solid upon which to build an account of truth in history.
The concept "truth" rests for him on the concept "rightness." Any attempt to explicate "rightness," however, must contend with the notions
of "historical inquiry" (what is one and how does one distinguish a legitimate one from an illegitimate one?) and "getting ahead" (does this
involve only the fact of further questions, or must they be practically
speaking answerable?). As noted earlier, Collingwood's own thoughts
seem to turn back to the question of evidence and do not linger on

truth. His account of truth shows the same inclination insofar as resting truth on rightness and rightness on making progress in a question-answer complex bespeaks almost a disinterest in "truth" from a theoretical point of view. He favors instead an understanding of the activity of doing history. For as inquiries change, so will the assertion which count as right answers, at least to the extent that an altered inquiry will also reflect changes in the relevant questions. If an answer no longer gets one ahead in his new inquiry, it is not right and consequently not true--for the new inquiry. Not that it is false; rather, the assertion becomes irrelevant. "True statement" and "relevant fact" become, if not exactly, then almost, synonymous. And what one calls true under Collingwood's account becomes a pragmatic consideration.

This much of Collingwood's case covers only half the battle, for the subject of truth appears on two related but separable levels. The half just given concerns truth as ascribed to propositions. Collingwood also wants to speak to the practice of referring to shole historical accounts as true or not. Here the distinctive criterion becomes coherence, not necessarily explicable in deductive terms, but instead describable as a narrative fittingness of the elements of an account on the order of Oakeshott's story with no lacuna.[27] Without belaboring the dubious *a priori* status Collingwood wishes to give a presupposed conception of universal history against which one measures his partial story (IH, 245), one can minimally recognize the question raised by his account, the question of what role, if any, coherence, connectedness, or other such concepts play in determining the truth or falsity, acceptance or rejection of historical accounts. As Waters has noted, we register disapproval of historical accounts more with words like "dubious" and "rejected" than with "invalid" or "disproved."[28] Collingwood, showing more concern for disapproval than for approval, would have us hold that narrative incoherence in an account, however warranted the individual assertions, counts against or gives us reason to doubt or reject an account.

On either level, Collingwood leaves little with which to work save a few questions and the suspicion that truth, like evidence, has pragmatic dimensions. With respect to a single historical assertion, any notion of correspondence dies as an operative account of truth. The very pastness of history's events precludes any clear sense in which an assertion might correspond to what is asserted, although nothing in that claim relieves historical assertions of the need to square away with the evidence on which they rest. Whatever its role with respect to narratives, coherence too lacks any force in accounting for the truth of particular historical assertions. Again, however, the assertions must square away with the evidence. Oddly enough, both "correspond" and "cohere" can be stretched to conversationally cover what I have termed "squaring away with the evidence." In such a tense use, neither term serves much of an informative role, for only by knowing in advance what it is for an assertion to square away with its evidence could one decide whether a stretched use sufficed to subsume a particular case under the traditional theory which in other places the respective terms denote.

Before turning away from the dead ends of these traditional accounts, one must note at least one role played by coherence in the generation of historical assertions. The primary role played by evidence gives way in the absence of relics to the interpolative process which Collingwood dubs historical imagination and which Danto calls conceptual evidence. One has no evidence for Caesar's journey but safely asserts it for the reason that the general was one here and soon after there. Such an assertion rests on conceptual grounds; moreover it rests on the factualness of the two enclosing assertions. To doubt Caesar's presence in Gaul *eo ipso* casts doubt on his having taken the asserted journey. Hence, although the ability to make interpolations goes here unquestioned, their propriety is dependent in every case upon some other statement or statements which have evidential justification, i.e., which are facts. Even here, then, the question of truth with respect to historical assertions leans upon the subject of evidence.

To center the discussion of historical truth on the notion of evidence presupposes some general considerations regarding the appropriate formulation of the so-called problem of truth. In as much as evidence, truth, and their relation comprise the elements of analysis, the correct question is "what makes an assertion true?" This is not the only possible question. One could ask what we mean or are saying when we say that a certain historical assertion is true. To such a question Ramsey was answering when he took as self-evident that "'It is true that Caesar was murdered' means no more than that Caesar was murdered."[29] Other answers have been given, but Ramsey's holds especial interest since the redundancy thesis opens immediately a further question: why repeat oneself, or what might one be doing in asserting "It is true that Caesar was murdered" or "That is true" that one is not doing with the original assertion "Caesar was murdered?" There appear to be many good reasons for repeating oneself with the proper locutions: to confirm a story, verify a report, corroborate testimony, and so on.[30] Each activity by its nature necessitates repetition of the assertion, but for reasons which constitute part of the aim of the activity. For example, if the activity is the confirmation of a story, it takes the story to have been given, a fact which occasions from locution of the order "the story is true" or a retelling of the story. In short, the use of "is true" and related expressions is pragmatically occasioned. There are grounds which warrant the activity, in the absence of which conditions the use of an expression like "That's true" or "The statement is true" is vacuous. These conditions will vary from activity to activity, and even within kinds of instances of an activity.

Whatever else the foregoing account has in its favor, its chief merit lies in leaving unaffected the question, what makes an assertion true? The line of work eliminates rather than creates a theory of truth. It puts forth neither new entities nor new relations to pre-

shape and predetermine the connection between the truth of historical
assertions and the evidence on which the assertions rest. Such a trend
of analysis does not even specify that there shall be only one possible
relation. This result is wholly desirable, for in answering the question of what makes a historical assertion true there remain no further
grounds than those for making the assertion itself. The grounds for
asserting "It is true that Caesar was murdered" consist of the same evidence as for asserting "Caesar was murdered." To the extent, then,
that the notion of evidence for an event or action is coterminal with
the notion of criteria for the assertive use of an event or action concept, the criteria which warrant the assertive or factual use of an
event or action concept "Q" are precisely those which warrant the assertion "S is true," where "S" is a statement to the effect that Q occurred. If Sheridan's hammering up the Pike on horseback, "his flat
hat waving in his hand, his bull voice bellowing . . . man, horse, and
little swallow-tailed red and white guidon with its two white stars
bobbing behind" should together provide sufficient grounds for the assertion that Sheridan was rallying his men,[31] then those same criteria
fulfilling facts also warrant the assertion "It is true that Sheridan
was rallying his men." They provide the grounds, but not the occasion
for the latter assertion. In addition to the considerations that entail this result, we may also note that the conclusion coincides with
the fact that historians are not mere story tellers; they make their
assertions to express facts.

Not all occasions for questioning the truth of historical assertions amount to straight-forward calls to re-examine the grounds used
to justify an assertion and find them fulfilled or not fulfilled. One
may find the evidence insufficient to establish something claimed as a
fact. One may also desire in cases of reasonable doubt independent
grounds for reaching the same conclusion. We may, if we have reason to
doubt that Sheridan's actions were directed toward rallying his men,
ask him or consult correspondence and other testimonial records. Such
a case does not arise automatically or universally, as Meiland seems to
believe in his attempt to define historical truth solely in terms of
agreement on a particular judgment made on the basis of different standards.[32] The situation demands, first, grounds for doubting the initial conclusion, and second, reasons to seek other grounds. The second
condition is fulfilled only where more than one criteria set--in the
example, testimony and the collection of observed actions--provides
sufficient grounds within the same context. If our doubts are strong
but records conflict, we reach not a judgment of truth or falsity, but
only an impasse.

Many denials do not equate with judgments of falsity. Instead,
they only entail a suspension of assertion. This follows from the fact
that criteria warrant the use of a concept but do not imply the concept
nor are implied by it. The crucial criterion for Collingwood's assertion that the Roman Wall was a sentry-walk was the existence of the remains of towers located along the coast. Assume that the towers had
left no trace: perhaps they had never existed or perhaps their remains

had been carted off, with the land being cut deep and reused so as to preclude discovery. For want of justification, one could not warrantably assert that the Romans had built a sentry-walk. Neither could one say that such an assertion was false. The thesis that the Romans built a sentry-walk becomes only more or less likely (or unlikely) depending upon the remainder of the evidence. Since criteria do not constitute necessary conditions for the assertion, the failure to fulfill a criterion, that is, the absence of a condition does not suffice to negate the assertion. In view of this feature of event and action concepts, one must beware of the ambiguous form, "It is not true that Q occurred." It may express either a falsification of "Q occurred" or only the lack of warrant for Q's assertion.

If the account so far given holds, then with respect to historical assertions of events, actions, and the like, "true" and "false" do not constitute necessarily the alternatives of a mutually exclusive bivalued set. While this consequence may go some distance in explaining some of the difficulty formal theory has when attempting to formulate rigorously various aspects of historical activity, it more significantly is consonant with other findings mentioned along the way. For example, Collingwood's seeming shortness with truth in the interest of other concerns becomes appropriate to the extent that his aim was to portray the activities of history. For "truth" in the formal sense does not stand as the goal of those activities; the goal is something else, which Collingwood portrayed overzealously as "certain" conclusions. Waters chose the more revealing side of the coin when he characterized bad accounts rather than good ones, because like the subject of justification, truth rarely becomes a consideration except under challenge. Bad accounts are dubious or implausible and they are rejected or impossible. The inability to find remnants of the towers would make the sentry-walk thesis implausible; a defensible assertion that there never had been towers along with the absence of any other criteria set by which to justify the sentry-walk assertion would make the thesis impossible. These suggestions coincide with the earlier note that historical assertions based on the inference from evidence are neither deductive nor inductive; the terms which best portray them are "permissive" and perhaps "eliminative."

VII. The Truth of History

Every assertion eliminates others. Of course, not every other assertion is eliminated by an initial statement. As Lord Acton notes of Charles I, "when, after the Petition of Right, he governed without a parliament, the problem is whether he did it for the sake of power or for the sake of religion." The two are not mutually exclusive; Charles could rule for the sake of both, either at different times or simultaneously. "It resembles the problem of the American Civil War, whether the confederates were fighting for State rights or for slavery."[33]

Still, every assertion does eliminate some others. To assert a
political revolution eliminates the assertion of aimless terrorism. To
assert a political assassination eliminates the assertion of unpremeditated murder or of accident. Where criteria sets may overlap, as with
terrorism and revolution, which assertion of equally justified pairs
that one chooses may follow from considerations other than warrant.
Those committing acts of violence call themselves revolutionists, while
their victims call them terrorists. Indeed, a class of low-level humor
has developed on the basis of just such possibilities, e.g., I am concerned; you are meddling; he is a preacher. In constructing a historical account, the writer must choose which of the warranted assertions
he will use. Assuming no particular bias (whether some form of bias is
a necessary feature of history comes under analysis in the following
chapter), the historian must find some grounds for selection. In general, he chooses the most plausible assertion.

The distinction between what is implausible and what is impossible, what is merely dubious and what must be rejected, often rests on
whether one assertion eliminates another in such a way as to preclude
fulfillment of the criteria for another or whether it simply takes precedence for various reasons over another also warranted assertion.
When one is said to commit a political assassination, then unpremeditated murder becomes an impossibility (without further information to
modify the situation). Such impossibility is neither purely conceptual
nor purely empiric. To assert a political assassination is tantamount
to denying that the assassin killed out of rage or other emotion on the
spur of the moment, which denial leaves an assertion of unpremeditated
murder without justification. To the extent that one is speaking of
unfulfilled criteria, the problem is conceptual; to the extent the non-
fulfillment rests on the evidence of a plan, of unemotional execution,
of political motive, the problem is broadly empiric. If one makes some
additions to the story, e.g., elements of hesitation, conversation, argument, the possibility arises that the assassin changed his mind, but
ultimately killed because the victim enraged him. Without decisive ev-
idence--say, a believable confession--both possibilities have some
plausibility. The historian's task is to choose the more plausible.
Unlike a judicial system, where decision is decisive, the historian may
stand ready to be corrected or to be convinced by a better case.

The sorts of facts which eliminate other assertions as impossible
or implausible do not form any sort of well-defined class. A general
whose birth records date him to 1903 could not *possibly* have fought in
the Boer War; one born in 1895 could not *plausibly* have been in the
war. The latter, given the practice of assigning rank at birth and
some set of circumstances to place the boy in a proper position, keeps
open the possibility of the boy's having been in the war, but it is not
a very live option. An emperor of Nero's ilk would *not likely* have
persecuted Christians for religious motives (it was not impossible, but
quite against character), but far *more likely* for political reasons.
It is far *more plausible* that Agrippina married Domitius out of family
and political duty than for love, because such dutiful marriages were

the rule rather than the exception in those days; too, the daughter of
Germanicus could have no love for a husband chosen by an emperor
(Tiberius) who had continually slighted her father. Love may be implausible, but as old wives tales have it, with love anything is possible. In these crude examples, the alternative assertions (he did
fight, he had religious motives; she loved) do not fall out as false or
impossible. Rather, given the varied sorts of evidence, they all became implausible. Just as facts make an assertion implausible, they
can also make it plausible once more.

Just such a point seems to lie behind Dray's category of "how-
possibly" explanations which, he notes, do not establish that something
did occur, but instead, rebut a presumption against its occurrence.[34]
To use his example, given a flyball twenty feet above the ground at the
wall, there is a natural presumption against an assertion to the effect
that the fielder caught it. A ladder left by workmen rebuts the presumption by allowing the possibility of the catch (leaving aside any
question of the legality of such a catch). So far, however, the catch
is only possible, since anyone who in fact could climb the ladder and
intercept the ball can be said to have caught the fly. But the catch
remains implausible insofar as climbing ladders takes more time than
any fielder would have to reach the fly. Other facts would also make
the catch possible, for example, a gale force wind occurring either
naturally or as a result of the stadium's peculiar construction. Given
this account, the catch remains implausible considering that the wind
would have had to force the ball to drop vertically. In short, more
than possibility must be allowable if the assertion is to play a role
in a historical account. Perhaps the fact that the fielder was already on the fourth rung of the ladder when the batter swung or perhaps
a conjunction of facts concerning wind currents in the park and the
towering laziness of the flyball: either may make the assertion of the
catch plausible. Thus, the assertion of a catch by an eye-witness or
the inference to one by a historian requires not only those means which
open a possibility, but as much more as will make the possibility plausible.

The case for plausibility presented here has relied upon opening
the way to two or more roughly equally plausible accounts (ladder or
wind). Dray's examples in support of how-possibly explanations involved but a single account. The change in strategy was undertaken in
order to avoid the danger of possible over-simplification. The danger
is signaled in part by Dray's failure to consider an additional requirement: the means, the "how," must not only be capable of occurrence; one must also have some reason to take the means as fact. Making the case comparative, to the extent that comparison suggests a
decision as to which means are the more plausible (any possibility is
equally possible with any other), hopefully clarifies the situation.
Whereas attributions of "possibility" are simple (something either is
or is not possible), "plausibility" is susceptible to comparative uses,
even where no other alternative account has been presented. We judge
accounts through locutions such as "not very likely," "almost certain,"

"quite plausible," and "highly improbable." None of these expressions, of course, entails anything like statistical notions. Rather, they constitute judgments concerning the justification of historical assertions which have less than the status of fully warranted facts.

The use in a history of any assertion which has less than a complete factual justification requires some account. Earlier in this chapter, reference was made to Collingwood's notion of historical imagination, through the use of which the historian fills in gaps in his account. Dray's how-possibly explanations perform the gap-filling function, and thus force an alteration to the analysis of Collingwood's own example of Caesar's trip. Whereas Collingwood's example was primarily a conceptual interpolation, an equivalent claim cannot be made for the sorts of accounts Dray appears to have in mind. Nonetheless, the gap-filling ability of the class of historical assertions under consideration here constitutes a necessary feature of their use. Any number of statements find partial justification in terms of the facts at hand. The grounds for limiting that number to a collection of historical possibilities, of which one then determines the relative plausibility, must come partly from the role the statements might play in a historical narrative. One might loosely generalize the test of having a fact-connecting narrative role under the name of coherence. If one then suggests that historical narratives differ from other rational systems, e.g., deductive logic, one might go on to suggest that history, the well-plotted story of human action, has a peculiar *a priori* form of its own which serves as a universal test of histories. Moving in such a direction takes one dangerously close to Collingwood's position on the truth of history (as distinct from historical assertions) (IH, 245). In raising the question of the function of coherence in attributing truth to historical accounts, the position simultaneously loses sight of the features of narratives which would enable one, at least in part, to answer the question.

If what counts as a gap-filling assertion or set of assertions—the imaginative reconstructions—depends upon the narrative in which it functions, then a few statements become appropriate with respect to the nature of coherence in this context. (A more systematic attempt to isolate elements of narrative "coherence" will be taken up in the final chapter.) Any gap in a narrative requires termini, although some cases require only one. The baseball example from Dray required a connective which cemented both temporally and conditionally separated states, namely, the situation of the ball in the air near the wall and the catch. The case of Agrippina has only her actions which want, in a tale devoting attention to "thought," motivation. One could give such a case an artificial second terminus in terms of Agrippina's character and Roman mores in general, for indeed, the reconstructive assertion of duty on her part must be consistent with both her actions in the given situation and her character as an individual and a Roman female. Such a second terminus may be useful and non-artificial to this extent: it shows clearly that not all gaps to be filled coherently involve logical or temporal progressions between categorically like terms. Oakeshott's story without lacuna and Collingwood's *a priori* complete history express too simplistically the far looser idea of making a story go on and also just making it go. A variation of the Oakeshott-Collingwood notion of coherence, equally over-simplistic, appears in Woodbridge's *The Purpose of History*. Historical "continuity," as Woodbridge terms it, explains only with respect to the question "What have been the antecedants of any given fact?" Even inquiry into the consequences of a "given fact" stems from "our habit of looking at consequences as derived from their antecedants."[35] Coherence, with respect to historical narratives has the thinnest of theoretic bases and relies mostly upon pragmatics, that is to say, a contextually founded understanding of a gap which needs filling and the kind of filling which suits the rest of the tale.

A case for pragmatics does not, however, eliminate all useful generalizations. From the claim that a gap, narrative or otherwise, entails one or more termini by which one judges it to exist and how best to fill it in the absence of fully warranted fact, one may infer that the notion of coherence, insofar as it applies at all, applies to accounts and not to singular assertions. As expressed, this may hold for all historical assertions since a single factual assertion of an event's occurrence supposes as fact that which fulfills the criteria for assertion. The present case, however, differs importantly from this sort of supposition; the termini with which a gap-filling statement must be consistent do not constitute evidential or linguistic criteria, nor does the gap-filling statement pretend to the status of fully warranted fact. Facts may be asserted without the prior existence of a gap. The assertion of a gap and the acceptance of a reconstruction involves in every case the termini and whatever fills the gap. Therefore, where one asserts a fully warranted fact, it takes precedence over any reconstruction; i.e., it takes precedence over coherence as a ground for inclusion in a historical narrative. The discovery that Agrippina loved Domitius would preclude duty as the contending motive for her actions (and, obviously, duty and love need not in all cases contend). Such discoveries often lead to new questions requiring new gap-filling reconstructions; in effect, they change the termini. In this hypothetical case, the question "Did she love?" or "What was her motive?" becomes "How could she love?"

Because history sometimes operates far into the region of reconstruction, with comparatively few facts for the scope of the work undertaken, many cases do not admit of such easy solution. We may become so attached to a favored complex reconstruction into which we have poured a lifetime of work that it seems wholly unreasonable that a fact should overturn the coherent tale we tell. Coherence may thus overide fact in affecting our beliefs. Concerning a neighbor one might ask, why would such a peaceful, upright son of an established community leader suddenly murder his wife? So unbelievable is the story that one refuses to believe it. No one can doubt that instances have occurred in which the refusal to believe has reached hysteric proportions, even to the point of acquittal in the face of overwhelming and unquestionable eviden-e. The reverse can also hold true. Perhaps Steinbeck's Lenny must die less for any crime than because his absolute physical strength makes innocence unbelievable. The law also provides clear instances of contesting reconstructions, for example, in a prosecution vs. defense struggle which pits circumstantial evidence against the defendant's character. That he did not commit the crime becomes inconsistent with the evidence; that he did commit it becomes inconsistent with his personality and every past action. Such contests of fact vs. coherence also occur in the activity of history, hopefully with some sense of detachment.

Emotional and otherwise motivated attachment can and does occur in history, but the fact of its occurrence does not speak to the logical necessity of its occurrence. That it is not a necessity emerges from the very language in which we ordinarily characterize history. History deals in evidence, produces facts, tells us what happened in the past. We tend to criticize any history which we catch distorting the facts in the service of some purpose, however noble. Whatever the outcome of the debate on the question of whether the enterprise called history contains unremovable stains of bias or subjectivity, we permit none that we are equipped to detect. We praise the objective, the fair, the balanced treatment. We rejoice over new relic discoveries, not for the reconstructions they permit—they regularly shatter more gap-fillers than they permit—but for the facts they reveal. In short, historical methodology places and must place a premium on facts. To reverse the precedence would leave no criterion by which to determine which one of multiple coherent accounts is most acceptable. Coherence and imaginative reconstruction without fact would lapse into mere arbitrariness. As Danto has noted, to know what "*in fact* happened, we require documentary evidence. Conceptual evidence, accordingly, at best supports a *plausible* account."[36]

None of these points argues for or needs to argue for an absolute standard of what counts as historical fact. One could allow the interaction of evidence and principles of evidence to keep historical fact ever open to change, and one could go farther to deny on epistemic grounds that historical fact ever get beyond the level of inference, all without affecting the soundess of the present argument. So long as the historian can have for any given period a body of assertions which he can reasonably term facts, the precedence of fact over gap-filling, coherent constructions holds. Moreover, the inability to ask a question or make an inquiry without already accepting something as fact which gives sense to the question and inquiry, entails a body of fact.

Despite the precedence of facts over imaginative reconstructions, the foregoing account of historical coherence may suggest that one can draw no hard and fast lines between fact and reconstruction. Both obtain Collingwood's *nihil obstat*, although at differing epistemic levels. Methodologically, the levels mix to one degree or other. How much justification a fact must have cannot be specified *a priori* in view of the absence of explicit criteria sets. Precisely what strength the connections between gap-fillers and the termini of a gap must have to be deemed acceptable or favored is likewise a contextually bound consideration. One can explicate the clear cases, as in the artificially simple examples, and such explanations can illumine the practice of history. Still, a clever soul can generate enough densely complex examples to befoul any analysis. This analysis is no exception.

NOTES

[1]Michael Oakeshott, *Experience and Its Modes* (Cambridge: At the University Press, 1933), p. 108; R. G. Collingwood, *The Idea of History* (New York: Oxford University Press, 1956), p. 204. Since I shall extensively cite Collingwood's works in this chapter, I shall use in the text the following abbreviations:

A   -- *An Autobiography* (New York: Oxford University Press, 1939)
EM   -- *An Essay on Metaphysics* (Oxford: Clarendon Press, 1940)
IH   -- *The Idea of History*
SM   -- *Speculum Mentis* (Oxford: Clarendon Press, 1924)
NAPH -- "The Nature and Aims of Philosophy" (1924)
LHK   -- "The Limits of Historical Knowledge" (1928)
PP   -- "A Philosophy of Progress" (1929)
PH   -- "The Philosophy of History" (1930)

The dates of the articles are of their first appearances, although references herein are to their collected source, *Essays in the Philosophy of History*, ed. William Debbins (New York: McGraw-Hill Book Company, 1965). In the text, (Ph, E, 136) means the article "The Philosophy of History," in the *Essays*, p. 136. (A, 109) would refer to page 109 of the *Autobiography*.

[2]Collingwood uses all three terms; see, e.g., IH, 293 and 296 for uses of the latter two terms.

[3]Debbins, "Introduction," *Essays in the Philosophy of History*, p. xxviii.

[4]E.g., Louis O. Mink, "Collingwood's Dialectic of History," *History and Theory*, 7 (1968), pp. 55 ff, or N. Rotenstreich, "From Facts to Thoughts, Collingwood's Views on the Nature of History," *Philosophy*, 35 (1960), pp. 122 ff.

[5]One may compare any number of Socratic productions, e.g., those of Taylor, Burnet, Guthrie, and Fuller, to name some in English, plus a number in German, such as that of Zeller.

[6]William H. Dray, *Laws and Explanation in History* (Oxford: Oxford University Press, 1957), p. 161.

[7]See, for example, Alan Donagan's extended treatment, *The Later Philosophy of R. G. Collingwood* (Oxford: Oxford University Press, 1962), esp. Chapter IV.

[8] *Ibid.*, p. 74.

[9] A. D. Ritchie, "The Logic of Question and Answer," *Mind*, 52 (1943), p. 28.

[10] Bruce Waters, "Historical Narrative," *The Southern Journal of Philosophy*, 5 (Fall, 1967), p. 214. See also John Passmore, "Explanations in Everyday Life, in Science, and in History," *Studies in the Philosophy of History*, ed. George H. Nadel (New York: Harper and Row, Publishers, 1965), pp. 18 f, and Dray, *Laws and Explanation in History*, pp. 20 and 98, for remarks on the pragmatic dimensions of the concept of explanation. That "explanation," "cause," and "evidence" should all have pragmatic dimensions (or all not have them) should not seem surprising given the interrelationship of the three in use. Anticipating the contemporary analysts and even Collingwood himself was Frederick J. E. Woodbridge, who remarked in his 1916 lectures, *The Purpose of History* (Port Washington, New York: Kennikat Press, Inc., 1965), p. 66, that "To explain anything at all, it is necessary to keep in mind the questions to which the proposed explanation is relevant."

[11] Cf. Haskell Fain, *Between Philosophy and History* (Princeton: Princeton University Press, 1970), p. 176: "The reason for the open endedness of the concept of the total body of evidence is that what one considers to be a part of the total body of evidence bearing on a certain event is, in fact, a function of how one conceptualizes the event, of how one interprets its significance and relationships to other events making up the history . . ." of the subject in question. But see also A. C. Danto, *Analytical Philosophy of History* (Cambridge: At the University Press, 1965), pp. 218 ff, on redescription and Charles A. Beard, "Written History as an Act of Faith," *The Philosophy of History in Our Time*, ed. Hans Meyerhoff (Garden City: Doubleday and Company, 1959), pp. 150 f, on history as "controlled inexorably by the frame of reference of the selector and arranger," for interpretations of Fain's ambiguous notion of "conceptualizing an event."

[12] For example, compare IH, 212-13 with A, 90 ff, and see also NAPH, LHK, and PH in the *Essays*.

[13] F. H. Bradley, *The Presuppositions of Critical History*, ed. L. Rubinoff (Chicago: University of Chicago Press, 1968), pp. 85-86.

[14] Danto, *Analytical Philosophy of History*, pp. 122-28, 226.

[15] W. H. Walsh, *An Introduction to Philosophy of History* (London: Hutchinson University Library, 1958), pp. 57-58.

[16] See a good example in Fain, *Between Philosophy and History*, pp. 144 ff. Contrast the attempts of Dray (*Laws and Explanation in History*, pp. 118 ff) and Donagan (*The Later Philosophy of R. G. Collingwood*, pp. 187 ff) to make good analytic sense out of Collingwood's conception.

[17] Cf. Waters, "Historical Narrative," p. 207.

[18] Rogers Albritton, "On Wittgenstein's Use of the Term 'Criterion'," *The Journal of Philosophy*, 56 (October 22, 1959), p. 856; Michael

Scriven, "The Logic of Criteria," *The Journal of Philosophy*, 56 (October 22, 1959), p. 865.

[19] J. H. Hexter, "Storm Over the Gentry," *Reappraisals in History* (New York: Harper and Row, Publishers, 1961), p. 148.

[20] *Ibid.*, pp. 141-43.

[21] J. H. Hexter, "The Myth of the Middle Class in Tudor England," *Reappraisals in History*, pp. 71 ff.

[22] Fain, *Between Philosophy and History*, p. 107.

[23] *Ibid.*, p. 106.

[24] The example is drawn from information in Preserved Smith, *The Social Background of the Reformation* (Part II of *The Age of the Reformation*) (New York: Collier Books, 1962), pp. 40 f.

[25] On distinguishing kinds of explanation, see Passmore, "Explanations in Everyday Life, in Science, and in History," pp. 17-18.

[26] R. Ernest Dupuy and Trevor H. Dupuy, *The Compact History of the Civil War* (New York: Collier Books, 1960), p. 350.

[27] Oakeshott, *Experience and Its Modes*, p. 143.

[28] Waters, "Historical Narrative," p. 207.

[29] Frank P. Ramsey, "Facts and Propositions," *The Foundations of Mathematics*, ed. R. B. Braithewaite (London: Kegan Paul, Trench, Trubner and Co., Ltd., 1931), p. 142.

[30] See P. F. Strawson, "Truth," *Truth*, ed. G. Pitcher (Englewood Cliffs, New Jersey: Prentice-Hall, Inc., 1964), pp. 45 ff, and "Truth," *Analysis*, 19 (June, 1949), pp. 90 ff.

[31] Dupuy and Dupuy, *The Compact History of the Civil War*, p. 350.

[32] Jack W. Meiland, *Scepticism and Historical Knowledge* (New York: Random House, 1965), pp. 105 ff.

[33] Lord Acton, *Lectures on Modern History* (New York: Meridian Books, Inc., 1961), p. 193.

[34] Dray, *Laws and Explanation in History*, p. 161.

[35] Woodbridge, *The Purpose of History*, pp. 66-67.

[36] Danto, *Analytical Philosophy of History*, p. 226.

CHAPTER FOUR

Selection, Purpose, and Objectivity

Three topics which bear too close a relationship for separate treatment form the core of the chapter. The historian's selection of events for inclusion in his account and his purpose in writing a history have both been associated with the debate on the question of history's objectivity. Although farther removed from the starting point of this study than the subjects of Chapter Four, these topics find relevance to the extent that they involve consideration of conceptual proposals and of the interrelationship of question and method. The first section of the chapter traces the trends in the history of philosophy which lead to Dray's attempt to find a place for non-objectivity in history via the need in a purely descriptive history to select events with respect to their "intrinsic" importance. In the next section, I argue that the elements of non-objectivity which Dray includes in a descriptive or non-explanatory history as a result of the need in such a work to create unifying concepts belong to the context of discovery or genesis of those concepts. Attention to the justification of these conceptual proposals provides grounds for a relevant possibility of objectivity. The third section explores the relation of purpose to objectivity. By distinguishing internal purposes (goals) from external purposes (uses) of history, one can separate those factors of historical use and abuse which are necessitated by historical method from those which follow contingently. The factors usually characterized as non-objective fall into the latter category. In the last section, positions which argue for history as non-objective by stressing the role of personal, subjective factors in the selection of events for historical account are rejected because of their dependence upon reference to personal facts and processes. Ignoring the interrelationship of method and purpose, they amount to genetic accounts of written histories rather than to inquiries into the justification of those histories. Only in the latter context does the question of history's objectivity appropriately arise.

No historian says everything. Yet we do not take the bare fact of omissions as a sign that he has flawed the work. Nor do we assume that his omissions result *just* from the fact that he cannot say, in this large sense, everything that happened in the piece of the past about which he writes. For we also say of the best of historians, and with-

119

out contradicting the earlier assertion, that he has said it all. Thus, it is for reason rather than philosophical whimsy that we sometimes ask and have to ask why one has left out such and so events. Why, for example, did a historian of the French Revolution fail to mention Burns' poetry on the subject? It would make interesting reading. Perhaps, since the historian's thesis concerned internal French affairs, mention of the Scottish poetry was irrelevant. Even should his thesis concern foreign opinion and influence on the events in and surrounding the revolution, the historian might still justify his omission on the grounds that the poetry had little or no effect; its mention would have been interesting but wholly digressive.

The fact that we routinely request justification for certain sorts of omissions correctly suggests that we also judge what the historian includes in his account. When he piles in irrelevancies, digressions, pointless collections of facts, we properly fault the work. Granted, since history constitutes a genre of written matter, we often excuse and even praise such departures from the main current of the narrative. We do so on literary grounds, just as we laud well done comic relief in a tragedy. Nonetheless, the historian's selection of events for his narrative remains a routine subject for question. While particular questions concerning the selection of events may strike a historian (for personal reason of his involvement in his work) as non-routine and perhaps nit picking, the general practice of selecting events and questioning selections seems to warrant little scepticism.

Besides holding its status as an everyday task for critical history, the question of on what grounds a historian chooses the events which flesh his narrative has periodically tantalized philosophy of history. Perhaps the subject earns its perennial budding because of its association with another: the question of history's objectivity or lack thereof. As the positivistic fixation upon historical explanation gave way to probings into the nature and function of historical narrative, both these thorny vines poked their heads above ground once more. Recognition of history's storied structure, acceptance of its artful as well as its scientific techniques, counterattack by those who claimed history for the liberal arts and humanities against those who would associate only with social scientists--all of these trends encouraged a review of the questions specifically centered on the anti-positivistic claims that the choice of events which make up a given historical narrative rests upon either a normatively evaluative base or a subjective base, or both. To the new humanists, the very denial that explanation serves as history's central purpose seemed to leave the field to subjective and normative considerations by default.

Default, however, usually characterizes an investigation ended too soon and short of its goal. This part of the present study seeks to discover whether the historian's selection of events need ever be value-laden or subjective in any dangerous sense. Obviously, the question concerns the logical necessity of bias, prejudice, and the like, rather than their fact. That biased, subjective, value-laden histories have existed and will continue to appear stands beyond doubt. Anything which can be done or used properly can also be done or used improperly. So much follows analytically from the applicability of the label "proper" to the subject matter. What concerns philosophers is whether history *must* rest on essentially non-objective grounds. That inquiry leads off the main path of historical concerns, where methods and their justification mark a relatively clear trail, into the by-ways of such murky fields as non-explanatory history, dead and live metaphors, and inventive colligation. Nonetheless, at the end--if the trail has an end--we shall find that even when stripped of explanatory purpose and its attendant methodology, historical narratives retain criteria for the inclusion of events. They may be non-scientific criteria, but they will satisfy relevant demands for objectivity. In that regard, my point will be less to pin on history some insignia of respectability (to be objective is to be respectable) than to see in what the objectivity of selection consists.

I.   Non-objectivity and Selection in Descriptive History

The historian's problem of selection--more precisely, the philosopher's problem with the historian's selection of events--derives in modern times from two myths, the American and German versions of Rankean historicism.[1] The polarization of empirical and rationalistic viewpoints produced overt charges by each camp which deprived the opposing side of any possibility of objective selection. Idealism, so went the attack, selected its facts to fit preconceived schemes having no historical or methodological justification. In the other direction, the separation of past event and present study supposedly prevented empirical fact-finders from achieving an epistemological warrant for their results. Such dialectical bedevilment engendered strange alliances, such as the coincidental one between the subjectivist Becker and the positivist Hempel: both claimed that history had so far been no more than the historian's intrusions upon fact. The only difference lay in Hempel's optimism bred from his faith in a historically applicable scientific method. Becker remained pessimistic.[2]

The fundamental problem can be stated simply. Granted that the historian must select from among the facts at his disposal,[3] how does his selection proceed? In such deceptively neat form the question obscures all the complexities of history: the procedural differences between defending a thesis and telling a story, the necessity for the historian to establish facts as well as to tell them, and so on and on. With equal deception, the simple question seems to admit of simple answer. A negative response condemns all history, while an affirmative one gives history but a slim hope almost universally dashed by the malpractice of historians. Affirmatively, history can be objective if it prepares for conversion to scientific ways; negatively, it not only fails to be a science, but amounts to the most fanciful of fictions unworthy of serious attention. The simple question and answer have thus never risen beyond the pessimism which besets history's eternal quest for epistemic respectability.

Despite the dark shadows, past attempts to condemn history on the grounds of non-objective selection have met with effective reply. A few examples from the near past illustrate this cause for at least a modicum of optimism.

Mannheimian cultural or ideological relativity, for one example, persists despite rather devastating criticism. Croce, Ortega y Gasset, and even Dewey have come near to embracing, if they have not actually embraced, this view.[4] Since all histories arise from cultures and societies, they must be written in and through the values of social groups. The historian, consciously or not, must select facts which express those values. Consequently, an objective history--one free of cultural or ideological bias--is simply not possible.

This direct charge and attribution to history of eternally unconscious bias and prejudice perishes in the chasm of vacuous alternative.[5] If we are to call these histories subjective or value-laden, we must be able to conceive an objective history. And (contrary to the denigration usually accorded him), Mannheim almost provides grounds for such a conception. In his "unmasking" process, one identifies the values contained in a history. However, Mannheim did not see that the ability to unmask did not imply a "scientific" procedure of "relationism;"[6] instead, it expressed an important logical point: The identification of anything as a set of values entails the identification of something as other than the set of values, to which other sets of values are not of logical necessity attached. The ability to unmask cultural values in a history thus entails the possibility that some portion of that history is not necessarily value infected. The mere possibility of non-valued facts suffices to nullify any serious consequence to the claims of necessary sociological subjectivity.

Moreover, the non-valued facts need not be "ordinary" historical facts; this is, facts about what events occurred on what dates with what effect. For one will still encounter cultural variations in the treatment of historical subjects. Rather, the claim for cultural variation in history, and its Mannheimian explanation in terms of value, entails an identification of the standards by which cultures made their assessments. But to say one culture used a certain standard and another used a different one is to utter a historical fact, one which cannot easily, if at all, be laid in the grave of ideological relativity. In short, the claims of a socially oriented relativity are self-defeating when carried to the level of universality and logical necessity.

Descending from the social to the personal level, Becker held that "the history of any event is never precisely the same thing to two different persons." The difference, the uneliminable "personal equation" or subjectivity, rests for Becker on a theory of facts as mental constructs, where "mental" represents a personal and private process closed to public scrutiny or agreement. On these grounds, even the agreement which historians may reach concerning "records" (as distinct from "histories")--the only form of agreement Becker supports--must become a logical accident dependent upon the mental acts of reading and understanding them. Subjectivity, in brief, is endemic to human nature.[7]

To this sort of view, Nagel has replied most succinctly: however many the personal problems, the historian's subjectivity remains a problem of contingent fallibility. Subjectivity entails the possibility of the ability to separate it from the objective. Too, it presupposes something to be called objective from which to separate the bias.[8] To characterize anything as subjective entails a recognition, and to recognize is already to distinguish and separate. Melden has made a similar point with a slightly different distinction: because facts can be used to tell stories, express values, propagandize, etc., it follows that facts are presupposed by and separable from their uses. Therefore, where a fact is asserted, it is separable from the values already in or brought to the assertion, even if those values constitute necessary elements in the value-expressive or propagandistic use of the fact.[9] By characterizing facts as themselves subjective, Becker has either created a contradiction or emptied the term "fact" of meaning; his mystic epistemology serves but to conceal his shift in use and the consequent emptying process.

Meiland has attempted to blunt the Nagel-Melden argument by countering that the possibility of correcting bias does not follow from the possibility of identifying it. His case rests upon treating all evaluations of evidence according to "values and standards" as cases of bias. Since history results from the evaluation of evidence, it is inevitably biased.[10] However, Meiland's notion of "bias" seems somewhat queer. To evaluate according to standards is generally what one is inclined to call an unbiased activity. It may in fact be the paradigm and, lacking that status, at least comprises the sort of activity one would cite to explain what an objective judgment might be. If one claims that the standards can be biased--as one might do in examining the earlier noted essentially contested concepts of Gallie--and can specify what it is for them to be biased, then one has merely admitted the Nagel-Melden point at a different level. That is, one has confessed that it is logically possible to identify bias in standards and hence equally possible to correct or remove it. Where Meiland ultimately goes wrong is in treating evaluation as a subclass of valuation, where in fact the reverse subsumption holds. Thus, evaluation, however necessarily general a practice, cannot itself make a case for necessarily biased history.

To this point, the positions for social and individual subjectivity or bias have not distinguished between two possible ways in which non-objectivity might be introduced: via the choice of events so as to slant a case or via the means by which the historian expresses the facts. Clearly, the Nagel-Melden argument collapses either alternative; which is to say, either form of bias is subject to correction.

123

Indeed, the weight of this argument has gradually narrowed the gateway for subjectivity and bias in history to the question of selection. The result has been a gradual sophistication of claims, for example, the subtle position which developed from such sources as Collingwood, Berlin, and Winch. Roughly, the position suggests that history is the history of human actions, which are themselves goal directed and value-laden, i.e., normative.[11] Thus, the historian cannot avoid value, for it lies within the very thing he studies, the actions he selects for his narrative.

In the first place, such a view uncritically compounds two notions of the normative or of rule-following in the blanket idea of goal-directed actions. We have value-laden rules, such as those for directing traffic or those assigning penalties for stealing, and we have non-valued rules, like those for putting together children's toys or those specifying the dimensions of a basketball.[12] Only by treating both as normative in the same sense can one arrive at a universally value-ridden history. However, to the extent to which the latter defines activities, the attribution of value is artificial, if not simply mistaken. In the second place, as Dray has correctly pointed out, the attribution of purpose to an act does not necessitate or amount to the historian's evaluation of that act. The problem for history is not the values *in* an act, but the values *of* an act, *viz.*, "that they are necessarily evaluated by the historian in the process of selecting them for a historical account."[13]

In large measure, the positivists--notably Nagel--removed from selectional evaluation the onus of value and subjectivity. Where the historian proposes a causal explanation of events, his purpose provides criteria for selection: he must include those events dictated by the methodology of his explanation form. In the positivist's view, those events must be such as to count as causes in a suitable covering law formula.[14] Similar considerations would apply *mutatis mutandis* to other types of explanations.[15] Thus, whenever explanation serves as the historian's purpose, objective grounds exist for his selection of events.

Whether or not the last point is exceptionless, it cannot--according to Dray--dissolve the relativist's case. By suggesting that there is "descriptive" history as distinct from "explanatory" history, he eludes the positivists' point to the extent that descriptive history does not seek to explain and therefore lacks methodological selection criteria. Instead, descriptive history tries to find some "unity" within the limits of the period and place studied, a unity usually expressed in terms of "main movements." The main movement of fifteenth century Italy, for example, was the renaissance of the arts and sciences.[16] Dray's views of descriptive period history coincide with those of Walsh (who does not use the label "descriptive history"): both hold that the historian's tasks include, either as a partial or as a separable whole endeavor, the discovery of what events of a given time or place made up. That they make up something--a golden age, an era of good feeling, a closing of the frontier--is in part a function of the historian's creativity and value judgments. He selects those events which are "worth noticing" (Dray) or "intrinsically important" (Walsh); then via metaphor, analogy or other device, he sees what kind of movement they can "intelligibly" constitute. His judgment in such cases is at worst purely subjective and at best normatively evaluative.

Dray sums up the case in the following way: "Now if it is allowed that the selection of 'main movements' . . . involves the historian's use of value judgments, and if it is allowed that it is legitimate to attempt the construction of histories of the period type at all, then the relativist case is surely a strong one."[17] To invalidate Dray's conclusion here, one need deny only one of the two conditions he sets forth. Since the second seems unassailable, attention will be confined to the first.

Many sources, conceptions, and philosophical notions underlie Dray's idea of "descriptive" history with its period-place orientation. The peculiar uniqueness of large scale historical "events," so ill-accounted for by Rickert and others, perhaps prompts the explanation in terms of value judgment and artistic device. Dray's tendency to treat facts as interpretations, conjoined to a distinction between chronicles or "basic" narratives vs. histories, provides clues to the impetus behind his dualism of explanatory and descriptive histories.[18] However, despite Dray's failure directly to connect the two conceptions, major theoretical support for the relativistic descriptive history resides in certain portions of Dray's analysis of "explaining what" and Walsh's notion of "colligation."

The relevance of colligation (the term here covers both Dray's and Walsh's very similar accounts) to descriptive history should be apparent. As noted in an earlier section of this study, colligation consists in the subsumption of known events under a concept, e.g., the events of fifteenth century Italy under "the renaissance in the arts and science," or certain events in Germany during the thirties under "Hitler's policy of German self-assertion and expansion." The concepts most relevant to colligatory analysis principally encompass those which designate human actions, group activities, mass movements, and other teleologically oriented affairs. Both Dray and Walsh conceive of colligation as in part, and perhaps chiefly, an intellectually inventive activity by which the historian generates new categories, a process to which analogy and other sources of organizing concepts are essential. The historian sees a group of events, actions, and conditions as something not previously seen. In doing so, he has added no "empirical" facts to history. Rather, his product enlightens the reader and intellectually satisfies the historian himself through the new organization, perspective, and understanding he has captured.[19]

The notion of colligation, however, comprises a partial account of the logic of event and action concepts.[20] For non-controversial or non-inventive cases of event, action, or movement assertion, the events, actions, and conditions which Dray sees as subsumed under the concept used actually amount to the events and other facts which constitute criteria instantiations serving to justify the concept's use in the given context. Perhaps the variety of uses, the multiplicity of criteria sets, the non-formality of their conventional existence, all of which preclude total and exact *a priori* analysis for any concept, has contributed some of the mysterious aura that surrounds such concepts. Yet, requests for justification speak to specific criteria and by-pass the mysterious elements. Even such cases as are contested on technical or normative grounds reduce to contests over criteria, and these contests are also subject to demands for justification.[21]

Consequently, that portion of colligatory theory which is analyzable in terms of ordinary assertions cannot support the case for a relativistic descriptive history. Moreover, common assertions like "There was a French Revolution" and "Lindberg soloed across the Atlantic" cannot count as the sorts of assertions in question, for however large or small the event subsumptions, they are not historical theses in the sense required by Dray's "unities." For no one would think of denying them. (This fact, of course, does not make the assertions logically undeniable or preclude their being possible theses.) Likewise, "Pompey crossed the Rubicon" and "Curie invented the polio vaccine" are not historical theses because no one would think of affirming them. The assertions Dray and Walsh have under scrutiny are theses, but of a particular kind: assertions which are made for the first time by some historian and which describe or assert the occurrence of an action, event, or movement in contradistinction from explaining the action, event, or movement. Yet, theses, of this or any other sort, do not comprise the whole of the assertions historians make, and the failure to attend fully to the ordinary, non-controversial assertions probably undergirds the attempt to put relativistic elements in the account of inventive "unifying" concepts in descriptive histories. They need not be there.

II. Justification and Relevant Objectivity

A historian may make perhaps two sorts of descriptive or non-explanatory assertions which might be considered to enlighten the reader without adding new facts to his supply. First, by attending to facts which others have known but ignored, he may apply a concept where it had not been previously applied. Thus, by noting in detail the activities among the court scholars of Charlemagne, a historian might justifiably assert--with the facts as his justification--that there occurred a Carolingian renaissance.[22] Here he fulfills the Dray-Walsh demand of organizing facts as they had not been previously organized. He may well have changed our understanding of the relevant period (if we agree with him, if we are in a position to agree rather than to give mere assent, and if the criteria for "renaissance" are not in question), insofar as what follows from "renaissance" does not follow from the bare presence of court scholars. He may also have changed our attitude, e.g., from disapprobation for a dark age to a milder neutrality for an age only gray. Interestingly enough, despite his enlightening thesis, the historian has made a factual assertion quite within the realm of uninventive and uncreative ordinary uses of concepts. That his thesis enlightened us in no way altered the logic of appeals for justification or of the grounds for assertion from those applicable to assertions which do not enlighten.

Second, a historian might create a new concept or alter the use of a present concept. These cases display more clearly the features of Dray's descriptive history. For example, the first historian to speak of Parliament's history as evolutionary may have had Spencerian theory in mind.[23] Like its biological counterpart, the social institution changed slowly with no individual accounting for more than a slight alteration and with each change arising in answer to specific crises, conditions, and problems. That is to say, for the purposes of the hypothetical example, the concept of "institutional evolution" might have originated on analogy to "biological evolution," however low its theoretical status. The case for "institutional evolution" seems also to be the case for "descriptive" history: the creative historian has produced a "new" unifying concept, the use of which enlightens to the extent that it provides a new way of viewing the events, objects, and periods in question. In specifying the criteria for the concept through application to Parliament, the hypothetical historian has indeed had to "determine what shall be *ruled in*" without recourse to any historically explanatory methodology. (Once used, of course, his creation becomes available for sundry explanatory uses.) Too, his creation rests on analogy, which along with metaphor "is no artistic ornament to historical inquiry: it is of its essence."[24] Examples such as "institutional evolution" appear to speak in favor of Dray's relativistic analysis of descriptive history.

The conceptual creativity of descriptive history cannot, nevertheless, make a case for value-laden or subjective event selection. Since the events, objects, and conditions cited by a historian are to stand as criteria for the assertion of an institutional evolution (or whatever the conceptual proposal in question), and since the proposal rests upon an analogy or metaphor, the historian must choose events, objects, and conditions which match those of the analogous concept. In short, the conceptually creative historian does have non-normative grounds for his selection of events. Should the historian's concept reach the stage of conventionality, the criteria for its use would lose their dependence upon analogy. Still, the selection of events, by virtue of the convention, would remain criterially determinate.

So long as a conceptual proposal rests or is based on an analogy, its criteria and hence the events selected by the historian using the concept are determinate without reference to value or subjectivity. In such a case, one should not confuse the creative historian's use of his concept with the justification of that use and of the criteria for such a use. Metaphors and analogies play a genetic or historical role in conceptual proposals; they suggest concepts and how to use them, but they do not justify them. One justifies proposals by reference to such matters as the need in the language for the concept and the ability of the proposal to accomplish its intended aim or purpose. The death of notions like devil possession and colored biles as connected to human behavior left a descriptive and explanatory hiatus between consciously motivated action and physically caused action. This gap Freud sought to fill by extending the concept "unconscious" or "unconscious motive" to cover those cases wherein the subject incontrovertibly denied intention for an act otherwise having the earmarks of conscious motivation.[25] "Institutional evolution" failed to serve the explanatory purpose which theorists like Spencer proposed for it, but the concept continues to serve a perfectly good descriptive or characterizing need. From such examples two points emerge. First, a concept's use does not depend upon its genesis. Second, analogies and metaphors, with respect to the birth of concepts, can be good or bad and can themselves need justification.

The notion of analogy and metaphor have long held a tinge of subjectivity and personalness due to their association with techniques of the poetic arts. That association, however, fails to make the requisite case as soon as one probes the role of metaphors and analogies in concept formation. In the past few decades, opposing views have solidified with respect to the relation of a concept's origin to its present use. Theorists like J. L. Austin have warned that philology can mislead as much as help the attempt to understand the use of a concept.[26] Contrarily, C. I. Lewis and others have argued that all language, save perhaps for that part which labels physical objects, is but dead metaphors.[27] To the extent that one may learn to use a concept without knowledge of its origins, e.g., to assert an institutional evolution without knowledge of Darwinian tenets, the metaphor-ites have the weaker case. Since the justification of a conceptual proposal rests not on the metaphor or analogy which suggested it, but on its having a usable and useful place in the language, that case disappears. None of this, however, denies the illumination and knowledge afforded by philological studies.

The separation of concept genesis from justification carries the consequence that the use and judgment of metaphors and analogies constitutes a subject which has little bearing on the historian's selection of events beyond the extent noted earlier. Metaphors and analogies, whatever their detailed properties, come into relevance in discussions of discovery, invention, and creation, not in questions of justification. The question of the historian's selection of events is precisely a question of justification. To ask why a historian chose or made a concept, what prompted it, how he felt about it, what "processes" engendered it is to go outside the range of logically relevant questions. More appropriate are questions which seek the grounds for the historian's (or anyone's) use of a concept, the reasons which warrant one set of criteria rather than another with respect to use, and the need or use for the concept created.

On the other side of the coin, it would be equally misleading to dismiss Dray's notion of descriptive history as so much word play and to denigrate any work fitting the category. The creation of concepts can serve important and far-reaching ends. To view the early Carolingean period as a renaissance is not merely to redescribe it; it is to change one's perspective toward the era or to give one a perspective. Some things which historian's might have formerly assessed as implausible now become plausible. Indeed, only with the demise of the label "Dark Ages" for the entire medieval period did philosophers and historians come to view scholarship on logic during those centuries as worthy of study, let alone as creative and insightful. This, in turn, has led to an enlargement of demand for scholars interested in the period and to at least a partial fulfillment of the demand. New work from the pens of these scholars completes a sort of circle, insofar as attention to the detail of that millenium now threatens the propriety of using a single term, even the insipid "medieval," in reference to these variegated centuries. Redescription can refocus interests and lead to the discovery that certain events, hitherto overlooked, are important. This observation, however, does not specify in which of many possible respects they might be important, and it does not say they were "intrinsically" important. Judgments of importance must also be justifiable.

Invented concepts do not invariably or quickly lose their attachment to their origins. Toynbee's "challenge and response," which attempts to draw an analogy between personal psychology and social studies, has yet to reach conventional status. Fundamentally, his concepts provide an initial redescription of events on a mass level. Also, the concepts seem more powerful than Spencerian biologically oriented concepts, perhaps because the parallel between group and individual psychology extends farther and with greater plausibility than that between individual and group physiology. Despite Toynbee's dozen volumes, what the analogy suggests we may plausibly assert about social groups has hardly been exhausted. The more extensive the analogy, the longer the period between conceptual proposal and conventional usage. And when one has discounted the personal attacks and other irrelevancies of debate, the central issue of "challenge and response" emerges: how useful and productive is it to treat social groups in these terms?

The ultimate acceptance or rejection of a concept born of analogy or metaphor, its eventual conventional status or disuse, only rarely depends on the overt argumentation raised at the time of its introduction. Even the most technical of terms in the physical sciences usually undergo extensive trial both by use and by argument before decision is rendered. "Aether" and the fundamental concepts of relativity still find themselves the subjects of debate and consternation. With respect to concepts in the liberal arts and disciplines--terms such as Toynbee's "challenge and response" or Freud's "unconscious motivation,"-- only after the clustering analogs have exhausted themselves (and new ones often crop up unexpectedly to give a dying term extended life) do the occasions for using the concept non-argumentatively determine its conventional function. The descriptive utility and theoretic vacuity of "institutional evolution" is by now abundantly clear; we know which uses of the terms are justifiable.

So far we have noted primarily the descriptive function of new concepts. Yet seldom, if ever, are terms introduced solely in order to describe or even, in Dray's term, to unify. Dray's own example--Hayes' volume, *A Generation of Materialism*--seeks not just to find a unifying descriptive concept for the generation preceeding the turn of the century, but as well to characterize and evaluate morally this period. (When have we ever approved of materialism?) Toynbee's "challenge and response" seeks to explain the historical genesis, course, and disappearance of societies in an "objective" and "scientific" manner. Perhaps critics have gone too far in claiming that his notions cannot explain at all. For explanations may be moral as well as scientific, and Toynbee has as much a lesson to teach as Eliot has in *The Wasteland*, and possibly the same lesson. It is a fact of language and not of empirical study that the term "explanation" does not automatically and absolutely attach to "science." Rather, it associates equally with "teaching," and to the extent that any subject, including morality is teachable, there can be explanations in terms of that subject.

The events which fulfill criteria with respect to one purpose may not be the same events which fulfill criteria with respect to another. The purpose of concept introduction determines in part what shall count as a justification of the concept, and the concept's use in terms of that purpose (as well as the analogy or metaphor, if applicable, on which the conceptual proposal rests) determines the criteria for application. A term introduced on suggestion from an analogy may not need, if the point of introduction does not go beyond description, to retain criteria perfectly analogous to those of the suggesting term. Because terms like "institutional evolution" have had explanatory purposes in the hands of some writers, explanatory purposes which paralleled those of known physiological explanations, the criteria have adhered closely to those of the analog so as to preserve the desired explanatory structure. Apart from such purposes, no need for post-introductory parallel exists, and many terms find themselves cut off from their suggestive origins. For questions of justification it matters not which came first, the orange of the orange or the orange that is orange. The events selected by a historian doing Dray's "descriptive" history thus do not merely fulfill criteria in a context; they fulfill criteria with reference to a purpose.

As one must note continually, even remarks as loose as these too readily formalize the process. To redeem the value of making them, one must also note that they do serve to indicate that colligatory descriptive history is neither simple nor isolated. Moreover, these reminders supply the necessary groundwork to release the selection of events in any descriptive historical assertion at any level from the burden of inherent subjectivity or value-ladenness. Wherever there is purpose in selection, there *can* be criteria for selection. Where a unifying or

colligatory term is new or where the criteria for it are novelly proposed, the use of the term lies open to requests for justification.

Neglect of purpose too often leads to the erroneous assumption
that certain concepts are inherently valuational, that their use always
entails an act of valuing on the part of the historian. Dray appears
to have lapsed into such a position when he took the difference between
"killing" and "murder" as that between a value-neutral and a value-
charged concept. He recognized at the same time that we do not merely
replace an evaluative concept with an objective one; instead, as he
puts it, "we . . . restrict our attention to those aspects of what
[someone] did which could be subsumed under the value-neutral word
'killing'. . . ."[28] The notion of "aspects" in Dray's view presents a
vagueness and perhaps an object-oriented view of event concepts which
almost allows the heart of the matter to slip by with the idea that
there are value aspects or parts of events which one may either mention
or not. A more adequate analysis of such claims would replace the notion of aspects with a list of events, conditions, and facts which in
an exemplary case would justify the assertion of murder. Some, but not
all of these events, conditions, and facts may in certain kinds of
cases also justify the assertion of killing, or as we say, a murder is
also a killing. Nonetheless, "murder" is not always an evaluative concept; rather, it is most often used for the purpose of evaluation. The
historian who records the Warren Commission conclusion that Oswald murdered Kennedy does not necessarily evaluate. Even where the differentiating criteria involve the breaking of a law or social rule, the assertion of murder may rest on the fact of breech and not on the evaluation contained in the breech for the society in which the murder occurred. Concepts *may be used* evaluatively, but even evaluative uses
have criteria. However obscure these criteria may be in sidewalk conversation, they comprise the historian's use when it is judicious.

These considerations should suffice to remove from the notion of
descriptive history the cloud of creative specialness which made it
suspect. The coinage of concepts may be creative, but it is not special. In fact, rather than being a peculiar branch of history, descriptive history turns out to be a part of the routine of writing history.
It is not the product of employing special methodological techniques,
but a matter of using language. It is not the whole, nor even a large
part of description. Nevertheless, Dray's colligatory descriptive history does not constitute either a useless or an impossible task. In
following general editor Langer's instructions to find "main movements," Hayes and his cohorts in the series which includes *A Generation
of Materialism* are charged with the sole task of ascribing to the period, place, and people assigned those unities which they can justifiably assert on the basis of well-established facts.[29] Although none of
the authors writes a purely descriptive history, the colligatory work--
is prominent. Where the characterization involves no new concept or
new use of a concept, it is justifiable or not on conventional grounds.
Where it necessitates something new, the characterization stands the
request for justification on the grounds appropriate to conceptual pro-

posals. Neither of these projects requires the introduction of value in any relativistic or subjective sense.

We may not prize the descriptive history so highly as other sorts of historical writings, but it has its uses. Although often preparatory to other kinds of studies, such works can be judged on their own ground. The historian, or anyone else familiar with the language, can judge whether colligatory assertions are justified. The historian's favored position consists, roughly, in these facts. He can judge the accuracy of the accounts upon which a progression of characterizations stands. He can judge the adequacy of the work; i.e. whether the writer has included all those events from which characterizations of as high a level can be made. He can judge the utility of any new concept for other historical writing. Such considerations nevertheless fail to convert an unremarkable feature of concept use and justification into a subjectively or normatively tainted methodology.

III. The Relation of Purpose and Method to Historical Use and Abuse

The entire division of explanatory vs. descriptive history, reflecting the supposed distinction between objectivity and non-objectivity in the historian's selection of events, over-simplifies the process of writing historical narratives. What Dray termed "descriptive," the production of unifying concepts designating characterizations or main movements, comprises but a small part of the historian's descriptive work and is only descriptive to the extent that the historian does not intend it to be explanatory, morally heuristic, etc. Whether or not the historian intends it, such descriptions or assertions may be explanatory. What has been analyzed, then, is less a kind of history than a kind of activity which may find service in the production of historical narratives. Occasionally, it may constitute the main point of a narrative. Not just explanation or description, but many other purposes may also serve as a narrative's point: for example, to evaluate, react, promote, teach, praise, condemn, complain, portray, report, characterize, destroy (as a myth or a thesis), create (as a myth), support (as a thesis), argue, dismiss, reconsider, inspire. . . . The distinction between explanation and description in history thus falls into the class of dangerous philosophical bifurcations which may have some limited utility in making a distinction but which too easily expand to encompass, simplify, and distort the subject matter.

A similarly dangerous bisection of history has been growing in recent years: that between history as a fact-finder or empirical science and history as a storyteller or narrative enterprise. The positivists had urged upon history a concern for general laws, prediction, and explanation under the supposition that history's central interest and purpose was the discovery and analysis of facts. In countering that view, some proponents of the narrative's primacy in history have stressed the non-fact-finding operations and features that go into a historical account. Thesis history, the boon and bane of American monographic historiography, has given ground to the narrative as the paradigm of historical writing.[30] However, the narrative could not stand for some writers as an end in itself, as could the scientific explanation. Mere narrative without a special purpose would permit the disreputably artful and fictional novel to claim a place beside the works of Ranke, Michelet, Beard, and Geyl. Yet, to rest the narrative on fact alone would be to retreat into the scientist's camp, to give history no more goal than sterile scientific explanations.[31] The consequence of this dilemma has been an effort to preserve the humaneness of history, to give it a "moral" purpose. History thus became "the story required by society."[32] In another version, it is the narrative that, with respect to the institutionalized portions of our lives, teaches us the limits of our possibilities, the attitudinal skills necessary to our actions, and the moral graces needed to face our situation.[33]

In order to distinguish the group of writers who support both the primacy of the narrative and the position that it has social or moral purpose from other investigators of the relation of the narrative to history, let us coin the phrase "social narrativist."

As difficult to uproot as are the epistemic origins of the positivistic portrait of history, the social narrativist's insistence upon the primacy of social and moral purposes presents a far greater challenge; the insistence appears to go back perhaps to the origins of history itself, to the practical, ritual, and moral teachings which are mixed with the predecessors of history. The transition from oral to written forms, the expansion of content from divine tribal and family trees to records of the recent past, the confusion of the memory of what was taught with the memory of what happened: these (and much more besides) comprise the beginnings both of history and of history's practical, social, and moral purposes. However, to argue that these remain history's only purposes would be to admit guilt of a massive genetic fallacy and to neglect the development of history into a relatively independent discipline. In as much as these purposes had fallen into temporary obscurity in the isolated concern for historical fact and explanation, their renewed celebration enlightened and informed. To use them in a theoretic war against positivism is to rend history unnecessarily in twain.

The social narrativist's case for history's purpose generally rests on the ambiguity possible with the concept "purpose" and on a misconception of the notion of facts. Taking the latter first, the narrativists have literally forced themselves to seek a non-historical purpose for history by virtue of having relinquished facts to positivistic, quasi-scientific, empirical (in the narrower philosophic use) theories. The standards for being a fact which these theories set forth prove incompatible with the kinds of subject matter historians traditionally and typically take up. Character, moral strength, force of will, mental attributes, intentions, and the myriad other factors historians must account for in adequately portraying and narrating a course of human actions and events do not succumb easily to empirical or positivistic analysis. One records mass movements, but does not observe them in any sense amenable to optical and instrumental notions. One can know someone's intention and character, but one cannot observe them or reduce them to observables. Despite his insights into the nature of historical facts, even Collingwood gives them up in his search for history's purpose. History is for human self-knowledge.[34] Unless the requisite knowledge consists solely in the record of what man has done, history must seek outside itself for a purpose which would justify its use of concepts that do not fit some one or another narrow theory of recordable facts. Such a maneuver as this becomes necessary where one so interprets the notion of "fact" in such a way as to make it in part or whole inapplicable to history. Only then do we feel a need to find a purpose for history which will justify both the factual and non-factual aspects of the work.

That sort of problem need not exist. In large measure, the classes of assertions which historians make that do not fit empirical and physical theory still qualify as fact. An assertion warranted by the fulfillment of criteria counts without possible objection as a fact. To question such an assertion in terms of criteria fulfillment is precisely to question it as fact. To the extent that what follows the assertion does not necessarily follow from the events, objects, conditions, and actions suffices to preclude any reduction of these facts to empirical or observable states of affairs. All this the preceding chapters have established. Also established was the wide range of relevant concepts and assertions to which criterial analysis applies. That range includes character, intention, mental attributes, mass movement, intellectual trends, group properties--in short, just those sorts of assertions narrative history relies upon and takes as its reason for seeking a goal other than fact. The need to invent such a goal disappears the moment such assertions are readmitted into the corpus of fact.

The view put forth here even has the consequence of admitting moral facts. No theoretic difficulty attaches to the possibility of such facts so long as any assertion or judgment can be justified by reference to fulfilled criteria. The problems which do arise are mostly practical rather than philosophic, although they remain primarily conceptual. For example, the judgment "Nero acted immorally in burning Rome" holds the portent of trouble on at least two counts. First it is in no way clear whether the judgment concerns Nero as a Roman or as "just a man," i.e., whether conventional Roman or conventional modern criteria form the basis of judgment. Second, it is not clear whether there is in fact a single conventional set of criteria covering the case either for Roman or for modern times. And if there is not, then one may relevantly argue on the question of which standard a historian should use. This second level may not admit of solution if moral concepts fit Gallie's category of the essentially contested. In no way, however, do these considerations prevent the historian from treating such judgments as Nero's immorality as factual, rational, and permissible in a narrative. Rather, the practical conceptual difficulties associated with these moral facts only make clear the requisite conditions for seriously treating them: the evaluation of such a judgment demands that the judge make clear the grounds on which he renders the verdict. Where the historian fails to make clear the criteria for moral and other judgments, a charge of subjectivity does not distinguish the absence of grounds from the critic's inability to find them. To that extent, "subjectivity" as a label has been accorded far more damaging an effect than it logically merits.

If the classes of assertions made by historians which do not fit certain theoretic empirical requirements still count as facts in perfectly non-controversial and respectable senses of the word, then the social narrativists could have opted to treat their stories as fulfilling a purpose of history without reference to other considerations. The facts of what happened constitutes a defensible goal of historical narrative, even when narrative is stripped of positivistic enthrallment with general laws, prediction, and explanation. Moreover, any of the earlier mentioned goals (e.g., evaluation, teaching, portraying, argument, etc.) may count as goals in addition to presenting the facts; that is, they constitute some proper uses of the facts. In the same vein, the purposes given by social narrativists—to serve society's demand, to supply moral grace, to impart self-knowledge—also count as uses of the facts.

Implicit in the untenable division of history into factual and human purposes, there is a more tenable distinction, one to be made between internal and external purposes of history. In viewing their position as an alternative to empirical or positivistic theories, social narrativists had covertly treated their purposes as counterparts to the quest for facts alone, and to this degree failed to realize the implications of the distinction which actually separated their goals from those of their opponents. Some of the difference may become clear with the help of two passages, one each from Herodotus and Nietzsche.

The Greek First:

> In this book, the result of my inquiries into history,
> I hope to do two things: to preserve the memory of the past
> by putting on record the astonishing achievements both of
> our own and of the Asiatic peoples; secondly, and more particularly, to show how the two races came into conflict.[35]

To paraphrase Herodotus' express purpose, he will arrive at and record the facts of what happened and why it happened. In contrast stands the lonely and disillusioned Nietzsche, who cries out thusly:

> We do need history . . . for life and action . . .
> We would serve history only so far as it serves life; but
> to value its study beyond a certain point mutilates and

degrades life.

> A historical phenomenon, completely understood and
> reduced to an item of knowledge, is, in relation to the
> man who knows it, dead. . . .

> History, so far as it serves life, serves an
> unhistorical power.[36]

However much one might like to dismiss Nietzsche as a mere aphorist,
his assertion is clear. We do not need history just to get at facts;
we engage in historical study to get at facts which are of some use to
us. To do history for its own sake is worthless. Regardless of the
problems associated with either statement or with either scholar, their
purposes clearly differ. One might well and correctly say that Herodotus (passing over the part about preserving memories) asserts something
about history's goal, whereas Nietzsche remarks on history's use.

More specifically, Herodotus' assertion of history's goal, its
"internal" purpose, amounts to the claim that the object of one's study
is to get at history, to ascertain the facts. To this end, one employs
the so-called methods of history, that loose collection of techniques
for the evaluation of artifacts and documents and for drawing inferences from them. Once the historian has said all that he can plausibly
or correctly say, he stops. His task is finished. The accomplishment
of his goal or purpose is logically a function of his methodology and
its application to what he studies.

As with all disciplines, in (possible) contrast to sciences, one
cannot specify generally and all-inclusively what shall count as historical methods. Certain techniques--of document study and relic dating, for example--invariably come to mind, because many, if not most,
historical studies and "objects" give rise to the questions that such
methods are designed to answer. But a list of representative or most-
used techniques of historical study neither orders nor limits the nature and size of a complete list. As noted in the preceding chapter of
this study, one cannot say in advance of a historical question what
will count as evidence or how it must be used. The absence of a codi-
fied body of askable questions, however, does not negate or endanger
the general point that history can be taken to have purely an internal
purpose, a goal whose achievement is a function of the appropriate and
successful application of history's methods. To the extent that one
can ask a historical question, have a means of answering it, and recognize a satisfactory answer, history for its own sake remains a viable
logical possibility.[37]

In contrast, Nietzsche upholds a position concerning history's use
or "external" purpose. His view asserts nothing directly as to history's methods. Rather, it speaks to the questions of how, for what,
and why one ought to use history's products, its facts, narratives, and
explanations. It may well be that the user of history may find some

gap which he must fill by doing historical research, that is, he may have to produce facts, but this sort of activity is to Nietzsche beside the point and preliminary to history's main purpose. The range of possible uses or external purposes is limited only the the nature of history's results: facts about past human actions and events, as the main though not sole concern of history, find extensive use for moral, political, and even economic enlightenment and edification,[38] but they seem to hold little relevance for the building of rocket ships, the discovery of cures for cancer, or the application of tourniquets.

The distinction between obvious cases of internal and external purposes, then, is not hard to make, nor are its consequences difficult to draw: one represents the aim or goal of applying historical methods, the other constitutes the use of the history gotten by the use of those methods. In a straight-forward way, described in the previous chapter, quests for historical fact directly affect methodology, insofar as a given question and the relics available to answer the question determine the techniques to be used in constructing a reply. Moreover, questions and relics which have hitherto held no relation may give rise to new methods. Internal purposes, then bear a direct relation to historical fact and method. Contrarily, external purposes *need have no* affect upon or consequences for method. Since they make use of one of history's products, the facts established by history, they are logically divorced from the methods by which the facts were established. For internal purposes, a change in aim or question may alter the method used to produce an answer; for external purposes, a change in aim need entail no more than a change in the collection of facts used to accomplish that aim.

A complication enters here to shut off any attempt to apply generally and generously such a simple and straight forward analysis. In point of fact, external purposes *can* and do carry implications for historical methodology. The most extreme and notable examples occur with the Christian historians from Augustine, Orosius, and Eusebius down through Bossuet. These writers sought (among other things) to justify Christianity in historical terms by a systematic deprecation of heathen acts and a consequent real or apparent appreciation of Judeo-Christian acts. Their need to discover comparable acts and events within both sacred scripture and the non-Hebrew world dictated, first, a method of chronology based upon traditional dogmatized datings of scriptural events and, second, the acceptance of raw myth as fact in order to meet the chronological and comparative goals. To Eusebius, Moses and Bacchus are equally historical figures.

Nietzsche recognized that external purposes influence historical method and that the influence is indirect, though powerful. His categories of monumental, antiquarian, and critical history characterize the uses of history made by certain types of men. In each of those uses there lies a danger: "historical study is only fruitful if it follows . . . , if it is guided and dominated by a higher force, and does not itself guide and dominate."[39] In these lines, Nietzsche notes

137

the human proclivity either to guide or to be guided, to lead or to be led. In his rejection of the latter alternatives, he refuses to countenance a history without a preconceived external purpose, not because such a history is impossible, but because it would fail to serve men of action. Without comment on Nietzsche's choice among possible external purposes, one may still note the recognition which his remarks implicitly contain: while the connections between use and historical method are susceptible to discovery and tracing, the occurrence of those connections is not a necessary condition for doing history. In Nietzsche's view, they are needed for doing "good" history, since history without them amounts to dead fact; nevertheless, that deadly factual history remains possible. Practical and contingent considerations--for Nietzsche, the need for human action; for early Christian historians, zealous dogmatism--led writers to alter fact and to wreak havoc with method. The blatantness of particular aberations often leads contemporary investigators to overlook the contingency of the connection. Nonetheless, that we judge particular uses by how and how much they distort fact and method suffices to establish that the connection is contingent. For any such judgment presupposes the ability to do history without external purpose and thus without factual distortion. The possibility of undistorted fact becomes a necessary condition to the judgment.

Considerations arising from external purposes, therefore, leave practical problems, namely, tracking down connections within a practice which, nonetheless, need not have occurred. Internal purposes, on the other hand, leave philosophic problem, some of which were explored at least tentatively in the preceding chapter. For example, the methods of history turned out to have no single philosophic principle or ground.[40] As an extension of this point, one may note the following. To the extent that the successful achievement of purpose is judged by the methods employed, purpose cannot constitute an absolute or basic consideration. Likewise, to the degree that what may count as a method depends upon purpose or what is sought, method is not absolute or by itself basic. The two notions are logically interrelated in a way parallel to the concepts of "knowledge" and "finding out." Ultimately, the issue devolves to one of pragmatics, for not until one formulates a question can one say what the appropriate methods of answer will be. In turn, the specification of methods sets limits to the range of possible answers and subsequent questions. A method which does not enable the answer to a question is an idle activity, and a question without, in principle, the means of reply is but the grammatical shadow of a question. The interlocking nature of history's fundamental concepts with respect to internal purpose denies application of traditional means of philosophic analysis, *viz.*, structural analysis in terms of axiomatized logics. No isomophism between a logic system and the practice of history is possible so long as none of history's questions, procedures, and purposes will hold still, i.e., have content apart from specific historical problems. In short, a wholly theoretic and formal treatment of history yields little as an analysis of historical practice.[41]

Complications of practice or principle, however, do not empty the original distinction between internal and external purposes of utility and thus of propriety. As one example, the distinction enables one to differentiate forms of historical abuse. Where a historian has solely an internal purpose, abuse comprises necessarily a misuse of method (where such misuse may also include neglect). With respect to a history's external purposes, abuse consists in the misuse of fact (without restriction on the ways in which fact can be misused). In practice, no sharp dividing line occurs, nor is one likely to find any clear cut cases exhibiting exclusively one or the other sorts of abuses. Moreover, to the extent that external purpose *can* influence method, abuse of historical fact *may* carry with it a misuse of method, but unlike the case with internal purpose, it *need* not. To use once more an example cited earlier, Taylor's little work on second world war origins finds itself in second thoughts compelled to analyze both sorts of error, first, to point out methodological abuse, e.g., that "dangerous" practice of deducing "political intentions from military plans," and second, to dispel certain legends about Hitler and his blameworthiness for the war in the "service of historical truth."[42] The conscious or unconscious desire of historians to give the subject his due undoubtedly engenders methodological malfeasance as well as factual finagling, but that, as noted earlier, holds neither dire nor necessary consequences for history as a discipline.

One minor significance of the distinction rests in its ability to help show where definers of history have substituted external for internal purposes, or worse, failed to make clear for which they opt. Renier, following Pirenne, treats history as "the story required by society."[43] The defining phrase contains a fatal ambiguity with respect to the idea of social requirements. A question for history may arise from a concern of a society, but in itself, that fact entails nothing about the answer. The facts alone may settle the matter, in which case, purpose may remain wholly internal. Or, some group may be seeking from historical precedent a guide to its own actions, i.e., the group may have an external purpose for history. By glossing the distinction between kinds of purposes, the Renier-Pirenne definition disables any attempt to follow out its implications. Although the ambiguity of the Renier-Pirenne definition holds great convenience for those who may be more concerned about history's reputation than its problem, it also carries the risk of obscuring just those facets of the subject which may enable a solution to problems.

Collingwood's "history is for self-knowledge" also tries to walk a line between the two sorts of purpose. Even his succeeding sentence gives no clue to which option he prefers: "It teaches us what man has done and thus what man is."[44] If self-knowledge amounts to something done *with* historical facts, e.g., an evaluative interpretation or the drawing of moral lessons, then it represents an external purpose. The implication of this option for any critical analysis of Collingwood's work would be that knowing history's purpose cannot help in determining the nature and epistemic validity of historical methods, methods inter-

nal to history. Yet Collingwood avers just such an aim: "What I am
attempting here is a philosophical inquiry into the nature of history
regarded as a special type or form of knowledge with a special type of
object. . . ."[45] Moreover, to the extent that self-knowledge as an external purpose functions to narrow history to the study of past human
actions alone, it sets unwarranted limits about the discipline, limits
which only internal purpose can determine.

If, conversely, self-knowledge comprises the history itself, if
understanding what man is logically equals understanding how he got
that way, then such purpose is internal, because it requires only that
history set out the facts of what happened and that it use methods of
the discipline appropriate to the production of those facts. Such an
option would demand, however, an account of how one comes to define
history solely in terms of human action. Any such definition lies open
to counter-example, since a definition of subject matter *eo ipso*
amounts to a definition of the limit and scope of methods.

Regardless of which troubled option one might prefer, the point of
raising the issue is less to reach a decision on Collingwood than it is
to see the peculiarities of the alternative treatments and the danger
of ambiguously stating the sort of purpose one envisions for history.
Indeed, in the practice of giving history a purpose lies much of the
confusion which sets false issues between narrative-oriented idealists
and thesis-oriented positivists.

The question of history's purpose and many of the issues which now
separate narrativists and positivists actually predate the contemporary
debate. In Woodbridge's 1916 lectures, for example, one can find an
anticipation of both modern groups (with a tendency to side with the
narrativists). Woodbridge distinguishes between "fact" and "understanding." Thus, history is "not simply the telling of what has happened; it is also and more profoundly the conserving of what has happened in order that its meaning may be grasped."[46] In a different
rhetoric, Woodbridge reiterates: "Conformably with the calendar and
with geography, we may be able to affirm that a given event was or is
taking place, but to tell what that event is in a manner which ensures
understanding of it, is to write the history of its career in time as
comprehensively as it can be written."[47] Accordingly, there are for
Woodbridge two senses of "truth." The term "may mean that the record
of what has happened is correct, and it may mean that the understanding
of what has happened is correct." In the former sense, correctness
yields "perpetual" truth; in the latter, it yields "contemporaneous"
truth.[48] Upon these distinctions Woodbridge builds for history a glo-
bal purpose which transcends "the conserving, the remembering, and the
understanding of what has happened." History "is also the completing
of what has happened. And since in man history is consciously lived,
the completing of what has happened is also the attempt to carry it to
what he calls perfection."[49]

Woodbridge's distinction between fact and understanding presages
similar distinctions made by social narrativists. Gallie, for one,
writes on the historical understanding, while Walsh, for another, ascribes to history the major task of finding "intelligibility" among
events. In each case, something occurs beyond discovering and record-
ing facts, something distinctly human. As argued earlier, however, it
is something of a category mistake to draw a line of demarcation between facts and "the human." For much of what we assert which falls on
the human side of the line is precisely fact. Thus, Woodbridge's fundamental distinction becomes suspect. Moreover, to say that temporal
and geographic criteria for event location are "perpetual," while those
of "understanding" are "contemporaneous," is to leave oneself open to
innumerable counter-examples. Perhaps merely asking the day of the
month of George Washington's birth will suffice to illustrate that
chronological fact is as open to changes in criteria as the humanistic
assertions fit for understanding. Conversely, what we understand, to
the extent it can be asserted, requires justification, just as do temporal and geographic facts.

One would be unfair to Woodbridge if one overlooked a second distinction he draws. It lies implicit in view that history written from
"the perspective of the time in which it happened" constitutes a "re-
strained exercise" of the historian's imagination.[50] More explicitly,
though still casually, Woodbridge separates "facts" from "our knowledge of them." The former he assumes to be fixed, the latter he
claims to be "progressive."[51] Part of Woodbridge's meaning appears to
be contained in the notion that there are things which a historian may
say which cannot be asserted by historical characters.[52] Burns is a
forerunner of, and partly responsible for, the Romantic movement: such
a claim could not have been made by the patron of the Kilmarnock edition at the time of publication, however significant he may have
thought the poetry to be. Nonetheless, that Burns is a forerunner of
the Romantic movement either is a fact or fails to be a fact in the
same way that his publication of the Kilmarnock edition is or is not a
fact. Either we do or do not have grounds for justifying each of the
assertions.

It is from the "progressive" knowledge of history that Woodbridge
finds it natural to move to the "completion" and perfection of history.
However, what seems most natural can often be a poor guide to the
grounds of justification for what we do. What we can say of the past
in any of the examples cited above is a logically separable task from
recommending future action. Historical facts of any of the sorts Woodbridge cites may contribute good reasons for certain courses of action,
but they in no way entail action. One may distinguish knowing facts
from understanding history along Woodbridge's lines if one does not
conflate the latter with understanding one's mission. Understanding
one's mission involves having the will to do it, and this is a matter
of an entirely different order.

The examination of Woodbridge's analysis has this consequence: it precludes attributing to history the special purpose of utilizing the past "as material for the progressive realization . . . of what we call spiritual ends" solely on the basis of the inherent nature of historical study.[53] Not just time and place, but as well causes, motives, intentions, influences, progressions, and continuities all fall among history's facts. That we race from the more human facts to conclusions about future thought and action does nothing to eliminate the logical distinction between what history produces and what we can or should do with that product. To suggest that history reveals "visions" such that "the fragments of existence are completed and illumined" is to suggest that either we or historians have a task in addition to doing history.

These remarks, of course, only set limits to the distinctions Woodbridge drew long before the debates of this decade. They do not negate the distinctions or the legitimate implications of them. Woodbridge's account of historical understanding and "progressive" knowledge goes a long way toward explaining why "the history of nothing is complete" and why it "has constantly to be rewritten."[54] Nor do these remarks proscribe recommendations for the use of history, whether for spiritual or mundane ends. Philosophical analysis seeks only to discover the logical status and foundation of such recommendations; it does not render verdict on their ethical propriety.

IV. The Role of Personal Factors in the Genesis and Justification of Written History

One more problem, already alluded to, needs further comment insofar as it has played a major role in many of the misunderstandings clustered around selection, purpose, and the objectivity of history. The difficulty concerns the already rejected position which views the problem of selection as a function of the historian as a person or as a knower. Within the realm of historical criticism, it is perfectly legitimate to seek out what a particular historian was looking for and on the answer to that reconstruct the grounds which he used in the selection of events for his narrative. However, subjectivists and relativists have attempted to transform this matter of historical practice into an epistemic precept. The particularity of a given historian's work becomes, in Becker's hands, a necessary uniqueness of perception and fact based upon the privacy of all epistemic functions. What the historian asserts, therefore, is not wholly subject to objective analysis.[55] More subtle is the Dray-Walsh position that some events are "intrinsically interesting" or "worth noticing." Since one can hardly make a case for treating worth and interest as a property or quality of the event, worth and interest depend upon the historian's perception and conception of the event.[56]

Such positions, and variations upon them,[57] place the key to the problem of selection in the psychic or epistemic nature of the individual perceiving historian. In so isolating the historian, theorists easily make plausible accounts to the effect that what a historian writes is a function of how he views events and comes to formulate his assertions. To the extent that these processes are not open to inspection, all history contains at least some unelimimable elements of either value or subjectivity (the former if one views the unanalyzable processes as valuational, the latter if one views them as merely private).

Walsh has attempted to avoid this isolation of the historian by insisting that "seeing the past with certain preconceptions about what is truly important in it is not in any sense a private matter: attributes of this kind can be, and indeed are, shared by large groups." He notes furthur that such preconceptions "can be argued for or disputed," and that they provide "criteria of importance that the expositor brings to history." Walsh's argument, then, amounts to this: preconceptions and judgments based upon them are open to rational justification.[58] Oddly, Walsh then goes on to say that judgments of intrinsic worth cannot be read "out of the facts."[59] If by this Walsh means that the fact of an event does not necessitate or entail a particular judgment and does not contain in it some quality or feature to be called "importance," then his point would be unobjectionable. However, Walsh has left his case and its formulation ambiguous in his attempt to explore the limits of "scientific history": one can also interpret preconceptions, not as being a source of criteria, but as being at least in part attitudinal. That which one cannot read out of the facts derives instead from attitudes possessed by the historian. If this much is true to Walsh's intent, then the shared-ness of the preconceived attitudes becomes a logical accident and rational debate over them becomes so much rhetorical exercise. For to make a judgment by reference to criteria *is* to read out of the facts, although it is not to equate the judgment with the facts. Thus, Walsh leaves us floundering between two poles of an ambiguity, one side of which suggests a strong alliance with the relativists and subjectivists to the extent that it treats the problem of selection-by-importance as a problem of historians.

With the notion of "decision procedures," Fain attempts to stand on both sides of the road, that is, to make the procedures by which we reach decisions with respect to historical questions both a matter of testing and a matter of personal choice. Indeed, for Fain, the former aspect has as its chief function the disguising of the latter. "I tend," says Fain, "to look upon decision procedures as the most important way by which man masks from himself some important realities of subjective choice."[60] By stressing alternately the terms "decision" and "procedure," Fain can shift his focus from the historian to the history produced by the historian and back again. Even this shift, however, is too much; it requires that one use the term "decision" ambiguously. The sense of decision relevant to decision procedures, as tests of historical fact, does not include the act of the historian, the process of deciding. Rather, it involves the elements of the test itself, by which a decision--if talk of "making" is at all relevant--"makes itself." What is decisive for historical fact is not an act of

the historian, but the procedure which justifies such an act. Therefore, to the extent that decision procedures can be said to justify the
conclusions of historians, whether taken on analogy with the analysis
proposed in this study or with some other, they are not mere "devices
for facilitating the making of decisions."[61] The act of making decisions and the use of facilitating devices have only a contingent connection; that they bear a relation is true or false in individual cases
and in each case amounts to a historical fact not unlike any other historical fact. In this respect, the question of historical decision
procedures is identical to the question of the historian's selection of
events.

To the degree, then, that the problem of selection holds philosophic interest, it is not a problem of historians, but a problem of
justification. An assertion becomes suspect when it lacks a means of
justification, not when it emerges from a particular process. Granted,
the philosopher has many occasions to use the expression "process," but
that fact derives from linguistic conventions which permit many uses of
the term without entailing any of the mechanistic and quasi-mechanistic
consequences that stem from uses in physical or even psychological contexts. Such contexts as do entail mechanistic consequences, where they
involve claims about a process, also entail the means of investigating
them. Otherwise, the assertions would be meaningless and the entailments would disappear. Philosophic method--the logic and allied tools
of conceptual analysis--can do nothing with processes in that sense,
although philosophic method is precisely tooled to investigate justifications, the "logical processes."

Moreover, that historians rarely justify and just as rarely can
give on request the grounds for including many of the details in their
accounts can make no case either for the positions of relativity and
subjectivity or for the idea that selection is somehow bound up with
peculiarities in the process of perception. Just as the question of
purpose was not a matter of the historian's intention, so too the question of justification is not a matter of the historian's ability to
rationalize.[62] The fact of an inability to justify or even to rationalize can only go so far as to affirm the *fact* of bias, prejudice, un-
explained preference, bad memory, or just plain ignorance of what a
proper justification should look like. It cannot, however, affirm the
necessity of such evils. Indeed, the very fact that one *can* recognize
good and bad, proper and improper, adequate and inadequate replies to a
request for justification entails that there are criteria for good,
proper, and adequate justification, criteria which are logically independent of the historian. If a proper justification stands independent
of the working historian, then too must the possibility of justification at all.

The question of selection, insofar as it is a philosophical question, is a matter of what *can* be justified. It does not concern why a
given historian chose a certain event, but whether the event is properly chosen. This point alone would suffice to make any reference to

verstehen, sympathetic understanding, re-thinking and other purported personal "methods" or "processes" of doing history wholly irrelevant to philosophic concern. It makes no difference whether one or all of these terms (and others which have from time to time gained popularity) designates a determinate process or whether they serve as mere place-holders for such out of vogue terminology as "insight," "inspiration," "revelation," or even "ignorance" in the sense of being unable to say why an event should be cited. The philosophic question does not end with *verstehen*; it only begins there. For one still has to answer, "Can this particular selection be justified?" More generally, the question becomes, "Can there be grounds to justify the historian's se-lections, or must at least some selections be groundless?"

The thrust of the present chapter has been that justification be-comes possible where one seeks out the appropriate framework. Dray's colligatory descriptive history could not acquire justification in terms of some explanatory methodology since the purpose of event selec-tions in this sort of history has nothing to do with explanations. However, given the purpose of the work, to make the highest large scale generalization possible over an assigned period, place, and people, there exist criteria by which to judge the selections. One must select those events which fulfill the criteria which warrant the grand charac-terization. In general, then, the determination of the grounds for ob-jective selection (and "objective" here becomes an otiose term in view of the reference to "grounds") becomes possible only in view of pur-pose, and wherever there is purpose, there can be grounds of selection. Purpose need here only include "internal" purpose, for any case of "ex-ternal" purpose which does not distort fact permits fact to count as an internal purpose (without restricting in this context the proper uses of the term "fact"). Purpose does not confine itself to the point of a historical work as a whole, but can and perhaps most often does refer to sections and passages of a work. Just as in a murder mystery, seem-ingly insignificant events may appear along the way, events whose grounds of inclusion do not become clear until the final pages when the detective ties them all together to point a finger at the butler, or until the historian ties them all together to make a case for his the-sis or theme, to the exclusion of all others. The question of selec-tion, then, is also a request for explanation: an explanation of the role played by an event which the historian has put into his account. A good explanation and a justification are here identical.

Viewed in the present manner, the question of selection admits of no single philosophic answer. Events may fill multiple roles, explana-tory, narrative, colligatory, evidential, and moral. Multiplicity of function never incriminates a piece of narrative so long as each func-tion meets the appropriate standards of success. More significantly, events do not merely fill roles; they fill them well, adequately, plausibly, partially, contingently, poorly, or better than other events. Different events, related to one in question, may substitute for, supplant, confirm, supplement, or counter the event in its given role.[63] The role-filling status of an event may depend in part on the audience: a present general text might include in its brief note on the general growth of technology in the 20th century the statement, "Lindberg was first to solo the Atlantic," whereas a writer in and for a later generation may have to add, "in an airplane," and a still later writer may have to explain what an airplane is or was. Or, in that far future, if technology continues to develop at its present pace, the Lindberg event may be omitted altogether. Its importance for aviation had not decreased, but space for that phase of transportation had shrunk too far to make room for it.

That criteria of inclusion change with time and circumstances does not imply that they are normative in any sense related to the relativist's charges against historical selection. The latter makes reference to judgments based upon a personal or social framework of values. To extend that framework so as to include any norm whatsoever only invites confusion. For valuation, as noted earlier, is but a part of evaluation. It may even be fruitful to reverse the relativist's maneuver and to note the objectivity with which valuations (like other evaluations) are and can be made. The judicious ascription of value can be justified, and events may appear in a history because they instantiate the standards which warrant the judgment. For the problem of selection, normative valuation counts as simply one more purpose for or within history.[64] The charges of necessary relativity or subjectivity which rest on the presence of value judgments become not merely false, but irrelevant.

Consequently, the most productive goal for philosophic inquiry is not a general characterization of the historian's selection of events, but instead an understanding of the grounds on which selection rests. Not "Is subjectivity or relativity of judgment necessary?" but "Does the selection of such and such events have good grounds?" In the event of a negative reply to the latter sort of question, the characterizations which hold more relevance than the charges of subjectivity and relativity include that the events in question are useless, merely dramatic, inessential by-play, personal trademarks of the author, or something else which informs one as to why they are present and what is wrong with their presence. A proper specification of what is in error provides the seeds of correction in a way that the charge of "subjectivity" with its attendant "make it objective" cannot do. Not all, perhaps few, unjustifiable selections are subjective, and many selections perfectly capable of justification are also subjective.

Not all cases in which one questions the selection of events can be settled. Judgments may be contested on technical, literary narrative, ethical, or even linguistic grounds. Indeed, the expressions, "criteria for selection" and "criteria for the use of a concept" coincide in this chapter only with respect to Dray's descriptive history. Neither is there a sharp line to differentiate the two generally. A dispute between two nations as to which of their representative teams is soccer champion and the requisite events supporting the respective judgments may involve a linguistic debate. It may also involve vested

146

national interests and pride, and lead to a small war.[65] Historians of
other nations may well discover that there are no grounds for decision,
no grounds for settling the dispute. Such a recognition and the consequent inclusion of all criterial grounds used by both sides comprises
(if one ignores putative uses of the term by the disputants) a model of
objectivity.

For the objectivity of any enterprise does not lie in reaching
answers. Rather, it rests in being able to set the problem and its
terms in the open, in understanding the grounds of solution or in understanding why no solution can be reached. A study may be fairly objective or not very; there may be lapses in objectivity. Judgments
that a particular selection of an event has been subjectively made become relevant where pertinent criteria have been contravened without
justification, where contradictory, contrary, or inconsistent criteria
(i.e., logically, non-criteria) have been used, or where canons of justification cannot be fulfilled. Only by neglecting such features of
the application of the label "objective" can one arrive at the simple
problem of selection: that selection should be either objective or
subjective, objective or relativistic. The conventional forms of the
problem of selection have concerned just these labels of approval and
disapproval,[66] and to that extent, they have ignored precisely the features of historical selection which in fact earn the appropriate labels.

The original problem, then, has taken an untraditional turn. The
relativists' question of whether selection in history, or in any parts
of it, is necessarily value-laden was narrow and short-sighted. Valuation is but one possible purpose for the historian, and even then, the
events selected to justify a value judgment are not themselves value-
laden. Even where the historian asks and answers questions raised by
his society, culture, time and place--thus in general expressing values
(or the hopes and fears) of his culture--his answers and the selection
of events which make up those answers do not become value-laden necessarily. "Caesar crossed the Rubicon" does not become an expression of
value just because Bede, Hegel, and I all might utter it from within
our respective societies. The subjectivists' version of the problem of
selection equally misdirects us insofar as it treats the logic of selection as a problem of the historian rather than as one of justification. A history need not be subjective, i.e., unjustified and unjustifiable, anymore than it need be objective (although it may be true
that "subjectivity" is parasitic upon "objectivity"). Nonetheless,
these general and summary remarks say little apart from considerations
that go into making particular judgments.

I should hesitate, for all this, to deny history a place for the
purely subjective, personal, and irrational. The verbal explosion of
a Nietzsche and the passion of a Tolstoy suggest much, including things
moral and historical, but they do not trouble us philosophically. Mere
drama and over-indulgent emotion are rendered logically harmless by the
very routineness of their detection.

147

There may even be a difference between what history logically must be and what makes a good piece of historical writing. Very often we stress the canons of research and forget the writing, or worse, we confuse the two.[67] Good history stands up to objective justification (a redundancy, since "subjective justification" is, if not a self-contradiction, then at least a philosophical cacophony). But, though they might be, historical works are not laboratory reports. At present, they are great books, inspiring books, comprehensive books, detailed books, as well as dull, useless, inaccurate, propagandistic, and pedestrian books. Such a profusion of diverse purposes and products opens dozens of questions more important and interesting than their general objectivity.

NOTES

[1] See George Iggers, "The Image of Ranke in American and German Historical Thought," *History and Theory*, 2 (1962), pp. 17-40.

[2] Carl Hempel, "The Function of General Laws in History," *Aspects of Scientific Explanation* (New York: The Free Press, 1965), pp. 233-34, and Carl Becker, "What Are Historical Facts?" *The Philosophy of History in Our Time*, ed. Hans Meyerhoff (Garden City: Doubleday and Company, Inc., 1959), pp. 131-32.

[3] See Frederick J. E. Woodbridge, *The Purpose of History* (Port Washington, New York: Kennikat Press, 1965), pp. 44-45 for an argument that selection "is not arbitrary, but necessary."

[4] Croce's *History: Its Theory and Practice*, Ortega y Gassett's *History as a System*, and Dewey's pragmatic view of thought in his *Logic* all hold positions short of relativity, but which lapse over when some consequences of their positions are driven hard.

[5] See Christopher Blake, "Can History Be Objective?" *Theories of History*, ed. Patrick Gardiner (New York: The Free Press, 1959), pp. 329 ff.

[6] Karl Mannheim, *Ideology and Utopia*, trans. Louis Wirth and Edward Shils (New York: Harcourt, Brace and World, Inc., 1959), pp. 329 ff.

[7] Becker, "What Are Historical Facts?" p. 132 and the entire piece, and see *Everyman His Own Historian* (New York: F. S. Crofts and Co., 1935), pp. 233 ff.

[8] Ernest Nagel, "Some Issues in the Logic of Historical Analysis," *Theories of History*, pp. 380-81.

[9] A. I. Melden, "Historical Objectivity: A Noble Dream?" *Journal of General Education*, 7 (October, 1952), p. 22.

[10] Jack W. Meiland, *Scepticism and Historical Knowledge* (New York: Random House, 1965), pp. 89-90.

[11] R. G. Collingwood, *The Idea of History* (New York: Oxford Univer-

versity Press, 1956), pp. 231 ff. Isaiah Berlin's *Historical Inevitability* (New York: Oxford University Press, 1955), sections IV and V, and Peter Winch's *The Idea of a Social Science* (London: Routledge and Kegan Paul, 1958), esp. Chapter V, reflect the same thrust.

[12]The distinction used by Rawls and Searle between constitutive and regulative rules is similar: John Rawls, "Two Concepts of Rules," *Philosophical Review*, 64 (January, 1955), pp. 3-33; John Searle, "How to Derive 'Ought' from 'Is'," *Philosophical Review*, 73 (January, 1964), pp. 43-58.

[13]William H. Dray, *Philosophy of History* (Englewood Cliffs, New Jersey: Prentice-Hall, Inc., 1964), pp. 36-37.

[14]Nagel, "Some Issues in the Logic of Historical Analysis," pp. 382 ff.

[15]See John Passmore, "Explanations in Everyday Life, in Science, and in History," *Studies in the Philosophy of History*, ed. George H. Nadel (New York: Harper and Row, Publishers, 1965), pp. 17-18 for examples of other types of explanations.

[16]Dray, *Philosophy of History*, pp. 29-35. The material here also appears in Dray's "The Historian's Problem of Selection," *Logic, Methodology and Philosophy of Science*, ed. Nagel, Suppes, and Tarski (Stanford: Stanford University Press, 1962), pp. 595 ff.

[17]Dray, *Philosophy of History*, p. 35.

[18]See Lincoln Reis and Paul Kristeller, "Some Remarks on the Method of History," *The Journal of Philosophy*, 40 (April 29, 1943), p. 243, on vertical vs. horizontal interpretation; W. H. Walsh, "The Limits of Scientific History," *Philosophical Analysis and History*, ed. William H. Dray (New York: Harper and Row, Publishers, 1966), pp. 54-74 as well as the other cited items of Walsh; and Morton White, "The Logic of Historical Narration," *Philosophy and History*, ed. Sidney Hook (New York: New York University Press, 1953), pp. 5-7 and p. 30, n. 4a on basic narratives.

[19]William H. Dray, "'Explaining What' in History," *Theories of History*, pp. 403 ff. and W. H. Walsh, *An Introduction to Philosophy of History* (London: Hutchinson University Library, 1958), pp. 59 ff.

[20]See earlier portions of this study plus my "Colligation and the Writing of History," *The Monist*, 53 (January, 1969), pp. 40 ff.

[21]Here W. B. Gallie's essentially contested concepts may play a role, *Philosophy and the Historical Understanding* (New York: Schocken Books, 1964), pp. 157 ff.

[22]In fact, Karl Stephenson and Bryce Lyon, *Medieval History*, 4th Ed. (New York: Harper and Row, 1962), pp. 163 ff, argue that reference to a Carolingian Renaissance is "somewhat exaggerated." They take a decisive cultural advance to be necessary in order to warrant that assertion and find that, although an advance was made, it was perhaps not great enough.

[23]The example here may not adhere wholly to historical fact, but that it is plausible suffices for its purpose.

[24]Dray, *Philosophy of History*, p. 20.

[25]A. C. MacIntyre, *The Unconscious* (London: Routledge and Kegan Paul, 1958), pp. 44 ff.

[26]J. L. Austin, "A Plea for Excuses," *The Philosophy of Action*, ed. Alan White (London: Oxford University Press, 1968), pp. 41-42.

[27]C. I. Lewis, "Bluspels and Flalansferes," *The Importance of Language*, ed. Max Black (Ithaca: Cornell University Press, 1969), pp. 36 ff.

[28]Dray, *Philosophy of History*, pp. 26, 28.

[29]Carleton Hayes, *A Generation of Materialism*, preface by William Langer (New York: Harper and Brothers, Publishers, 1941), p. x.

[30]See, e.g., Gallie, *Philosophy and the Historical Understanding*, p. 66; A. R. Louch, "History as Narrative," *History and Theory*, 8 (1969), p. 54; Glenn Morrow, "Comments on White's 'Logic of Historical Narration'," *Philosophy and History*, p. 286, Morton White, *Foundations of Historical Knowledge* (New York: Harper and Row, Publishers, 1965), p. 4 for views which associate history with narrative either essentially, typically, or identificationally.

[31]Some writers view the narrative as essentially explanatory, either as a form of covering law explanation or as a unique form of explanation. See, e.g., Louch, "History as Narrative," p. 58; Gallie, *Philosophy and the Historical Understanding*, p. 108; A. C. Danto, *Analytical Philosophy of History* (Cambridge: At the University Press, 1965), p. 251. For a review of the views of history's relation to narrative and narrative's relation to explanation, see William H. Dray, "On the Nature and Role of Narrative in Historiography," *History and Theory*, 10 (1971), pp. 153-171.

[32]G. J. Renier, *History: Its Purpose and Method* (New York: Harper and Row, Publishers, 1965), p. 87.

[33]Gallie, *Philosophy and the Historical Understanding*, p. 127.

[34]Collingwood, *The Idea of History*, pp. 9-10.

[35]Herodotus, *The Histories*, trans. Aubrey de Selincourt (Baltimore: Penguin Books, 1965), p. 13.

[36]Friedrich Nietzsche, *The Use and Abuse of History*, trans. Adrian Collins (Indianapolis: The Liberal Arts Press, Inc., 1957), pp. 3, 11, 12.

[37]See, for example, H. B. Adams, "Leopold von Ranke," *Papers of the American Historical Association*, 3 (1888), pp. 104-05, and the entire American empirical tradition stemming from von Ranke.

[38]The list, of course, is not exhaustive.

[39] Nietzsche, *The Use and Abuse of History*, p. 12.

[40] Collingwood makes the same point for a different purpose, *The Idea of History*, p. 248.

[41] This remark does not, of course, speak to the issue of whether a particular theoretic approach can propose or recommend for history questions, procedures, and purposes which may prove to be in one or more sense "better" than present practice.

[42] A. J. P. Taylor, *The Origins of the Second World War*, 2nd Ed. (New York: Fawcett Publications, 1961), pp. 278, 282.

[43] Renier, *History: Its Purpose and Method*, p. 87.

[44] Collingwood, *The Idea of History*, pp. 9-10.

[45] *Ibid.*, p. 7.

[46] Woodbridge, *The Purpose of History*, p. 23.

[47] *Ibid.*, pp. 23-24.

[48] *Ibid.*, pp. 27-28.

[49] *Ibid.*, p. 89.

[50] *Ibid.*, p. 25, italics mine.

[51] *Ibid.*, p. 28.

[52] Danto, *Analytical Philosophy of History*, pp. 151-59 and chapter VI.

[53] Woodbridge, *The Purpose of History*, p. 4.

[54] *Ibid.*, pp. 14, 29.

[55] Becker, "What Are Historical Facts?" pp. 132 ff.

[56] Dray, *Philosophy of History*, p. 33; "'Explaining What' in History," pp. 406-07.

[57] For example, Mannheimian cultural relativity has been treated as a matter of psychic conditioning.

[58] Walsh, "The Limits of Scientific History," pp. 63-70.

[59] *Ibid.*, p. 66.

[60] Haskell Fain, *Between Philosophy and History* (Princeton: Princeton University Press, 1970), pp. 178 ff.

[61] *Ibid.*, p. 178.

[62] Toynbee's twelfth volume, in which he replies to his critics and expands upon his ideas and views on various technical points, manages to confuse matters by its numerous inconsistencies with not wholly self-consistent material in volumes I through X. In many cases, rationalization, excuse, and second thought by the working historian only makes things worse.

[63]The lists in this and other paragraphs are intended to be suggestive, not exhaustive.

[64]Attempts such as Robert C. Stover's, *The Nature of Historical Thinking* (Chapel Hill: University of North Carolina Press, 1967), to divide historical thinking into two standpoints (that of natural order intelligibility and that of living in the world) thus appear to suffer from over-simplification, a feature which too readily overlooks differences (e.g., within deterministic frameworks, see Chapter II, esp. pp. 27-32) and equally too readily creates differences beyond the point at which matters actually differ (e.g., Stover's creation of a special viewpoint for evaluation wholly on the living in the world side without attention to the justificational aspect implicit in his admission that there are standards or principles, see Chapter VII, esp. pp. 162-65). Such schemes thus become simply unconvincing. A personal viewpoint, i.e., the standpoint of living in the world, is possible, but to the extent that it holds philosophical interest, the question concerns justifying the conclusions reached on that basis, and to the degree that one stresses the personal, the standpoint holds only a contingent connection to conclusions reached in doing history. (What is being contrasted here amounts to two different sets of presuppositions guiding different sorts of studies, Stover's and my own, hence, the placement of these remarks among the notes rather than in the text.)

[65]Gallie, *Philosophy and the Historical Understanding*, pp. 158 ff.

[66]Rebels have been known to revel in adopting and approving precisely what the establishment disapproves: against essentialists and positivists stood proudly the relativists and subjectivists. But they still wrote respectable history.

[67]See J. H. Hexter's interesting *The History Primer* for a volume devoted to the writing of history.

CHAPTER FIVE

Narratives and Arguments

The present practice of history is marked by the
widespread, if not predominent, use of the narrative form.
The fifth and last chapter of this study attempts a contribution to the investigation of the narrative form in
history by showing that narrative structures are generated
by virtue of certain features of concepts and of statement
forms. As a necessary preliminary, the first section of
the chapter rejects three major theses which have from time
to time been associated with historical narrative: a. that
history is to be identified with narrative, b. that narrative and explanation have a necessary connection, and c.
that a historical narrative must have a central subject.
Separation of narrative form from the control of these
theses provides freedom to explore narrative as a structure
for a certain mode of discourse and to explicate elements
of concepts and of sentence forms which supply what shall
be called "narrative organization." Using and expanding
upon suggestions made by Danto, sections two and three
attempt to elicit the features of "past-referring terms,"
tensed sentences, "narrative sentences," and "temporal
structures" which permit time progressiveness and continuity of content, the foundations of narrative. Since the
"narrative-organizational structures" noted in these
sections supply structural elements of narratives, but do
not themselves amount to complete narratives, the fourth
section attempts to distinguish among various relations
which may occur within a narrative and which provide criteria for successful narratives. The relations to be
distinguished include narrative consistency, the relation
of non-narratively expressed facts to narrative-organizational structures; narrative congruency, the relation
between two (or more) narrative-organizational structures;
narrative unity, the relation of narrative-organizational
structures to an entire narrative; and thematic unity, the
relation of a narrative to a central theme or subject. One
major consequence of delimiting the structural elements
designated by the relationships mentioned in section four
is that narratives need not be, nor need they contain,
arguments. Insofar as an argument is essential to some
pursuits in which historians engage, e.g., proving a thesis
or illustrating a theme (not to mention certain forms of
explanation), it becomes necessary to investigate the
conditions of compatibility between narratives and arguments.
The condition of compability, that there be produced or

153

producible a series of statements narratively consistent
with the story and argumentatively consistent with the
operative mode of argument, suffices not only to establish
a relation between narrative and argument, but as well to
explicate the manner in which theses, morals, and arguments may be said to be drawn from narratives which do not
themselves argue.

Throughout this study, the use of concepts has served as the
starting point for the analysis of questions and problems within or related to the philosophy of history. Hopefully, the conclusions which
resulted from the analyses have vindicated the choice of starting
points and the particular view of concept use which was developed. Important to the vindication is not only the contribution which a study
of concept use can make to the particular questions and problems
raised, but as well the establishment of the limits of that contribution with respect to the totality of considerations relevant to each
question and problem. To restate what must be obvious, written history
does not consist solely of a series of factual assertions to the effect
that such and so events occurred.[1]

Historians not only make factual assertions that events have occurred; they also use factual assertions to do other jobs, to accomplish other tasks for which factual assertions are a part of the means
to accomplishment. Without claiming either completeness or mutual ex-
clusiveness, one can note at least these two sorts of tasks which historians from time to time perform: they argue and they narrate. The
canons of formal argument, deductive and inductive, comprise a large
part of philosophical history and need no rehearsal here. However,
narration and narratives have only in recent years come in for inten-
sive study, especially with respect to their use in history. Moreover,
the relation between narrative and argument has scarcely been touched
by more than suggestion. Whereas the relation between narrative and
explanation supplies a subject for numerous well-developed positions,
the relation between narrative and argument has not offered itself for
detailed scrutiny. To choose a random example, Dray has suggested that
narrative history may have as one of its goals a "synthetic unity."[2]
Following Mink, this synthetic unity would have as its goal the deline-
ation of a complex of relations which "are *represented by the narrative
order itself*," which are "*exhibited* rather than *demonstrated*," and
which constitute "ingredient" rather than "detachable" conclusions.[3]
The effect of this position is to draw an implicit contrast between
formal argument with demonstrations and conclusions and something else
which narratives can do. Whether Dray and Mink identify the use of
narrative to produce synthetic unity with argument or whether they hold
that it bears a relation to argument (and whether such a relation would
be to formal or informal modes of argument), there remains an important
question: if Dray and Mink have reported with factual accuracy, what
in the nature of narratives permits such a goal to be achieved? In
this question and its answer, I believe, lies a fruitful approach to

determining both some of the basic elements of narratives and the relation of narratives to arguments.

Because the question presented by Dray's and Mink's suggestion is typical rather than unique among the questions presented by analyses of the goals of narratives, the central investigation of this chapter will concern the nature of narratives without specific concern to answer only the Dray-Mink question. Among analysts of narrative form, agreements are few and perhaps can be summarized in this way: narrative is the form in which stories occur; the events of a narrative show a temporal progression (however modified for dramatic or rhetorical purposes), but the simple "then and then and then" of temporal progression does not suffice to make a collection of events into a narrative; in addition, some form of continuity is required to relate the events contextually. What remains precisely in question in this preliminary characterization of narratives is what sort of things count as contextual relations and by what means are the twin requirements of temporal progression and contextual relation achieved. Making use of some remarks which Danto makes concerning narrative connections that appear to be built into the language of present and past referencing statements, I shall attempt to explicate the relevant portions of the structure of narratives. The explication will consist of differentiating several relations which 1. are peculiar to narratives, and 2. provide the means for both the temporal and contextual continuity which have been taken to be the hallmarks of the narrative. Following the explicatory work I shall contrast the structure of narratives with that of arguments. The contrast provides grounds not just for arguing that narratives and arguments have disparate structures, but also for determining what are the conditions of compatibility between the two.

I. Narratives, Explanations, and Central Subjects

The premise upon which this investigation is built, and that which may distinguish this investigation from others, is that narratives are not to be treated as first and foremost whole stories about which one can make only general comments. Rather, narratives have a structure whose key elements are to be found within relations which are a function of kinds of concepts and statements out of which narratives can be built. The investigation of the kinds of concepts and statements which inform narrative structure will occupy the succeeding sections of this chapter. In this section, however, I think it important to note some of the immediate consequences of the initial premise, for it entails the rejection of several theses which have formed the basis of other studies of the narrative. By noting some of these theses, confusion in later sections may hopefully be prevented.

First, since narrative structures may be built out of elements of language without regard to the factualness of the resulting statements or series of statements, and since history may be written in forms other than narrative form, history cannot be identified with the narra-

155

tive form. As Dray has correctly argued, the relation between history and narrative is contingent, despite the large role narrative plays as the predominant form in which written history is presented: "I shall," writes Dray, "proceed on the assumption that the construction of narratives is an admissible and prominent, although not universal, aspect of historiography."[4] The effect of rejecting the identification of history and narrative is twofold. It forces, first of all, a rejection of positions held by a wide variety of contemporary philosophers, for example, that of Morrow, who states that history *is* narrative, that of Gallie, who takes history to be a *species* of narrative, that of Louch, who holds narrative to be *essential* to history, and that of Danto, who takes narrative to be a presupposition of history.[5] The effect of rejecting the identification of history and narrative is, second of all, to reject certain immediate implications of the position. If history and narrative are identified in part or whole, then it becomes a temptation to associate with narrative form what history has as goals, and equally to associate with history what narrative form enables. For example, if history is coterminal with narrative (or coterminal over the relevant extent of both history and narrative), then one can ascribe to the narrative both argument and explanation, since historians do argue and explain. However, the ascription must for the time being be rejected insofar as, with respect to the present investigation, the relations of argument and explanation to history are open questions.

The identification of explanation with narrative form constitutes a popular position which too must be rejected in virtue of the premise from which the present investigation begins. That one may be inclined to say (with or without sufficient justification) that a narrative does explain an event does not suffice to create a necessary connection between explanation and narrative. Such a connection has been suggested by Louch, who takes narrative to be a *kind* of explanation, by Danto, who views narrative as a *form* of explanation, and perhaps even by Gallie, who sees narratives as *self-explanatory*.[6] Any position which would hold explanation and narrative to be in part or in whole identical would have first to specify those features which the two hold in common. Since the aim of this investigation is to specify certain essential features of a narrative, the question of whether a narrative is a form of explanation in any respect must remain open until much later than this point. (Then, at the suitable place, I shall suggest that we have good reason not to identify the two, although we do have grounds on which to understand a claim that a particular narrative is explanatory.)

The third thesis of which the premise of this study forces rejection is that a historical narrative must have a central subject. This thesis has been no less pervasive in philosophical studies of history then the preceding two, but has less often received explicit statement. Fain, for one, does assert that "narratives must be *about* something; a story requires a subject."[7] He then utilizes this position to formulate a necessary condition of stories, namely, that they have a "narrative unit of reference to tie the incidents together."[8] Obviously, the condition only holds if the initial assumption, that a narrative is a story and thus must have a subject, is true. Without imitating Fain's unqualified universality, White similarly concentrates "on those narratives or histories which are histories *of* something like a nation, a society, or even a person insofar as biography may be considered a form of history."[9] The danger underlying both positions, i.e., of taking historical narratives which do have a subject, is that one all too easily may read into the structure of all narratives those features (e.g., unity of reference) which belong only to narratives which in fact have a central subject. To do so is unjustifiably to ignore the question of whether there can be a narrative without a central subject, and if so, whether such a narrative can be a suitable or warranted form for a history.[10] However, if the procedure is reversed, that is, if one first investigates the structure of narratives, then the question of whether a narrative must or can have a unitary subject, and the further question of what role such a unitary subject plays in a narrative, specifically in a historical narrative, can be answered on the basis of supporting considerations rather than assumption. The desire to answer questions in this manner counts, I think, as at least a partial justification for the procedure to be followed in the ensuing investigation.

Some further consequences of rejecting as suppositions the three theses noted above can be seen by attending to a particular aspect of White's study, namely the fact and manner in which the theses interrelate.[11] White attempts to distinguish between chronicles and histories: chronicles are a "conjunction of noncausal singular statements which expressly mention that subject [the central subject] and which report things that have been true of it at different times"; a history, in addition to meeting the condition for being a chronicle, also contains "causal statements."[12] If one does not accept White's restriction of one's consideration to narratives having central subjects, then his definitions of chronicle and history, insofar as they depend on reference to a central subject, cannot be sustained. Moreover, to the extent that causal statements may be intended to associate explanation with historical narrative necessarily, the definitions contain an element which needs support before it can give support. It may be true, as Waters notes, that "the familiar 'cause' of practical discourse is completely adaptable to the office of explanation in history."[13] Yet that fact in itself is not sufficient (nor does Waters claim it is) to establish that "cause" is the only concept which provides either narrative or explanatory connections. If there are other modes of narrative connection, if a history need not be a narrative whose continuity is provided solely by causal statements, and furthermore if a narrative need not be explanatory, then nothing is left of White's definitional distinction between chronicle and history other than the fact, perhaps, that a chronicle is a collection of true statements about occurrences and a history is a collection bearing a continuity which one might call narrative continuity. But what narrative continuity might consist of, what might be its structural features, becomes the open question. It is just this question which I have been suggesting should be the first question, rather than the one which follows on a set of assumptions or positions.

The set of theses which have been rejected as suppositions can, if adopted in whole or part, lead one to the position that there is no such thing as a peculiarly narrative structure. For example, in attempting to reduce fundamental schemes of intelligibility to two, Stover argues that "we look in vain for a fundamental scheme of intelligibility peculiar to the narrative form itself, a way of accounting for happenings in terms of interrelationships among occurrences." Narratives must rely upon "determining conditions."[14] Unfortunately, Stover has, prior to his look at narrative form, already committed himself to theses which prevent him from asking a question about narrative structure openly, i.e., without presuppositional commitment to a certain order of answers. His commitment is to a version of convering law determinism. Stover goes so far as to say that the reason historical narratives appear unlike scientific explanations is that narratives "are characteristically so casually structured."[15] But when pressed, the casualness of structure he finds is with respect to the criteria for causal explanations, not to the criteria for being a narrative. For example, the notion of the interrelationship among occurrences within Stover's context must be restricted to that provided by such things as causal laws, i.e., by relations which preserve the logical independence of the occurrences related so as to preserve their plurality. Hence concepts which may organize (as opposed to laws which organize) are never considered either as having a role in narratives or as relating events.

Even if one does not assume the theses which have been rejected, one does not gain automatic access to a clear analysis of the structural features of the narrative form. In asking whether there are any structural ideas related to narratives, Dray analyzes both Gallie's model and what he would take as additionally his own. In the process he finds the following: a. contingency (that some events are not predictable); b. necessary conditions (that some events do have determinable conditions); c. continuity; d. reasons (that some events occur as products of rational consideration); e. opportunity: f. (possibly) purposive order; and g. synthetic unity.[16] What the list includes amounts to a roster of some kinds of concepts which perform structural duties with respect to narratives; but in fact the nature of the structural duty they perform is not specified by Dray. Until structural duties have been specified, one cannot even judge whether the list is complete or whether it is inexhaustive or redundant.

The upshot of all the considerations in this section is that the task of investigating narrative form must be started afresh, and that the standpoint of the following investigation will be that narrative form results from the use of certain structural features inherent in certain kinds of concepts and statements already in the language. Given this sort of starting point, one does not thereby commit oneself to the position that every unit which employs or makes use of the structural possibilities of the concepts and statements in question is a narrative. Therefore, the terms "narrative" and "narrative form" shall be restricted to use in connection with bodies of writing which we should agree are narratives, i.e., anything we might call a story (but perhaps not just stories). When speaking of the structural features that make narratives possible, I shall speak of "narrative organization." It shall be the task of the following to find some of the basic features of narrative organization within concepts and statements; hence there shall arise terms such as "narrative organizational statement" or, when referring to conceptual and sentential possibilities without discrimination, "narrative organizational structure." Although the terminology does not lend itself to rhetorical flourish, hopefully it will not be so ponderous as to obscure the points being made.

II. Past-Referring Terms and Tensed Sentences

Perhaps the most basic work on the logic of narrative writing comes from Danto. His *Analytical Philosophy of History* contains abundant insights into various features of narratives, many of which contribute to the solution of problems just now coming to be understood. Unqualified acceptance of Danto's views, however, cannot be given, because he has unfortunately chosen to link his insights by means of certain general theses which center around, first, "an inexpungable subjective factor" which supposedly pervades narrative organization (p. 142),[17] and second, the identification of narrative with explanation (p. 201). As a consequence of these theses, Danto gives undue attention to the concepts of "causation" and "description" and emphasizes certain forms of narrative organization which are inherently causal (and hence explanatory) at the expense of others. Alternative views of either "causality" or "explanation" would have obviated the unbalanced treatment. For example, treating "cause" as independent of general laws in Waters' manner,[18] or conceiving explanation in the puzzlement removal fashion of Passmore,[19] would loosen the grip on historical narrative of the still influential covering law theories and variations. Freedom from such theories would allow a look at narrative organization for its own sake.

This last, the attempt to explore narrative organization and connection without subterranean theses on causality and explanation, seems a more productive route than detailed criticism of Danto's views.[20] Accordingly, this and the following section will review some of his insights with sufficient commentary to counteract the causal orientation and to open further possibilities. The goal will be to see how the conceptual and sentential structures noted by Danto accomplish their work of providing temporal and contextual continuity without presupposing that the work must be done in one and only one way.

"Our language," writes Danto, "is saturated with past-referring predicates. . ." (p. 73). Such predicates necessarily refer not only to a present object or event, but also to a past event. Being a scar, for example, necessarily refers to a prior event such that if the whitish, shiny mark "was not caused by a wound, it just simply is not a scar" (p. 72). Terms such as scar contrast to temporally-neutral predicates, which stand independently of past-referring terms. On the other hand "past-referring predicates are not independent of temporally-neutral predicates (p. 73)." The absence of some mark would preclude the application of "scar," although not every whitish siny mark is a scar. Furthermore, non-recognition of a past would not only eliminate past tense sentences, it would falsity or make senseless many present tense sentences, namely those employing past-referring terms (p. 74).

The importance of Danto's remarks lies in his realization that single terms can make reference to time separated events in such a way as to organize them progressively. "Scar" does not just refer to past and present events and conditions, but organizes them, however rudimentarily. The wound, or whatever left the scar is (tautologically) prior to the scar. In effect, then, the use of the term in a sentence, e.g., "John has a scar," already shows some characteristics of a narrative. Narratives flow, i.e., no assertion in a properly constructed narrative stands out as an isolated fact. This perhaps captures what is meant by the common assertion that narratives tell stories. No connective is needed between, say,

    a. John was wounded,

and

    b. John has a scar,

as might be required between a. and

    c. John has a whitish shiny mark.

The connective for a. and c. is

    d. The whitish shiny mark was left by the wound.

Sentence b., then, does the work of both c. and d., which work is not just to assert facts but to organize them.

The organizing potential of past-referring terms becomes apparent without reference to what Danto calls an "obvious causal relation" (p. 72). The wound may be a "cause" in the relatively vacuous sense of being an antecedent of or the reason for having a scar, but it counts as neither a necessary nor sufficient condition of a scar. Many wounds leave no scars, and many scars result from other than wounds, e.g., acne, smallpox, cysts, etc. One tends to say a wound, acne, poc, or cyst leaves a scar rather than causes it. But whether scar and wound bear a causal relation, and whether, even if they do, one has said anything special by admitting the relation, the most striking feature about past-referring terms remains their narrative-organizing function. Moreover, terms without the least causal connotation succeed in organizing past and present events or conclusions. Being a "two-year old" organizes a present condition with respect to a past event, one's birth, but one would be loath to argue that one's birth causes one to be a two-year old.

That one can admit the organizing feature of past-referring terms without a necessary commitment to causal theses effectively blunts Danto's attempt to reduce "future-referring" terms into temporally-neutral ones. Were the only or primary use of future-referring terms to explain and predict, Danto's efforts would be well placed, for indeed being a "father-to-be" does not entail any future event (p. 75). If being a father-to-be depends upon anything at all, it is upon present and past events. Having said that, however, one still owes an account of the dependency. Danto writes: "Thus, X is a father-to-be in the case where X has impregnated Y and Y has not yet delivered the child. And nothing more is required" (p. 75). True, nothing more is required to justify the assertion that X is a father-to-be (assuming he is not expecting a miscarriage: note how cruel it would be to call X a father-to-be when he knows a miscarriage is imminent). Nonetheless, fulfilling the requirements for warrantably calling X a father-to-be does not reduce the term to those requirements. For, as noted throughout this study, the criteria for warranted use do not equate with the term whose use they justify upon fulfillment.

    The assertions
    e. X impregnated Y
and
    f. Y has not yet delivered
organize a past event and a present condition. The assertion
    g. X is a father-to-be
organizes past and present (if we assume, not always safely, that Y is involved) and also future, whether or not the future materializes. That such expressions organize activities in a time period beyond that essential to their justified utterance becomes clear from their use in the past tense, e.g.,
    h. X was a father-to-be.
Given h., no further connective is required to organize X's subsequent actions, for example, buying out a toy store, increasing his life insurance, *et al.* (it was his first child). Not as accomplished actions, but as expected, anticipated, dreaded, hoped for, probable, and unlikely actions, g. also organizes within a time period beyond that essential to justified assertion. The title "father-to-be does not logically depend upon what the future brings" (p. 75), but it does determine to a large measure what the future holds. Otherwise expressed, it determines in part what one can sensibly say of the future. Moreover, it does so in a way that merely being the impregnator of undelivered Y does not: "Father-to-be" is a socially and psychologically based title, not just a medical one. One could claim justice in calling X a father-to-be just by watching his shopping spree, without seeing Y or even knowing X and Y planned to adopt a child.

    What seems most to color Danto's account of terms like "father-to-be" is perhaps his urge to call them "future-referring" and thus to raise the synthetic dust of future reference. In the supposed clearing of the dust, the narrative organization accomplished by such terms disappears along with the hopeless project of saying how a word might refer to what does not yet exist or has not yet happened. Still, as noted in earlier chapters, event words do not refer in the past tense either, unless it is by virtue of already having an event word to serve

161

as grammatical referent. The ability to organize temporally is equally grammatical and not ontological; hence, future organization holds no more logical terrors than past. "Father-to-be" shows as much narrative structure as "scar."

Not just words, but sentences also and obviously play a role in temporally organizing events and objects. Danto rightly recognizes the analogy between past-tense sentences and past-referring terms. Just as the use of a past-referring predicate presupposes that a temporally-neutral predicate can be appropriately applied, so too a true past-tense sentence presupposes that a temporally-neutral sentence is also true (p. 73). "Caesar died in 44 B.C." supposes the death of Caesar, and further, it relates the event to the time of utterance (p. 55). The relating portion of the sentence, notes Danto, does not stand in conjunction with the untensed portion; for if the untensed part were false, then the tense-bearing part would become neither true nor false, but functionless. "How can I stand in any temporal relation to a non-existent event?" (p. 57). If one must disect a tensed sentence, then the portion which relates the event to the speaker is perhaps best treated as an "operator-variable which takes tenses as values" such that T(p) cannot be true unless p is true and p cannot be false unless T(p) is also false (p. 58).

From this sort of analysis, there follow several consequences for the narrative. First, the organization of past events is not independent of the events asserted. While it is possible to assert facts tenselessly, it is not possible to assert tenses factlessly. In narratives, then, organization occurs as a part of asserting facts, rather than being something brought separately to them. No tenses wait in the wings for application to previously asserted tenseless facts; we either assert facts tenselessly or tensed. If we do so tenselessly, then no narrative can result, for not even the "then-then" condition is possible. ("Caesar dies 44 B.C., then Antony dies 30 B.C." substitutes for tenses and accomplishes the same end insofar as the mention of the later date entails that a dateless version of "Caesar dies" would correctly take the past tense.) In short, a tensed sentence constitutes a form of temporal and narrative organization.

The complex tensing possibilities which exist within language acquire function not by locating events in the simplistic past, present, and future, but by relating events to one another. Note the following:
   i.   Caesar dies and Antony died.
   j.   Caesar died, then Antony died.
   k.   Caesar having died, Antony died.
   l.   Caesar had died, and Antony died.
Of the four, only i. expressed no organization between events (although the very use of a past tense relates the events to the speaker temporally). The latter three, j., k., and l., relate the mentioned events in serial order, though in different ways, each perhaps appropriate to various contexts and purposes. To the extent that tenses and other grammatical devices in the language relate and organize events in a

temporal progression, then examples like j., k., and l., show narrative structure (while i. does not). But of course, j., k., and l., do not tell much of a story, if any at all.

Second, the organizing function of tenses occurs even in future-tense statements. For some cases of future-tense sentences, the tenseless assertion would be neither true nor false; hence the tensed-statement could not be true. Thus,

m. World War III will begin in three years

is not true because the tenseless assertion that World War III begins is not true (or false). Such an analysis does not apply to all cases.

n. Lincoln will have been dead two centuries in 2065

is true, though the case involves a computational method which analytically guarantees the future-tensed statement if the implicit past reference is correct. In addition to statements which cut across past and future, many activities invoke the use of future tense statements and their organizational function. Preparations for battle might include the assertion,

o. At 0630 the bombers will be gone and we will attack.

In a narrative, no further connectives are required to permit a present- or past-tense report of attack. Further, nothing in narrative organization forbids crossing from past to future and back.

p. Having reached the first point, they decided they would go only as far as the second before camping

might occur in a narrative about a mountain climb. Again, no additional connectives are required to make sense of assertions to the effect that they reached point two and camped or that they had (or have) six miles to go before stopping. In fine, when causal and predictive theses are set aside, the organizational function of tensed sentences becomes the key element of their use in narratives. That tensed sentences can serialize events, regardless of the order of mention, suffices to capture their central role in narratives.

However, serialization does not alone suffice to produce an extended narrative or a historical narrative. That narratives proceed sequentially or progressively (whatever the literary devices one uses dramatically to alter the progression) amounts to but one of the many features which characterize narratives. (Sequence and progression here refer to the connected succession noted early in this chapter, not to a random selection of events temporally ordered.) Connections other than sequence alone connect the time separated events and objects. The mountain claiming example (p.) referred to a decision, the attack example (o.) to a requisite condition for the next step in a plan, the Caesar-Antony examples (j., k., l.) to a common occurrence. Something more than temporal succession is needed, though not necessarily cause. Danto, in providing insight into two further narrative phenomena--the narrative sentence and project verbs,--has provided means for further exploring the range of narrative connectives.

163

III. Narrative Sentences and Temporal Structures

"Narrative sentences'," notes Danto, "refer to at least two time-separated events, and describe the earlier event" (p. 159). Such a sentence is "Aristarchus anticipated in 270 B.C. the theory which Copernicus published in A.D. 1543" (p. 156). Numerous other examples can be found in actual historical writings. To give just one case, Goethe apparently analyzed Aristotle's *katharsis* as a "relationship within tragedy itself" instead of as the more usual "psychological effect." Here, noted Monroe Beardsley, Goethe "strikingly anticipates a recent reinterpretation of Aristotle by Gerald Else. . . ."[21]

Narrative sentences such as these not only assert facts (implicitly and explicitly), but also organize them or create a relation between them. As with any relation, notes Danto, it is falsifiable by the denial of either or both the relata. With respect to organizational features these sentences resemble 1. above, but with additional features of note: they require completion of the second event before assertion can be warranted. They are members of a class of sentences which only historians (or others in their after-the-fact position) can utter. One could not meaningfully use such a sentence during Aristarchus' lifetime or even after it prior to Copernicus' publication (pp. 156-157). Moreover, "anticipates" may be predicted of Aristarchus, but it is not something Aristarchus intends or could intend. Likewise, Piero da Vinci can intend to beget a son Leonardo (although he may be thwarted by genetics), but he cannot intend to beget "a universal genius" (p. 157). (Nothing stops him from hoping to do so.) Thus, many verbs which organize events narratively are not available for use while the events are occurring.

As valuable as are Danto's remarks concerning the structure of narrative sentences, they retain his characteristic ambivalence with respect to certain conceptual problems. It is possible to say that "anticipate" is something Aristarchus *did* and "beget a universal genius" is something Piero da Vinci *did*. Of this situation Danto wants to assert that there is an event E in each case which descriptions (whose applicability becomes proper only after some other event) refer to and which makes possible the narrative sentence (p. 157). That the event referred to is "the same" event as that under a different description in a non-narrative-sentence remains an intuitive fact in Danto's account, and nowhere does one discover what counts as being the same event. As noted in an earlier chapter, the notation "E" becomes very elusive and perhaps illusive with respect to events. Illusions of identity in turn breed problematic positions. For example, Danto says, "What Aristarchus did may in no sense have caused Copernicus to discover the heliocentric theory, but in a very definite sense it caused Copernicus to re-discover the heliocentric theory" (p. 156). It is difficult to imagine any sense wherein one could seriously say that Aristarchus' work caused Copernicus to rediscover. For Copernicus' theory rests on grounds independent of Aristarchus' work. The only "cause" here seems to be conceptual: consideration of Aristarchus' work provides grounds for historians to use the verb "re-discover" rather than "discover" (although where one intends no slight to Greek insight, "discover" works as well). Grounds for word use decision appear to go beyond even what such a loose term as "cause" will bear. Moreover, if Else did not read the relevant passages of Goethe, the only connection between the reinterpretations of Aristotle would be the fact that they were similar. To say that Goethe (or Goethe's analysis) causes Else to rediscover (or causes the rediscovery) would be to come very near to committing a fallacy *post hoc ergo propter hoc*.

Danto's treatment of E as an event which one then goes on to describe leads to other difficulties. He had characterized narrative sentences as referring to two events and describing the earlier. Later, he says that sentences using project verbs resemble narrative sentences in their referential and descriptive aspects, although without requiring for truth the occurrence of the later event (pp. 164-65). Holding aside the nature of project verbs, one still cannot help noticing the problem engendered by such an account of project verb sentences, namely that of referring to the future without requiring a future, of having reference without a referent. Danto shows no urge to develop an artificial referent (e.g., out of such notions as "potentiality"), nor does he require the occurrence of a future event for the truth of project verb assertions. In short, no future reference occurs. If this is so, then the characterization of project verb sentences cannot be correct if it requires "reference to two time separated events." This conclusion, in turn, reflects serious doubt upon whether a past event is "referred to" by the use of event concepts in narrative sentences.

One may eliminate the need for reference by taking narrative sentences to *assert* two events and to *describe* (or predicate something of) the former. (One requires a slightly different solution for project verb sentences.) Thus not Aristarchus, but his discovery anticipates Copernicus' work, which is to say that an event word "discovery" takes a predicate like "anticipates." The example asserts not only the event, Aristarchus' discovery, but as well a later event, Copernicus' discovery. Note, however, that Copernicus' re-discovery is not anticipated: for that to be the case one would have to be able to assert a further heliocentric discovery prior to Aristarchus. Hence, Copernicus' re-discovery and discovery are not just the same E under two descriptions; nor is that mode of characterizing narrative sentences helpful in explicating the logic of narratives.

Far more useful and enlightening to the subject of narrative organization is Danto's notion of a temporal structure. A temporal structure consists in a conceptual link of discontinuous events, e.g., writing a book or planting roses or anticipating one discovery by another (p. 166). The events making up the structures have interludes between them when no part of the structure can be said to occur. Examples are the periods when a writer sleeps, when the gardener eats dinner, or when Aristarchus has ceased to discover through (at least) the

birth of Copernicus. Each of the kinds of narrative devices mentioned
thus far fulfills the criteria for being a temporal structure, although
the case of past-referring terms may be less than obvious. The apparent difficulty with past-referring terms emerges from Danto's wish in
his example causally to connect the scar and wound, a condition which
by his Humean analysis requires conjunction and contiguity (pp. 242-
43). However, whether wounds leave or cause scars, the constant inter-
vening presence or visibility of the scar is to assert a present mark
and a past event in an organized way. Moreover, if continuity and
cause serve any function at all, they do so only for certain concepts.
For many others, their consideration is otiose.

The chief classes of temporal structures which Danto elicits are
the narrative sentences already noted and project verbs. Project
verbs, e.g., "planting roses," exhibit a structure similar to that of
narrative sentences, i.e., reference to two time separated events with
a description of the earlier (p. 159). While the occurrence of the later event was a condition for the truth of narrative sentences, no
analogous condition exists for project verbs. Thus, one does not require fulfillment of the reference to roses in order to say truly that
someone is planting roses (p. 164). Rather, one observes one of "indefinitely many sorts of behavior" which may be covered by the term,
for example, digging holes, setting seedlings, filling holes, watering,
fertilizing, playing Bach. In effect, Danto seeks to explicate a subset of Ryle's "polymorphous" terms, terms which cover the display of
disparate forms of behavior under differing circumstances. Danto re-
stricts his attention to those terms which make reference to the future: "obedience" would count for Ryle, but not for him.[22]

More correctly, the feature which delimits Danto's subset of
Rylean polymorphs is their temporal organizing function. For the rejection of future reference noted above does not imply that "planting
roses" and other such concepts lose their organizing ability, and in
fact one need not even go so far as to deny reference entirely. The
reference which occurs with the use of project verbs, however, is not
to future events, but to goals, aims, hopes, plans, plots, projects,
and any of a large number of outcomes which play a role in human action. Outcomes are not only built into many terms marking out personal
endeavors, but as well into concepts indicating socially institutionalized rule-governed behavior. Danto himself, in another connection, argued that one cannot reduce the statement "The bank-teller certifies
the withdrawal slip" to "The man makes marks on the piece of paper"
(p. 273 f). The first sentence, unlike the second, looks both backward
(withdrawal slips, but not pieces of paper, require prior acts) and
forward (one withdraws the money). Forward reference is not to the
yet-to-occur event, but to a goal which would end the game or activity.

Replacing reference to future events with goals and aims does not
clutter up the world with ontologically suspect entities. About goals
one can say something similar to what was said of events: we have
grounds for asserting them, and once asserted, we can refer to them.

The latter act becomes possible insofar as goal terms fill the grammatical role of substantives. As little as goal terms add to nature's furniture, they do reflect upon the grounds for asserting the truth of a project verb statement. A man is not planting roses when we see him tamping down the earth unless it is his plan, hope, aim (or other applicable "end" word) that roses arise. (We can, however, plant roses--i.e., rose seedlings--without a goal and still be planting roses, but such is not a project in the present sense.) The use of such terms organizes events in a forward direction, as Dray has put it, by seeing what events lead to.[23] Notably, narrative sentence verbs demarcate generally what one cannot intend, as Aristarchus could not intend that his work anticipate Copernicus' theory, but goals and aims cover precisely the sorts of things which can (though they need not always) be intended. One need not know, however, that a person in fact intends or plans or hopes for a given end, i.e., have first hand testimony. Where certain patterns of actions occur, one can sometimes assert that a person does intend, hope, or aim, since the patterns of actions themselves fulfill the criteria for the assertion. In other cases, the goal is of an act rather than of a person: roses are (tautologically) the goal of planting roses. Moreover, patterns which justify goal attributions change with time. Playing Bach is not now a "part" of planting roses, but someday might be. Consequently, understanding how people generally went about things in a given day and age plays a role in learning what counts as a case of a project or activity. The so-called limited laws of Joynt and Rescher seem to be more often of this variety than of the "causal" sort.[24]

The organizing ability of action words, specifically those making reference to ends, turns out to be a good bit more variegated than Danto's examples would lead one to believe. Nonetheless, they retain the essentials of narrative organization to the extent that they relate time-separated events and thus determine what one can, without further connectives, say of both the past and future. For historical narrative, the use of such concepts rests not on the future (the goals and aims) of the historian, but on that of the historical figure. What counts as a goal may be some event which occurred (e.g., Hitler planned to invade France and did) or an event which did not come to fruition but for which the historian has grounds for assertion as a goal (Dewey wanted to be President, ran, and lost). In part, these constitute Walsh's colligations under an organizing concept, and--following Walsh further--ends and directions serve to organize even where one cannot appropriately mention intention.[25] The Romantic Movement in English literature organizes discontinuous events under a concept of social-literary direction. Given the kind of movement, one can then characterize some works or writers as steps in the direction, e.g., Burns or Blake, others as mainstream, e.g., Wordsworth, and others still as transitions to a new direction, e.g., Carlyle. Such assertions gain part of their sense from the justified assertion of the movement; they do not apply as descriptions of the writers in isolation. Moreover, movement and project attributions sometimes license narrative sentences. Alone, Burns may presage other writers; given the Romantic Move-

167

ment, he can presage an era.[26] In addition, some of the examples that
Fain cites in order to illustrate the manner in which "showing how one
event leads to another, how one event generates another," produces
"narrative coherence," appear not to fit precisely the categories of
project verbs or of narrative sentences. One event is said to be the
occasion of another, others lead up to, generate, or make more probable
following events, all "without supposing that they are related to each
other as cause to effect."[27] The result, then, is a large collection
of concepts which, either by themselves or in use in certain kinds of
sentences, supply the temporal and contextual continuity which enables
the narrative.

In every case, conceptual criteria govern the use of narrative-
organizational assertions, and this fact counts against Danto's worries
over an "inexpungable subjective factor" and "an element of sheer arbitrariness" (p. 142) in historical narrative. Those worries apparently
stem from Danto's discovery that "no *a priori* limit" can be set to the
number of different narrative sentences, and hence no limit may be set
to the number of different temporal structures within which historical
organization of the Past will locate E (p. 167). Which organization we
choose seems to have no grounds except the historian's interest (p.
167). There is a limit, however, and whatever its scope, it bears the
power of exclusion. Even though the number of narrative organizational
structures possible in the language is very great, not all apply to any
given event. A historian may assert only those narrative organizational structures for which he has grounds as fulfilled criteria. What he
says must be justified or it does not count as history. That the possibilities at his disposal allow more than just causal organization
does not count against history, but against those who place the onus of
objectivity on causality rather than justification. "Retroactive re-
alignment of the Past," as Danto calls it, "does indeed occur and does
alter the relative significance we ascribe to events" (p. 168). But
here Danto speaks of two things at once: what we are justified in asserting and the evaluations we are justified in making. The interests
of historians may well hold genetic power over the shapes of histories,
but they do not alter the fact or method of justifcation. That justification is possible suffices to make Danto's worries over whimsy themselves whimsical.

IV. Narrative Consistency, Congruency and Unity

Any catalog of the narrative-organizational structures possible
within the conceptual framework(s) available to the historian cannot
exhaust the subject of narratives. Even the brief list given here,
which has rested upon the common features of members and paid too scant
attention to their differences, raises the question of what holds a
narrative together. While assertions such as "here is a scar" and
"Burns presaged the mainstream Romantic writers" exhibit the essential
characteristics of narrative organization, one can hardly take this
much to be the whole story with respect to narratives. The question

168

naturally arises of how the structures made possible by these conceptual and sentential features of language fit into larger narratives, e.g., into the history books. As a first try, one might suggest that the larger narrative is a mere concatonation of narrative-organizational structures. The trial answer, however, raises objections on at least two grounds. First, larger narratives contain many sentences which do not fit the genus of narrative-organizational structures. "Washington had ill-fitting false teeth" and "Scott married Charlotte Carpenter" fall as naturally into narratives as do any of the narrative-organizational assertions illustrated in the preceding sections. Their place requires some account. The unity of narratives, an oft-mentioned but ill-explicated feature, also counts against concatonation theories. Books have beginnings and endings, and, whether prejudice or truth, one likes to think of books as beginning and ending the same thing. Some few works, like the Hayes volume mentioned in an earlier chapter, have a single theme or large scale colligation to hold everything in place, but colligation alone scarcely suffices to encompass the conditions of narrative unity.

In order to answer the relevant questions just raised, one can make some distinctions among the ways in which the elements of a narrative relate to each other. 1. Let us call the relation of facts to a narrative-organizational structure "narrative consistency." 2. "Narrative congruency" will designate the relation of one narrative-organizational structure to another. 3. The relation of narrative-organizational structures to the whole narrative can be called "narrative unity." 4. Finally, let us hold out as an important non-structural feature "thematic unity."[28]

1. The four named conditions, I think, will go a long way toward distinguishing the peculiar features of the narrative without introducing elements which conflict with ordinary logic principles such as non-contradiction. The "smallest" of them, narrative consistency, concerns the relation between non-narratively expressed facts and narratively expressed facts. A non-narratively expressed fact I shall take to be any fact which does not depend for its assertion upon the use of a narrative-organizational structure of the sort described above in sections two and three of this chapter. This class of facts includes, as well as true statements, assertions that have the form of facts but turn out not to be true; what is in question here is not the truth of an assertion, but its relation to some other assertion. The choice of the phrase "non-narratively expressed fact" rests on the need to distinguish between the class of facts designated by the term, which encompasses perhaps the bulk of what one may wish to call facts, and the class of facts which are asserted or presupposed by narrative-organizational statements which do make use of the temporal and contextual organizing structural possibilities described in the preceding sections. It would be judged a flaw in any narrative to make or presuppose assertions which are inconsistent with those made or presupposed by the use of narrative-organizational sentences. Thus, narrative consistency becomes a necessary condition of a successful or proper narrative. Even

this much, however, still leaves the conditions of consistency imprecise. The conditions take at least two forms, because non-narratively expressed facts can stand to a narrative-organizational sentence in separable relations: either as criteria for them or as tautologous (or contradictory) to them. (Of course, given any single narrative-organizational sentence, innumerable statements automatically become consistent with it by virtue of having no particular relation to it at all. These statements hold no interest yet, since at the present level they can create no difficulties.)

In a hypothetical historical narrative, one might find statements like one or more of the following (not all of which happen to be true statements):
1. Leibniz anticipated Newton's discovery of the calculus.
2. Leibniz never completed his work which, had it been developed would have yielded the calculus.
3. Leibniz and Newton worked at about the same time, and given the communications and political situation of the day, could not have been expected to be aware of each other's work.
4. Newton developed the calculus as a necessary part of his mechanics.
5. Leibniz finished his calculus in the year T.

What holds interest here is not history itself, but the relations among the five sentences, using 1. as the keystone. Sentences 1. and 2. are not only inconsistent, but 2. contradicts a fact presupposed by 1., namely, that Leibniz developed a calculus. If 2. is true, then 1. cannot be true, and if 1. is true, 2. cannot be true. The relation between 1. and 3. does not emerge with the simplicity of that between 1. and 2. The criteria for using the concept "anticipate" in historical contexts ordinarily includes something to the effect that the anticipator precede the anticipatee by a significant time span. The assertion of 3., taken as true, provides strong grounds for asserting that the criteria for asserting a case of anticipation are not fulfilled. Sentence 3. does not definitely deny anticipation, for "about the same time" may allow for temporal precedence by Leibniz. Whether the time is significant would require further information not supplied here. However, the failure to fulfill criteria does make 1. and 3. inconsistent, but not contradictory. In order to make 1. consistent with 3., one might drop the term "anticipation" and assign Leibniz and Newton equal status as independent, co-temporal authors of the calculus. Statement 4. is a fact logically consistent with 1. and related to it via repetition of the fact (whether treated as explicit or presupposed) that Newton developed a calculus. Statement 5. bears a similar relation to 1., but contains an additional element, the date T of Leibniz's work. Given an additional "fact," i.e., that Newton finished his calculus in the year T + 40, then 5. would be not only logically consistent with the presupposition in 1. (that Leibniz finished a calculus), but in addition would fulfill a criterion for the assertion of anticipation. Thus, it would become both logically and criterially consistent with 1.

170

The examples do more than just explicate the notion of narrative consistency. They show how it is possible to incorporate within a narrative consistent assertions and series of assertions which in themselves have no narrative-organizational structure. To the extent that 4. is positively consistent with 1. (i.e., to the extent that it contains material the falsification of which would render 4. inconsistent with 1.), any statement which is consistent with 4. in a non-narrative way (i.e., logically) is narratively consistent with 1. Thus, any exposition of elements in Newton's mechanics in which the calculus plays a role represents a non-digressive but non-narrative piece of writing which could hardly be denied a place in histories of the period which find a place for 1. and 4. As noted in another connection in an earlier chapter, the writer of a narrative need not confine himself solely to temporally progressive narration. Indeed, the present analysis confirms the naturalness of expecting that much of the historian's work should be devoted to laying the non-narrative factual ground work which supplies the justification for his narrative-organizational assertions, especially the novel or potentially controversial ones. To choose an example from fiction, without the chapters on whales and the whiteness of the whale, one can hardly follow Melville's later narrative. More specifically of historical interest, without the passages describing the peculiarities of American geography, one can hardly understand narratives of the westward movement in United States history.

2. So far, the discussion has ranged over the relation between single narrative-organizational assertions and non-narratively expressed facts. It might be possible for a historian to write within the bounds set by the relation, perhaps in the format of a short article. In any event, narrative consistency will take on further importance later in this chapter. For the present, however, one may grant that many, if not most, histories follow one narrative-organizational assertion with another. The relation between any two of these assertions which abut was tentatively designated narrative congruency, i.e., the form of consistency which permits one to judge serial narrative-organizational structures, and the narrative constructed thereupon, as unflawed. Thus, generally, narrative congruency becomes a necessary condition for a successful or proper narrative wherever two or more narrative-organizational assertions abut. Again, this much of an account only sets a demand for explicating narrative congruency.

Illustrations by way of sentences from a hypothetical historical narrative again provide the best means of explanation.
1. Washington entered Independence Hall some twenty minutes before Franklin.
2. As Washington entered, Franklin shouted a friendly greeting from his place.
3. Before Franklin took his seat, he awaited with impatience the arrival of Washington.
4. As soon as Franklin arrived, Washington began the six-hour session.
Using 1. as the keystone, 4. clearly meets the test of congruency,

171

which is to say that no logical, criterial, or narrative difficulties
arise from placing 1. and 4. in successive positions within a history
(assuming them both to satisfy fact, of course). One might imaginably
place 4. first and withhold 1. a bit, perhaps to interject some material on Washington's manner with respect to Franklin, finally letting
everything become clear via 1. Whatever the dramatic effects of such
an arrangement of 1. and 4., it in no way alters their narrative order
or relation. Sentence 1. is congruent with sentence 4. to the extent
that the temporal order and relation established by it are not thrown
into question by 4., nor are the explicit and implicit facts of 1. contravened by those of 4.

The relation of 3. to 1., however, plainly displays an incongruency between the two narrative-organizational structures. Given an un-
extraordinary reading of the two lines, 1. places Washington's arrival
at time T, and Franklin's at T + T', an order which 3. reverses. Otherwise put, some of the facts of 3. (not those about feelings of impatience) warrant the assertion that Franklin's entry preceded Washington's, an assertion inconsistent with one warranted by some of the
facts in 1., namely that Washington's entry preceded Franklin's. (In
this example using 3. and 1., a historian might consistently use both
statements on the condition that he insert material, say, that would
have Washington leave and re-enter; in such a case, the two assertions
would no longer be incongruent, but, too, they would no longer narratively abut.)

The relation of 2. to 1. presents an interesting situation insofar
as 2. would not ordinarily count as a narrative-organizational assertion. The events asserted by it, Washington's entrance and Franklin's
greeting are not temporally separated. However, if what one questions
is the relation of 2. to 1., then 2. cannot be treated as a simple non-
narrative fact. The reason for denying non-narrative status to 2.
within the present context is that the assertion clearly entails or
supposes a narrative-organizational assertion which would place Franklin's arrival prior to Washington's. That supposition--and any assertion resting upon it--is incongruent with 1. Examples such as this
prompt the conclusion that assertions, which out of context appear to
warrant the label non-narrative, can be put to narrative uses. For another instance,
    5. Washington and Franklin entered arm in arm,
is non-narrative in response to the question, "How did Washington and
Franklin enter?" In the context of 1. and in conjunction with it, on
the other hand, 5. becomes narrative-organizational to the extent that
simultaneity suffices to deny a time-separation and to produce thereby
an incongruency.

The examples given so far have stuck to relatively simple relations, *viz.*, definite assertions concerning temporal precedence. Actual cases of incongruency rarely take this form: a well-schooled writer rarely makes the simple mistake. Something a bit more subtle (al-

172

though very likely still too easy to catch the practicing historian)
might be the following:

> The entry, bombing, and scooping of the money were all
> parts of his plan to rob the bank. After sneaking in
> through the rear window at midnight, he planted the bomb.
> Having set the timer, he scooped up the money from the
> teller's cage, only to be caught by the blast just as he
> leapt through the window. The blast, incidentally, failed
> to dent the safe, despite the great quantity of other
> destruction it created.

Something mars the tale. The lead sentence ascribes to the villain a
plan with a definite goal--bank robbery. The ascription of a plan supplies a temporal sequence to the events and constitutes a narrative-
organizational structure. Yet, the other assertions of the story are
not congruent with the initial assertion, though most of them also constitute narrative-organizational assertions. (The last assertion, as
non-narrative, would be narratively inconsistent with the lead sentence
rather than incongruent with it.) Facts, such as a bomb which does not
open the safe (plus the open and possibly unanswerable question of
whether the villain through it could), the order of setting the timer
and then scooping up the money from the teller's cage, *et al.*, do not
mesh with the sequence established by the assertion of a bank robbery
plan. Additionally, midnight money in a teller's cage suggests, besides inconsistency with good banking practice, alternative conceptions, such as a windfall. In turn, more plausible lead narrative-organizational assertions suggest themselves so as to preserve both congruency and consistency, e.g., "For political reasons he sought to bomb
the bank and fell prey to his own plan by the unexpected opportunity
for wealth." The thin lines of the story do not leave this as the only
plausible alternative. But the story does show realistically enough
the setting in which incongruency is likely to occur and to dissuade
one from either discounting the notion as simplistic or from treating
historical narrative as too complex to be subject to canons of justification.

3. Insofar as both narrative consistency and narrative congruency
fall under what one generally and loosely categorizes as consistency
tests, little appears to be gained by the use of separable terms. The
terms, however, designate separable tests. Narrative consistency
matches non-narratively expressed facts to those facts implicitly or
explicitly contained in a narrative-organizational assertion and thus
deals only in the "timeless" content of the questioned statements.
Narrative congruency, while necessarily involved with the non-narrative
aspects of narrative-organizational statements, concerns also, and perhaps primarily, the temporal structures, relations, and sequences established by the use of two or several such statements. The orders,
relations, and sequences, of course, do not function independently of
content; rather, both order and content must coincide in relevant pairs

of statements to provide the temporal and substantive progression which delineates the narrative from other forms of written discourse. One may call both tests matters of consistency, but only at the risk of confusion.

Transitions alone obviously do not supply the entire means by which a narrative achieves its unitary wholeness. Consequently, one can inquire into the relation of narrative-organizational structures to the whole narrative, be it book, article, monograph, or tract. Like narrative consistency and congruency, narrative unity lends itself to broad categorization under the title of consistency. Yet, there is good reason for retaining the term "unity" insofar as the question involved aims specifically at uncovering the necessary conditions for a large narrative hanging together as a unity. The argument given here, by necessity, tends toward generality, because its liability to example demands minimally a chapter length piece for adequacy. Nonetheless, one can say, I think, something not too outlandish on the subject.

Two sorts of large narratives come to mind as relatively extreme cases: first, the tightly structured story which covers a small time period, localized spatial position, and narrow range of topics; second, the broad, multi-faceted history of world civilization in so many pages or even volumes. Certainly many or even most narratives fall between these extremes, but the end points of the continuum, especially the broad end, hold interest here. I am inclined for the moment to overlook arguments to the effect that world history is impossible or at least very difficult, or that it tends to achieve mediocre results even in the best of hands. For it remains fact that such narratives do get written regularly, that people read and judge them, and that we judge them good enough for freshman classes. In short, the narrative so large as to cover major portions of time and space constitutes an oft-realized possibility. Such "big-stories" cover many events and many kinds of events. They often separate contemporary events into categories or subsections. They lack themes to bind the whole together.[29] Still, they show no want of overlap between chapters and parts of chapters. On pages 199 and 200 of a representative text, we hear of Henry I (the Fowler) and receive warning that Henry's illustrious son Otto I (the Great) will reverse a certain policy of his father. After many pages of other matter, we pick up the story on page 243:[30] Henry's son Otto registers dissatisfaction with his father's sort of situation. Well done!

The moral: if we choose the compact, tightly knit, restricted narrative as our model, we miss the minimal condition for narrative unity by being offered too much. Thematic unity, briefly discussed below, has advantages and pleases aesthetic tastes, but it does not comprise a necessary condition of holding together a narrative and its multitude of narrative-organizational assertions, as well as its non-narrative facts. The key to narrative unity is the overlap just noted, although the relation of "overlap" to narrative-organizational assertions needs further specification. Nonetheless, one can say that a narrative is unified if every narrative-organizational structure is related to at least one other narrative-organizational structure within the larger narrative.

Unfortunately for the sake of simplicity, one cannot *a priori* enumerate the possible means by which the relation occurs, except to note the repetition of one "term" of a narrative-organizational structure within another, either directly or indirectly. This I take to capture the point of Olafson's remark on time extended actions, "The consequences of that action must after all be described in terms that will permit them to serve as the premises of the next expisode in the story that is being told. . . ."[31] Outside of some preference for a different terminology, the only exception one could take with Olafson here would be to note that the connection may not be so direct as he implies. For narrative-organizational structures take many forms, as both Danto's examples and the additions herein suggest. A may cause B, and B anticipate C, and C accompany D, which gives E reason for going through steps F, G, and H to achieve I, and I forms the motive for J to do K which has the consequence L, the beginning of an M, which ends when N marks the shift to O. . . . The alphabet(s) end long before the list of narrative connectives. Moreover, O may be a criterion along with P and Q for asserting R, which one then asserts to have caused S.[32] In this sort of instance, because the criterial relation is non-narrative, the narrative unity only indirectly sustains itself. The very feature which leads to the view that narrative closure is theoretically impossible, though practically necessary, i.e., the illimitability of narrative relations, also makes possible narrative unity. This much takes a long stride from the simplistic "then and then and then" formula, and it does so without reforming narratives.

To the extent that a narrative which satisfies the condition of unity can stand without introducing further requirements, narrative consistency, congruency, and unity constitute sufficient conditions of a proper or successful narrative. If this is so, then certain perspectives from which analysts such as Danto view narratives turn out to be unnecessary. For example, Danto wishes to believe that "a narrative is a *form* of explanation" (p. 237, cf. p. 130). The grounds for this claim include that a narrative "is a structure imposed upon events" (p. 132) and as such may be regarded as a kind of theory. Now it is one thing to claim that a narrative can be *used* to explain; that assertion stands beyond denial. Something quite different, however, informs the claim that a narrative *is* a kind of theory and form of explanation. For one thing, such a claim could apply only to historical narratives, i.e., to those based upon fact. Yet, factual stories and fictional stories, insofar as they are stories--time extended progressions of actions and events--are both just stories. A narrative may be consistent, congruous and unified without being factual; which is to say, the criteria of proper narratives do not include factuality and hence cannot include theory and explanation. Second, the variety of connectives which enable even the simplest sort of narrative (e.g., A through S above) removes warrant from the designation of every narrative as a theory. For theories do not merely impose a structure; they impose a structure having some degree of uniform method and connection. The minimal standards of narrative lack just this feature and perhaps thereby permit one to distinguish among histories so as to identify the one which presents a theory from those which do not.

Finally, the imposition of structure upon events does not suffice to mark out narratives as theories. Rather, that imposition of structure, and its particular nature, only suffices to identify narratives themselves. At best, narratives have this feature in common with explanatory theories. The organization of events in narratives occurs by conceptual and sentential means using concepts without extraordinary criteria of application. To this extent, every assertion organizes and imposes structure, some narratively, some non-narratively. If one is to leave anything at all to the realm of the non-theoretical and non-explanatory (and one must, lest he logically preclude the request for explanation), then organization and structure, even qualified by temporality, fail to label anything as *eo ipso* theoretical. Narratives are a tough enough nut to crack without the addition of further impenetrable layers.

Just because narratives are not necessarily theories or theoretical, it by no means follows that narratives which meet the conditions of consistency, congruency, and unity cannot be theoretical. The concept of "synthetic unity" by which Dray characterized Mink's description of a particular form of historical narrative, may be apt (if I read both Mink and Dray correctly) at just this point. Although a theoretic history is not necessary at this level of unity presently under discussion, it seems perfectly possible to meet the conditions set out by Mink using the narrative structures and relations so far noted in conjunction with an appropriate set of facts. A narrative presented under the conditions of consistency, congruency, and unity would not argue, but indeed, would exhibit its conclusions in the form of narrative assertions (and any non-narratively-expressed facts which are consistent with the narrative-organizational statements). The conclusions drawn by the historian, "articulated as separate statements in the grand finale, . . . are not conclusions but reminders to the reader (and to the historian himself) of the topography of events to which the entire narrative has given order."[33] The narrative itself constitutes the conclusion of the historian, that is, his justifiable ordering of the events.[34] To this end, the narrative may be considered theoretic, but not a theory (for nothing in Mink's or Dray's requisites for synthetic unity require the unity of method of ordering which marks theories). In contrast, the conditions of narrative unity which Danto sets out, namely that the narrative have a central subject, and that the narrative contain no material extraneous to the explanation of changes in the central subject (p. 251), represent an imposition of conditions in addition to the ones set out so far. These conditions, in view of the discussion of narrative consistency, congruency, and unity, cannot constitute requisites for all historical narratives; instead they apply to a particular form of historical narrative, the chief characteristic of which is the presence of a central theme or subject.

4. Whatever formal justification narrative unity provides, it does not necessitate the sort of orderly, purposive tales one thinks of as narratives. Because narratives having no single purpose or aim do exist, one cannot argue that one-themed tales constitute either the paradigmatic or the genuine case of narratives. Nonetheless, the phenomenon of historical narratives having single themes occurs often enough to warrant some account of its peculiarities. The appropriate term to describe the sort of unity involved is "thematic," for the terms and nature of the unity lie beyond the limits of purely structural grounds and necessarily include elements of content or subject matter. In consequence, very little of perfect generality can be said about thematic unity. Still, if anything narrative answers to Danto's attempt to assimilate narratives under theories, it will come from the thematic unification of stories.

No single device and no single category of devices grant thematic unity to narratives. The "colligatory" descriptive history noted by Dray and examined under the topics of purpose and selection (in Chapter Four) represent a version of thematic unity, whether the overall characterization is chosen in advance of writing history or is "discovered" or uncovered in the course of doing history. Where factors are plentiful and conclusions fairly obvious, one may select a controlling and unifying theme from a stock of acceptable ones (acceptable to the profession, but perhaps new in application to the period and place in question) before writing. One may also develop a theme in the process of writing, i.e., discover what the main movement of the period was, discover what broad colligatory concept is ascribable on the basis of available facts.[35] These controlling ideas, for which Dray and Walsh show great fondness, function here with unquestionable legitimacy.

The fact of having a unifying concept or conception (not all unified narratives have one-word labels) does not in itself specify what sort of connectives will then supply the narrative unity required as a necessary condition to having a successful or proper narrative. One may have a thematically unified narrative which fails to attain narrative unity. Ordinarily in such cases, the writer will have also failed to warrant the implicit or explicit narrative themes ("narrative themes" because there are other sorts of themes not subject to narrative requirements). It is tautological that a mere collection of facts, however inherently categorially similar, cannot justify a narrative theme, just as temporal structure cannot guarantee categorial similarity.

Within the confines of these conditions, any number of distinguishable kinds of themes arise to provide the grounds for the appropriate modes of narrative unity. The simplest sort of theme seems to be the broad historical unit called a movement and traditionally exemplified by the Renaissance. A history of this movement demands for its unity that each event mentioned be narratively consistent or congruous with some other event which meets the criteria for being termed "renaissant" or be such an event itself. One requires no purposive or causal links to satisfy the terms of the theme, and categorially disparate events may quality.[36] Thematic unity does not supply narrative unity; it supplies the grounds for choosing which sort of narrative will appropriately fit the given tale. Thus, themes which take a form differing from that of the Renaissance dictate other means of narrative unity. Stories of social movements, for example, can employ both causal and purposive connectives, but each as appropriate to the class of events mentioned and (in histories) true of the specific events. Some kinds of events permit either sort of attribution: one may intend to create a riot or one may intentionally or unintentionally cause a riot. In general, large scale events do not admit of individual intentions as a sufficient unifying theme. (Perhaps, at bottom, this conceptual point underlies Taylor's complaint against other histories of World War II.) Nor do we feel comfortable taking some small event as the cause of a large scale event; we treat Lincoln's ascription of war causation to Harriet Stowe's book as more rhetorical than factual. To the extent that causal statements in narratives function to provide temporal structures and not scientifically (or otherwise) to explain, we do not go so far as to demand with Tolstoy or Descartes that the cause somehow equal the event. Even the division between causal and purposive connectives does not suffice to encompass all the devices of narrative unity appropriate to a theme. "Events which prepared the way for . . ." typifies the sort of expression which appears ambiguous when laid against the bifold categories of devices, but which with suitable themes precisely unifies events within a narrative. Not such expressions, but our habits of categorization are ambivalent here.

But not all narratives are unified with respect to a theme. Concern for the notion of historical evidence earlier raised the question of puzzlement and gaps in historical (and by extension, other forms of) narratives, gaps which the writer closes with "conceptual evidence." The substance of those remarks and their peculiar, almost unique, relevance to the narrative, as opposed to other forms of disclosure, can be clarified by the present discussion of the varieties of narrative relations. For the sorts of gaps, puzzlements, and questions which arise in a narrative follow directly upon the sorts of narrative requirements a writer has breached. Only to the extent that such requirements are uniquely narrative will the kind of puzzlement aroused also be uniquely narrative. A lapse in consistency, insofar as it includes possible non-narrative elements, will overlap problems found in other modes of writing. Likewise. the failure to fulfill criteria for a concept's use removes the warrant for that use whether the use be narrative or not, whether the concept be distinctly narrative or not.

Narrative congruency and unity, however, if not exclusively concerned with narrative elements, are more tightly bound to the fundamental requirements of narratives than to other forms of discourse. Moreover, they display in cases of failure to meet their requirements the

features previously ascribed to narrative puzzlements. The very assertion of consecutive or serial events within a narrative raises questions of congruency and unity which deny mere consecutiveness or seri-
alness the name of narrative. In practice, not an entire series, but
pairs or small groups of events, actions, and conditions form the subject of these multifaceted questions. To be aware of a gap in a narrative is to demand a connective, one which meets not only the temporal
conditions of the items to be connected, but which also fits with whatever theme the narrative may have. Since it is a condition of narratives to show temporal progression, the termini of the gap ordinarily
(but not necessarily) will mark out a time span. Placing Caesar in two
places separated by a distance and an appropriate time span calls for
the assertion of a journey--if one assumes the most common sorts of
context, i.e., those which do not in principle legislate against voli-
tional actions and the like. Raising the time span to several years
disallows the journey, that is, makes its assertion less plausible.
(Teleportation remains a logical possibility for all time spans, but is
categorically implausible for all of them.)

What fills the time span is not merely a user of time. Substan-
tially, it must also meet criteria of relevance for which no *a priori*
generalization can substitute. It may be well that an auto trip provides formal congruency between Caesar's acts in Gaul and in Rome, but
it wants for material justification as an appropriate "gap-filler."
Moreover, in extraordinary contexts, e.g., those having special methodological requirements, both an auto trip and a horseback ride might
fail, say, to the extent that both count among volition acts. Understanding the material and methodological possibilities, as well as lim-
itations, constitutes one advantage the practicing historian has over
the layman in constructing answers to narrative questions for which no
direct evidence exists. This advantage, of course, obtains only for
cases more subtle and technical than the examples used here. Conversely, the layman with a technical specialty can often offer to history a
connective hitherto overlooked.

That the historian, as a trained professional, holds greater expertise in the use of investigative methods in no way implies the existence of an irreversible heirarchy from common sense to historical inquiry. As Dewey has described concerning the relationship of science
to common sense, the two--to the extent they can be separated--also in-
teract. To quote with, I think, justifiable adjustment, "(1) [Histor-
ical] subject-matter and procedures grow out of the direct problems and
methods of common sense, of practical uses and enjoyments, and (2) react into the latter in a way that enormously refines, expands, and lib-
erates the contents and agencies at the disposal of common sense."[37]
Dewey actually said this of science, confident that he could show more
or less directly in the history of human thought the process by which
science became "increasingly remote" from common sense and conversely
the process by which science influenced a "revolutionary change" in the
"contents and techniques of common sense."[38] Such cross influences
probably cannot be shown for the relationship between history and com-

mon sense, because the closeness of the two makes details at best subtle, at worst invisible. Nonetheless, some cross influences can be
noted. Problems of religious faith and doctrine gave rise to techniques for the internal criticism of manuscripts, techniques raised to
high levels by scholars. Both techniques and results have returned to
the public to widen their range of questions and their appreciation of
materials to which such methods have been applied. Thus, while it
would be an error to suggest that history has effected a divorce from
common sense, especially to the degree attributed to physical science,
what separation does exist fails to prevent communion between the two.

In any event, the narrative tests outlined in this section flesh
out to some degree what has been called the pragmatic dimension of constructive history. For this reason, narrative coherence alone amounts
primarily to a negative test, or perhaps more loosely but positively, a
formal test corresponding to the question of whether a given narrative
has fulfilled the conditions of consistency, congruency, and unity.
Matters of material justification, methodological consistency, and thematic unity stand beyond the limit of that for which one can issue comparative standards of success and plausibility. The task of ranking
formally qualifying contenders for the role of "gap-filler" belongs to
historical expertise and falls subject to the same alterability of
standards as historical evidence. Consequently, the task can never become immune to disagreement. Historians, however, can settle upon the
grounds for disagreement.

One consequence of this discussion is that it becomes necessary to
view the special requirements which Danto posed (p. 251) as conditions
of narrative unity as going beyond those which thematic unity can demand. The requirement of a central subject may be seen as an alternative formulation of thematic unity. However, to demand that what the
narrative then does is explain changes in the central subject, and to
demand further that the notion of explanation be causal in some sense
compatible with one or more variations upon covering law theory, is to
impose upon the conception of a narrative a set of requirements which
apply to only a particular subset of narratives. The position that
history then does or should adhere to all the conditions of the subset
would require a further specific argument. The existence of historical
narratives which do not meet all the requirements of the subset suggests that such an argument would have to provide grounds that history
should meet them, and the reasons for arguing in that direction will
necessarily involve a set of methodological or metaphysical commitments
(e.g., those which might be said to underlie a consistant positivistic
or covering law theory) to which this study has neither a commitment
nor a lack of commitment. Such commitments simply go beyond the bounds
of the present field of study.

The discussion in this section has aimed at showing the sorts of
structural or formal requirements adherence to which produces narratives. The peculiarities of narrative form and the kinds of special

materials out of which one builds narratives have too long evaded independent treatment, perhaps because there exists no yawning chasm between narratives and other forms of discourse by means of which one can
make a point or build a case. Narrative and argument have never seemed
incompatible nor even separable in more than casual ways. The far more
extensive work which logicians have devoted to argumentation has produced the implicit supposition that proper narratives must meet the
standards of argument. Such a view has survived the most trenchant
counter-claims that narratives tell stories and do not argue. The supposition seems clearly to underlie Hempel's position that historical
narratives amount to explanation sketches.[39] It worked its way to the
surface in Danto's overt attempt to salvage a version of the covering
law theory of explanation and to bind it intimately to his own work on
narrative structures.[40] It remains to be seen, however, whether the
supposition has earned its existence. Given the modes of internal narrative relation outlined herein, the relevant question might take this
form: what are the necessary conditions for compatibility between narratives and argumentative forms?

V. The Compatibility of Historical Narratives and Arguments

     In order to explore the conditions of compatibility between narra-
tive and argument, it is first necessary to make some distinctions so
as to preclude confusion. The notion of argument, as applied to history, generally denotes a wider variety of activities than it does when
philosophers or logicians use the idea. "Synthetic unity," with its
ingredient, undetachable conclusions which are exhibited rather than
demonstrated, turned out to be, insofar as it is a possible activity at
all, a narrative activity, that is, a way of presenting history which
need only make use of narrative techniques and need not make use of
techniques which are argumentative in the sense or senses ordinarily
countenanced by philosophers. Indeed, one effect of Mink's exposition
is to distinguish between the philosopher's narrower view and the historian's wider view of argument; hence, the various lines he draws between applicable descriptive terms, e.g., between demonstrating and exhibiting conclusions.

     The question which concerns the conditions of compatibility be-
tween narrative and argumentative forms constitutes a request for the
terms of the relation between narrative on one hand and, on the other,
argument in the narrower rather than the extended sense. As such, the
question entails the supposition that historians can (and do) argue;
more specifically, it entails that one could write a history without
making use of narrative-organizational structures. Although it would
be difficult to find a pure example of such a history, that is, one
which made no use of narrative-organizational statements, it seems
equally difficult to deny the possibility that such a history could be
written. Two forms of history in which narrative-organizational structures would seem to play an incidental role most nearly approach the
realization of the possibility: for convenience I shall call them the-

181

sis history and theme history. In thesis history one attempts to prove, argue, or otherwise make a case for a point either of fact or of theory. In theme history one tries to illustrate some "truth" or "reality" of a general nature by reference to historical examples. Both sorts of histories warrant the title argumentative history. Minimally, both differ from narrative history to the extent that narrative organizational assertions play a secondary role in their formal structures. The point of an argumentative history may be a timeless generality or the occurrence of a single event, an ascription to an event, place, period, or movement, an attempt to order the facts (e.g., economic, demographic, cultural, etc.) for a given time and place, or still yet some other conclusion for which argument is relevant. Some theses or themes are amenable to temporally structured assertions. "The population dwindled in the countryside of England during the early years of the Industrial Revolution" is a narrative-organizational statement and yet may be the conclusion of a historical statistical inquiry and argument. Nonetheless, neither amenability to nor actual use of narrative-organizational assertions constitutes a necessary condition of being an argumentative history. Indeed, the question is whether and how forms of argumentative history are compatible with narrative history.

In speaking of forms of non-narrative history, the best terminology for now may be the loosest, not so as to be able to build a case on vagueries, but to be able to note certain features of historical argument. Truistically, the subject matter of history in any of its forms centers around human affairs. Social, ethical, political, cultural, and other normative enterprises hold at least equal interest with those non-narrative areas which especially tantalize theorists. Making a case or arguing a point may thus involve more than simply deductive argumentation. An argumentative history may include, besides statements of fact, assertions of rules, mores, conventions, principles, and imperatives. To whatever extent these sorts of assertion lie beyond the bounds of deductive argument, that far outside the same bounds will lie argumentative history. Whatever the other consequences this condition may have, it enjoins against taking too narrow or deductive a view of historical argument. The condition does not, however, commit one to the sort of extended view of argument set aside at the beginning of this section.

Within these loose confines, a historian who argues for a thesis or illustrates a theme must produce an account which meets standards of internal consistency. One may call a proper or adequate argumentative history, i.e., one which meets such standards, argumentatively consistent. The standards will include, as applicable, deductive validity and soundness, inductive propriety (in any and all its forms), and other such formal requirements as may apply to matters of fact when they include normative considerations. It may be the case that some or even all of these concerns overlap with those relevant to historical narratives, but one need not assume they overlap. To the extent that narrative features such as those outlined earlier need not be present in argumentative history, overlap represents an unsupportable assumption. Consequently, whatever the degree of overlap in specific cases, i.e., however much an author manages to combine forms, there exists sufficient reason to distinguish narrative consistency from argumentative consistency.

Insofar as one may distinguish narrative from argumentative consistency, the conditions of compatibility between narrative and argumentative history must be other than an overlap of expository technique. Where the two in fact overlap, then obviously they are compatible. In such cases one can lift sentences and perhaps larger units from one sort of history and insert them intact in the other. Yet, if the two forms are compatible, as intuition and practice suggest, even the absence of overlap should not isolate them from each other.

Narrative-organizational assertions which inform narrative history not only assert fact, they also presuppose facts or contain them implicitly. The former sorts of facts consist in temporal structures which connect events, events whose factual assertion is presupposed by the structuring. To say that Franklin arrived before Washington arrived is to relate temporally two arrivals which are, depending upon context, either taken or asserted as factual by the statement. Within any narrative, then, there exist a large number of both narrative and non-narrative facts, many expressly given, perhaps still more implicitly present. If the narrative in question meets the standards of success or adequacy, these facts will be narratively consistent with the narrative-organizational assertions by the use of which one forms a narrative.

Argumentative history, too, has need of facts by which to form the grounds, premises, and other bases of its conclusions. Because history does not require tenseless facts for those grounds, premises, and bases, there is no need in this discussion to work to a level of tenseless facts. Nonetheless, to the extent that tensed assertions logically depend upon tenseless assertions, while the opposite dependency does not obtain, the reduction of facts in argumentative history to a tenseless condition present no problems. For, to the same extent, one can treat the facts of narratives as tenseless, whether these facts be the ones which narrative-organizational structures assert or contain or whether they constitute the criteria for the organizational structure.

At this point, we may assume a sort of "worst-case" analysis, that is, one in which a historical narrative consists solely of narrative-organizational assertions and a thesis history consists solely of tenseless assertions of principle and the minimum number of tensed assertions to permit a historical conclusion. In this case, we may even stipulate that no direct overlap of assertions exists. It remains possible, nevertheless, to establish conditions of compatibility. The condition would be that any fact asserted or supposed by the narrative be argumentatively consistent with the thesis history and that any fact asserted or supposed by the thesis history be narratively consistent

with the historical narrative. The same condition may be expressed ob-
versely (and abbreviatedly): no fact in the narrative shall be argumentatively inconsistent with the thesis history, and no fact in the
thesis history shall be narratively inconsistent with the historical
narrative. Where a given fact appears in both forms of history, self-
consistency obviates all problems. Likewise, where a fact of one form
of history bears no relation at all to any fact of the other, inconsistency cannot arise. Such obvious cases do not always prevail, and one
may have to perform individual tests with the appropriate canons of
consistency.

The points developed in connection with the compatibility of narrative and thesis history also permit an account of how and under what
conditions it is possible to draw theses and themes out of narratives.
Those conditions do not include the narrative's having to contain an
assertion of some particular thesis (any more than it is necessary for
a novelist to proclaim a "philosophy" in order for a scholar to explicate the "philosophy" in that piece of literature). Argumentative work
may stem wholly from the constructive abilities of one who reads a narrative. In order for one to claim that a narrative contains, holds, or
yields the argument, it is a necessary condition that there be produced
or producable a series of statements which are narratively consistent
with the historical tale and argumentatively consistent with the the-
sis-making case. Moreover, the consistency must be positive in the
sense noted earlier, that is, the series of statements must be such
that falsification of one (or more of them) would render it (or them)
inconsistent with either or both the narrative or argument. The absence of such a series of statements would, under this "worst-case"
analysis which supposes no argument in the narrative and no narrative
in the argument, entail that the respective forms were logically isolated. Failure to meet the specifically relevant consistency tests would
defeat a claim that a narrative contains, holds, or yields the prof-
fered argument.

Moreover, the necessary condition is in present practice a sufficient condition for many, if not most, instances. In fact, we assert
that a historian holds a thesis when the statement series consistent
with both the narrative and argumentative forms is small, and we do so
for perhaps no other reason than that past scholarly efforts supply no
precedent with respect to how large the series must be to warrant thesis claims. Rather than a standard, one encounters phrases such as
"conclusive," "well-documented," "reasonable," "plausible," and "hardly
plausible" in the judgment of theses which are drawn from narratives.
From Muir's account of the Enclosure Acts, industrial production, and
improvements in communication and transportation, plus his assertion
that "It was not merely an economic change that was thus beginning; it
was a social revolution," one might conclude that the author holds the
thesis that social events causally follow economic events.[41] Whether
or not he does, it is more significant that one could also hold the reverse or deny both with only the narrative information given here.
(Similar cases of multiple possible positions which rest on single nar-

ratives exist for philosophy in literature, with one writer finding four "philosophies" in Kafka's *Trial*.)[42] Multiple "interpretations" become possible by virtue of the absence of standards for the series of mutually consistent statements with respect either to its length or to its content.

The notion of "worst-case" analysis serves no other purpose than to simplify and isolate the relevant considerations for getting to the root of narrative-thesis compatibility. By assuming no overlap of logical structure beyond the use of facts, an assumption prompted by the peculiarities of narrative structure, compatibility turned out to be possible without requiring overlap. Historical narrative, however, rarely occurs pure, that is, without elements of argumentative history, and likewise, argumentative history rarely, if ever, excludes all elements of narrative. Consequently, besides meeting the minimal condition of compatibility, the two forms often end up within the same pair of covers. Such was the case with Muir's thesis concerning social revolution, which occurs in the midst of his (brief) narration of political and economic history. Overlap thus permits a greater amount of point by point consistency. Whatever the advantages of overlap, it remains the prime significance of the argument herein to have shown that compatibility can be achieved without it. That much alone points out the presumptive flaw in analyses which link narratives and arguments by holding the former to be argumentative. Narrative and argument are compatible but need not be convertible. To combine the two under one rubric is necessarily to commit the historian to more than is his due.

Before closing this sketch of narrative considerations, the subject of histories and other narratives with morals deserves brief mention. That narratives can be and are written for purposes is by now well established. That some histories have moral purposes also goes unquestioned. What has been ill-understood is the relation of such purposes to a narrative. Many a writer tells his tale in the most unobjectionable of non-subjective, non-biased terms and ends by disclaiming any attempt to provide a lesson. To the extent that one can exclude and avoid the use of evaluative, heuristic terms in a narrative, the author must be allowed his disclaimer. Nonetheless, someone inevitably finds a moral, an ethical argument, or a lesson in life to undercut the writer's best intentions. Such situations incline the hardiest objectivist to confess against his will that history hides a subjective worm in its heart.

Moral, political, and social lessons or philosophies are, like thesis and theme history, argumentative. They consist, in rough outline, of a theory, thesis, or theme supported by suitable facts and principles. As with all human affairs "argument," the form more often resembles legal case building than it does deductive argument. The logical requisites, then, for drawing a moral, political, or social lesson or philosophy out of a historical narrative exactly parallel those which establish the relation between thesis and narrative history. In brief, the necessary and sufficient condition for a moral lesson or philosophy to be said to be contained in a historical narrative is that there be a series of statements which are narratively consistent (in a positive manner) with the history and argumentatively consistent with the lesson or philosophy.

Since no *a priori* limit exists for the size of the series, a minimum of one satisfies the condition set out. And perhaps some interpretations of narratives might lead one to believe that this little constitutes the entire basis for the reading. Such a problem, however, falls into the realm of practical fault, not theoretic. The viability of one moral interpretation as opposed to another, whether done by the author and included or intermixed with the narrative or whether done by a critic, often rests on the size of the series: the greater the number of statements, the more plausible the interpretation. The existence of such a list, extracted from the narrative or generated by eliciting its presuppositions, provides a necessary condition of the interpretation, because voiding any member of the series (and thereby creating a different series) ordinarily suffices to falsify part or all of an interpretation. That such a list comprises a sufficient condition for argumentative interpretations has the consequence of accounting for the fact that little explicit citation of a narrative is required for "critical" readings. Extricating those facts contained in or supposed by the narrative-organizational structures provides all the grounds necessary to an argumentative explication.

Similar arguments can be applied to other purposes for which one writes a historical narrative, though by no means to all purposes. Moreover an analogous argument appears able to establish the relation between a work of narrative literature and what some call "philosophy in literature." In that connection, the argument has the merit of allowing scholars to find "philosophies," usually moral, social, or political arguments, in the least openly philosophical works. The analogy holds because the relata, narrative literature and arguments over the range of human affairs, parallel the relata of history: narrative and argument. Were the analogy not to hold, scholarship would find itself hard pressed to justify its sometimes stretched readings of literature. A detailed argument in favor of the analogy would, however, also have to include some account of the relation between factual and fictional narrative, for it is one thing to establish conditions of compatibility between factual narratives and factual arguments and it is quite another to suggest immediate compatibility between fictional narratives and factual arguments. The necessary additions to the argument, which involve intrinsically interesting issues which I think can be successfully resolved, go far beyond the bounds set for this study. Philosophy of literature as a field for analytic endeavor still lies in infancy.[41] Literary investigations still want for the analytic study which would unveil some of the logic and justification of fictional narratives.

****

All of which carries us far from the field of history, the erst-
while center of this study. The fact of dispersion illustrates that
history does not stand isolated from other disciplines. Overlap, however, does not result from history's dependence upon others for methods
and principles; rather it stems from the fact that some concerns central to history share similar positions in other fields of study.

The analyses of this chapter cannot hope to have closed the subject of narratives. At best, they extend and moderate previous work
and lay a basis, positive or negative, for future work. Perhaps, even
if by accident, they have elicited some of the salient features of narratives and their relation to history. Similar remarks apply to work
in the preceding chapters. In all philosophical work, however, intention and disclaimer are never desiderata. Therefore, I shall take it
as sufficient for any issue if I have managed to confuse it in a new
and eventually useful way.

NOTES

[1] A series of factual assertions to the effect that such and so
events occurred does not even meet White's criteria for a "chronicle,"
which requires a central subject and a "conjunction of noncausal singular statements which expressly mention that subject and which report
things that have been true of it at different times." Morton White,
Foundations of Historical Knowledge (New York: Harper and Row, Publishers, 1965), p. 222.

[2] William H. Dray, "On the Nature and Role of Narrative in Historiography," *History and Theory*, 10 (1971), pp. 168 f.

[3] Louis O. Mink, "The Autonomy of Historical Understanding," *Philosophical Analysis and History*, ed. William H. Dray (New York: Harper
and Row, Publishers, 1966), pp. 180-181.

[4] Dray, "On the Nature and Role of Narrative in Historiography," p.
157.

[5] Glenn Morrow, "Comments on White's 'Logic of Historical Narration'," *Philosophy and History*, ed. Sidney Hook (New York: New York
University Press, 1963), p. 286; W. B. Gallie, *Philosophy and the Historical Understanding* (New York: Schocken Books, 1964), p. 66; A. C.
Danto, *Analytical Philosophy of History* (Cambridge: At the University
Press, 1965), p. 142; see also Dray, "On the Nature and Role of Narrative in Historiography," pp. 154-57 for a good review of the position
here rejected.

[6] Louch, "History as Narrative," p. 58; Danto, *Analytical Philosophy of History*, p. 251; Gallie, *Philosophy and the Historical Understanding*, p. 108; see Dray again for a review of the extent to which
the position has been held and the extent to which it is viable.

187

[7] Haskell Fain, *Between Philosophy and History* (Princeton: Princeton University Press, 1970), p. 209.

[8] *Ibid.*, p. 211.

[9] White, *Foundations of Historical Knowledge*, p. 221.

[10] See for instance Rolf Gruner, "Mandelbaum on Historical Narrative: A Discussion, 2," *History and Theory*, 8 (1969), for a position which denies the necessity of a central subject while adhering to another of the theses rejected here: "Although it is true that a history of *a* can only be a story of *a, not all works of history are histories of something* . . . ." p. 284.

[11] For another example of the theses developed in an interrelated and interlocking manner, see Danto's criteria for narrative unity: "Thus, if *N* is a narrative, then *N* lacks unity unless (A) *N* is about the same subject, (B) *N* adequately explains the change in that subject which is covered by the explicandum, and (C) *N* contains only so much information as is required by (B) and no more," *Analytical Philosophy of History*, p. 251. A set of reasons for rejecting Danto's use of the theses in question would too closely resemble the ones given for rejecting White's use to bear setting out.

[12] White, *Foundations of Historical Knowledge*, pp. 222-23.

[13] Bruce Waters, "Historical Narrative," *The Southern Journal of Philosophy*, 5 (Fall, 1967), p. 206.

[14] Robert C. Stover, *The Nature of Historical Thinking* (Chapel Hill: University of North Carolina Press, 1967), p. 70.

[15] *Ibid.*, p. 71.

[16] Dray, "The Nature and Role of Narrative in Historiography," pp. 166-70.

[17] All parenthetical page numbers in this chapter refer to Danto's *Analytical Philosophy of History.*

[18] Waters, "Historical Narrative," p. 206.

[19] John Passmore, "Explanation in Everyday Life, in Science, and in History," *Studies in the Philosophy of History*, ed. George H. Nadel (New York: Harper and Row, Publishers, 1965), p. 18.

[20] For wider ranging criticism of Danto, see, for example, Frederick Olafson, "Narrative History and the Concept of Action," *History and Theory*, 9 (1970), pp. 265 ff.

[21] Monroe Beardsley, *Aesthetics from Classical Greece to the Present: A Short History* (New York: The Macmillan Co., 1966), p. 260.

[22] Gilbert Ryle, "Thinking and Language," *Proceedings of the Aristotelian Society*, Suppl. 25 (1951), pp. 67-69.

[23] William H. Dray, "'Explaining What' in History," *Theories of History*, ed. Patrick Gardiner (New York: The Free Press, 1959), p. 406.

[24] Carey B. Joynt and Nicholas Rescher, "The Problem of Uniqueness in History," *Studies in the Philosophy of History*, pp. 8 ff.

[25] W. H. Walsh, *An Introduction to Philosophy of History* (London: Hutchinson University Library, 1958), p. 61. See also Maurice Mandelbaum, who argues that "the relation which I therefore take to be fundamental in historiography is . . . a relationship of part to whole, not a relationship of antecedent to consequent," "A Note on History as Narrative," *History and Theory*, 6 (1967), pp. 417-18.

[26] Cf. Fain, who notes that "in fact, most of the key concepts historians employ have a narrative function (for example, the Renaissance, the Frontier, the Reconstruction Period); they serve as principle elements in the organization of the historian's story line," *Between Philosophy and History*, p. 214. Although Fain's claim seems partly correct, his examples appear to be proper names rather than concepts. A renaissance or a reconstruction period may organize, but one must then treat "the Renaissance" as an instance of renaissances rather than as a name (and indeed, although it is nowhere mentioned, Fain may have in part intended this).

[27] *Ibid.*, pp. 302, 296.

[28] The choice of terminology for this section is more than anything a matter of convenience. Terms like "unity," "continuity," and "consistency" have all been used to designate very generally whatever it is that holds narratives together in their peculiar way. Herein I have chosen terms to designate (and to discriminate among) various sorts of ways in which narratives are held together. So long as the distinctions are made, it perhaps does not metter much what we call each way if the term used is not too misleading.

[29] The existence of such histories suffices to falsify Fain's claim that narratives must have a central subject, (*Between Philosophy and History*, p. 209) unless he insists on analyzing such big stories as collections of smaller stories.

[30] Karl Stephenson and Bryce Lyon, *Medieval History*, 4th Ed. (New York: Harper and Row, 1962).

[31] Olafson, "Narrative History and the Concept of Action," p. 278.

[32] See also Fain's examples of ways in which events lead from one to another without needing the notion of "cause-effect," *Between Philosophy and History*, p. 296. Note also, however, that "cause-effect" as a means of narrative organization is not excluded.

[33] Mink, "The Autonomy of Historical Understanding," p. 181.

[34] Dray, "The Nature and Role of Narrative in Historiography," pp. 169-70.

[35] William H. Dray, *Philosophy of History* (Englewood Cliffs, New Jersey: Prentice-Hall, Inc., 1964), pp. 30-31.

[36] This point may perhaps suffice to mark out weaknesses in Fain's account (*Between Philosophy and History*) wherein he apparently con-

flates narrative and thematic unity. He argues, for one thing, that narrative coherence "depends, at bottom, upon showing how one episode leads to another," (p. 298) and cites examples of leading terms such as "generates," "makes more probable," and "leads to." For another thing, he argues that "the key concepts historians employ have a narrative function . . . ; they serve as principle elements in the organization of a historian's story line," and he cites as examples "the Renaissance," "the Frontier," and "the Reconstruction Period" (p. 214). Unfortunately, Fain does not make it clear whether he construes the organizing function of key concepts as being the same as, similar to, or different from the notion of narrative coherence. The distinction suggested herein between narrative unity and thematic unity is designed to differentiate the two notions of unity in historical narratives.

[37]John Dewey, *Logic: The Theory of Inquiry* (New York: Henry Holt and Company, 1938), p. 66.

[38]*Ibid.*, pp. 66-78.

[39]Carl Hempel, *Aspects of Scientific Explanation* (New York: The Free Press, 1965), p. 238.

[40]See especially Danto, *Analytical Philosophy of History*, pp. 251-55.

[41]Ramsey Muir, *A Short History of the British Empire*, II (London: George Philip and Son, Ltd., 1923), p. 123.

[42]Stephen Ross, *Philosophy and Literature* (New York: Appleton-Century-Crofts, 1969), pp. 113-36.

[43]For exceptions, see, among others, the following: John Hospers, "Implied Truths in Literature," *Journal of Aesthetics and Art Criticism*, 19 (Fall, 1960), pp. 37-46; Margaret Macdonald, "The Language of Fiction," *Philosophy of Art and Aesthetics*, ed. Frank A. Tillman and Steven M. Cahn (New York: Harper and Row, Publishers, 1969), pp. 617-30; and D. H. Mellor, "On Truth in Fiction," *Ratio*, 10 (December, 1968), pp. 150-68.

Tolstoy, Leo N.--147; 178
Toulmin, Stephen E.--40; 46, n 51
Toynbee, Arnold--4; 26; 129; 130;
  151, n 62
Trawick, Buckner B.--45, n 30
Trevor-Roper, H. R.--99
Turner, Merle B.--45, n 33

Urmson, J. O.--39; 46, n 48

Walsh, W. H.--7; 11, n 3; 19; 29;
  44, n 10, n 20; 77, n 3; 92;
  116, n 15; 124-126; 141-143;
  149, n 18, n 19; 167; 177;
  189, n 25
Waters, Bruce--88; 116, n 10; 157;
  159; 188, n 13
Weiss, Paul--31; 45, n 28
Whewell, William--77, n 3
White, Morton--78, n 10; 149, n 18;
  150, n 30; 157; 189, n 1; 188,
  n 11
Winch, Peter--124; 148, n 11
Wittgenstein, Ludwig--39; 47;
  77, n 1
Woodbridge, Frederick J. E.--113;
  116, n 10; 140-142; 148, n 3

DATE DUE